Romantic Agency

Romantic Agency

Loving Well in Modern Life

Luke Brunning

polity

Copyright © Luke Brunning 2024

The right of Luke Brunning to be identified as Author of this Work has been asserted in accordance with the UK Copyright, Designs and Patents Act 1988.

First published in 2024 by Polity Press

Polity Press
65 Bridge Street
Cambridge CB2 1UR, UK

Polity Press
111 River Street
Hoboken, NJ 07030, USA

All rights reserved. Except for the quotation of short passages for the purpose of criticism and review, no part of this publication may be reproduced, stored in a retrieval system, or transmitted, in any form or by any means, electronic, mechanical, photocopying, recording, or otherwise, without the prior permission of the publisher.

ISBN-13: 978-1-5095-5152-1
ISBN-13: 978-1-5095-5153-8 (pb)

A catalogue record for this book is available from the British Library.

Library of Congress Control Number: 2023946993

Typeset in 10.5 on 12.5pt Sabon
by Fakenham Prepress Solutions, Fakenham, Norfolk NR21 8NL

Printed and bound in Great Britain by CPI Group (UK) Ltd, Croydon

The publisher has used its best endeavours to ensure that the URLs for external websites referred to in this book are correct and active at the time of going to press. However, the publisher has no responsibility for the websites and can make no guarantee that a site will remain live or that the content is or will remain appropriate.

Every effort has been made to trace all copyright holders, but if any have been overlooked the publisher will be pleased to include any necessary credits in any subsequent reprint or edition.

For further information on Polity, visit our website:
politybooks.com

Contents

Acknowledgements vi

Introduction 1

1 Modern Romance 9

2 Opening Up 25

3 Romantic Agency 58

4 Shaping Intimacy 71

5 Realistic Conversation 89

6 Romantic Risks 103

7 Jealousy 130

8 Grasping the Good 167

Conclusion 179

Notes 189
References 204
Index 216

Acknowledgements

Thank you to Pascal Porcheron for taking this project on at Polity Press, and to Ian Malcolm, Ellen MacDonald-Kramer, Leigh Mueller, Chantal Hamill, and Maddie Tyler for helping me to reach the finish. I would also like to acknowledge the two anonymous reviewers who helped me to improve the text.

This book is the product of my time at the University of Birmingham, and the University of Leeds. My colleagues at Birmingham, especially the ethicists and junior staff, supported me through several temporary contracts, the pandemic, and were kind.

The IDEA Centre in Leeds has been a wonderfully supportive environment over the past year. Thank you for the warm welcome Alice, Andy, Carl, Chris, Graham, Jamie, Jim, Josh, Kathryn, Liz, Merel, Nick, Paula, Rachael, Rob, Robbie, Robbie, Sarah, Sean, Sophie, and Tash. I also appreciate the contribution of everyone who commented on my work in the love reading group, the emotions workshop, the research seminar, the work-in-progress seminar, and other events. I have never had so much friendly criticism, and this book is stronger for it. Special thanks to Jamie Dow for nurturing IDEA's research environment.

PRHS colleagues at Leeds have also been fantastic. I have learnt from their incisive comments at workshops and events, and benefited from their efforts to cultivate a healthy community. Special thanks to the Bini Brew crew for small-town solidarity.

Sophie Goddard and Ruby Hornsby have been amazing in helping Natasha McKeever and me to set up the Centre of Love, Sex, and Relationships and organize events. Without Alice Burn and Rachael Bowerbank, we would have struggled to make things happen – thank you.

I would also like to thank audiences at the 'Love etc.' workshop in Leeds, the MANCEPT workshop on the 'Future of Love', the MANCEPT workshop on 'Equality in Intimate Life' (especially Esa Díaz-León for engaging with my work on compersion); Angie Pepper for an invitation to speak with people from the University of Roehampton; Suzanne Whitten for the invitation to speak with people from Queen's University Belfast; Nikhil Krishnan for the invitation to speak to an audience at Cambridge University; and Francesca Miccoli for an invitation to speak with people from Università degli Studi di Milano; and everyone who asked me questions. I would like to thank Herj Marway for conversation when this book was at an early stage; and Alba Cercas Curry, Sophie Goddard, Tom O'Shea, Joseph Saunders, and Margot Witte for some comments on earlier material; and all the other people whose questions or remarks have shaped my thinking over the years.

Few people make philosophy as fun as Pilar Lopez-Cantero. I have learnt much from her work on love, narrative, and the self, and her influence is visible throughout this book.

Natasha McKeever deserves special thanks. Her constructive feedback made this book better, and her encouragement helped me to finish it. She has done so much to make the study of relationships more visible, both at Leeds and beyond, and is a joy to collaborate with.

Thank you to my family Gary, Rosalind, Laura, Rosie, Gill, Ian, Ali, and Ryan. You've put up with my antics and kept me going. Thank you to Plosh, Honey, and Minnie for the constant amusement, and for not walking on my keyboard.

Most importantly, Jenny. You show me what it means to nurture and to be delighted by the world. Thank you for your love.

Introduction

Transformations

> Love approximates a space to which people can return, becoming as different as they can be from themselves without being traumatically shattered, it is a scene of optimism for change, for a transformational environment.
> (Lauren Berlant)[1]

This book is for people who like to think about romantic life.

We live in a time of growing openness to new kinds of intimacy and curiosity about romantic flourishing. Although things are far from perfect, we are less tolerant of miserable relationships, and are more creative in how we live and love. Divorce and remarriage are common; blended families thrive; television dating shows now mention queer desire and non-monogamy.

This openness is exciting. We have greater hope that we can build relationships which suit us, and increasingly feel this is more important than sticking to traditions or following trends. The enforced closeness of the pandemic heightened these feelings as we reflected on our intimate arrangements.

But the growing spotlight on personal flourishing can also create anxiety. We might be unsure what kind of romantic relationship we want, let alone what would be good for us. Even if our desires are clear, our insecurities may leave us doubting whether we can act on them. Will we miss the familiarity of an exclusive relationship? Can we cope with jealousy? What if we are not supported by our friends or family?

This anxiety is not helped by our shifting romantic landscape. Apps and websites have transformed our dating habits in ways which increase our choice, but also our disappointment. Using them can feel like work, tiring but necessary. Worse, the many options to adjust our filters, write a better bio, or just switch from Tinder to Hinge only reinforce the idea that, ultimately, our romantic happiness is down to us – not a nice feeling when yet another date sucks, or we are dumped for someone else.

Dating apps help place the idea of compatibility at the heart of modern romance. Narratives within dating shows or films also reflect this. The underlying thought is that if we can only get things right at the start and find 'our person', someone with the same desires and values, then the relationship will flow easily from there. This can be a hard thought to resist since it fits nicely with consumerist instincts: diligent research is supposed to guarantee our satisfaction.

I take seriously this mix of optimism, curiosity, and anxiety. At its heart is the core tension I shall be exploring in this book, which is that we might not have the romantic agency to bring our desires to life. Romantic agency is the name I give to the bundle of abilities which allow us to direct our romantic lives and relationships as we wish. The appeal of unconventional intimacies can make it easy to forget that relationships are ultimately sustained through activity, and that this requires various skills.

These abilities are often acquired slowly, and can be easily undermined. We learn to cope with repressed childhoods, restrictive social norms, or oppressive government policies in ways that can obstruct our flourishing. Even if we are lucky and avoid these problems, unhappy relationships, messy break-ups, or abuse can shape our personalities in ways which make it harder to thrive. These changes are often slow and lie outside of our conscious control. If we step back, we might notice our confidence fading, our insecurity rising, or that we avoid vulnerability by being evasive or aggressive.

Similarly, by focusing on compatibility we can overlook the ways we are changed in our relating to others. We mostly develop our romantic agency when being nurtured by romantic partners. As a result, our desires, values, and character may evolve in surprising ways. These changes can enrich our lives, even if we end up unlike the person we initially described to others in our dating profile.

I will argue that we need to take seriously our romantic agency, and that of our partners, and make choices to protect those abilities. Doing so sets us on the path to flourishing relationships. This process requires us to be realistic, and may leave some desires unsatisfied for now, but it helps us to navigate the tumultuous world of modern romance.

So how do we nurture romantic agency? A full answer would consider political policy as well as personal effort. My focus in this book, however, is mainly on the latter – on the traits and practices which help us to foster intimacy. I will provide arguments to favour a specific way of looking at romantic life, and to embrace several key traits. There are no shortcuts to cultivating those traits, or simple rules that could take their place. Relating well to other people is ongoing and difficult.

Romance

Before summarizing the argument of this book, it helps to clarify what I mean by romantic life. I understand romantic life broadly, since we experience intimacy in many ways. Romantic life includes our sexuality, dating practices, and relationships. Romantic love, specifically, is a contested idea, and is not a feature of all romantic relationships.[2]

Similarly, sex is a feature of some but not all romantic relationships. Some asexual people, for instance, who do not experience sexual attraction to others, have little or no sexual activity with their romantic partners.[3] Other people are celibate or cannot have sex. For others, sex occupies a minor part of their romantic lives.

We do not need to be in a relationship to have a romantic life. Single people have sex, go on dates, talk to potential partners, and process break-ups. Much of romantic life lies outside socially recognized relationships. The partnered perspective, usually that of couples, may be socially dominant but is one of many perspectives. As the prevalence of infidelity indicates, our romantic attention can easily be directed to people outside our recognized relationships.

This may seem counter-intuitive, but my understanding of romantic life also includes people who identify as aromantic. 'Aromanticism' is a label used by people who experience little to no romantic attraction. Although most aromantic people have little interest in romantic relationships, many enjoy sexual intimacy.

I am often asked how to draw a boundary between romantic life and other forms of intimacy but I am not sure there is one. Counter-examples are available for every candidate feature we can consider, from bodily intimacy to sharing projects or domestic space with someone. Asexual romantic couples, non-cohabiting spouses, platonic co-parents, aromantic sexual partners, friends with benefits: these configurations exist and complicate any attempts to define romantic life. Appealing to romantic love does not help either. Not all romantic entanglements involve love, and it seems unlikely we can define romantic love in a way which makes it radically distinct from love of friends or family.[4]

If pressed, my preferred approach to the boundary question is to say that romantic life is distinct not because of some special experience involved, but in virtue of how we locate our experiences in a web of social meanings. Our social world is animated by labels and stories which shape how people interpret what we are doing.[5] These patterns of meaning are imprecise, contested, and local to specific social contexts. But they have momentum. If you have sex with someone you love, for example, chances are other people will 'read' your intimacy in romantic terms. You could disagree with them, but the need to disagree and to define yourself against their interpretation points to the social reality of the meanings in play. We understand what counts as romantic not in terms of some essential feature, but in terms of the stories and labels we reach for to make ourselves understood.

I will shift between talking of romantic life, in general, and relationships in particular. Talk of relationships is not intended to imply they are all long-lasting or socially recognized. I will also talk of relationship configurations and policies. A configuration is the broad set-up of the relationship, for example whether it is monogamous, heterosexual, or domestic. A policy, in contrast, is a specific rule or expectation which we might have within a relationship, such as agreeing to use contraception or to share finances.

You might think that, rather than focusing on romantic life, in particular, it would be better to focus on intimacy as a general feature which can be present in different parts of life, from the family to the workplace. No doubt this would be a valuable project. Understanding what *intimacy* is, for example, is no easy task.[6] Some of what I say below also applies to intimacy more broadly, and it would not be a stretch to have named this book 'intimate agency'.

That said, romantic life demands independent attention. Here I am influenced by my own experiences. Romantic relationships have a tendency to engage our desires, emotions, and bodily presence in ways which are sustained and intense. Living with someone, or spending lots of time with them, shapes our personalities more strongly than many friendships.

Our attitudes towards romantic life are also more ambivalent. It is hard to reconcile the ideal of relationships as the place where we can be most ourselves and resist tradition with the reality that social pressure seems greatest in romantic situations and we are often held back by our habits and entrenched feelings.

A final reason to focus on romantic life concerns our relationships. Even if intimacy is common to many areas of life, we often pursue romantic intimacy in defined relationships. The idea of a relationship helps us to organize and make sense of our actions with other people. We make many decisions by thinking about our relationships: how are we to spend our time, what shall we do, where shall we be, how shall we behave, what are we prepared to miss out on? There is a sense, then, in which each romantic relationship is entered into as an 'experiment in living', to use John Stuart Mill's phrase. Even if we are happy with our own experiment in living, there is value in exploring other experiments because other people may have stumbled upon a better arrangement or come to understand a familiar value, such as commitment, in a new way.[7]

Argument Summary

This book divides into two parts. The first four chapters aim to tidy our thinking about romantic life by describing our situation, replying to some concerns about unconventional relationships, and then focusing our attention onto the idea of romantic agency. The rest of the book provides an account of some traits and practices that nurture our romantic agency.

In chapter 1, I present my understanding of modern love. Although our romantic practices are changing, and new attitudes are forming, they are still structured around several entrenched romantic norms about love, romantic exclusivity, and sex. Together, these norms can be disorienting.

One response to the disorientation of modern love is to explore possible alternatives. Non-monogamous lifestyles, such as polyamory where we have multiple intimate relationships, offer a vision of unconventional intimacy. Yet discussions of non-monogamy remain morally polarized. Some think non-monogamy is obviously immoral; others, that monogamy is. In chapter 2, I cut through these debates. After defending non-monogamous lifestyles from the worry that they are impractical, greedy, or unfair, I argue that some kinds of intimate restrictions can help us to sustain relationships.

Chapter 3 focuses on romantic agency. I show how these abilities are formed alongside other people, can be undermined, and might not be enough to help us satisfy our desires. Chapter 4 then explores the impact of different relationship dynamics on romantic agency, with their benefits and pitfalls. I explore the idea that exclusivity is a useful form of intimate specialization, and that non-monogamy might keep alive romantic appreciation, increase oversight, or offer us new relational practices.

The second half of the book begins, in chapter 5, with a discussion of realism. We can struggle to understand ourselves, our partners, or our relationship dynamic because we are defensive or fixated on a romantic ideal. Overcoming these gaps in understanding helps us to be more realistic, which, in turn, helps us to make choices that suit our romantic agency. We achieve this through conversation with others, not romantic negotiation.

Realism has its limits because we may struggle to understand how we will react in unfamiliar situations. Will opening up a relationship, for example, be satisfying or overwhelming? To require us to know how we will react entrenches traditional relationships, so is there a good way to take romantic risks? In chapter 6, I suggest that integrity and playfulness help us here. Understood correctly, integrity makes us reliable; we consider other people and make amends for our inevitable missteps. Playfulness helps us to explore, be serious but flexible, and accept that other people mess up.

Turbulent feelings such as jealousy are common barriers to intimacy. In chapter 7, I explore jealousy in detail and argue that, since jealousy can play a variety of roles in romantic life, we should be wary of blanket calls to remove it. We are better off trying to manage jealousy and we do this through, amongst other things, the compression of our feelings, and efforts to 'hold' other people experiencing challenging emotions.

We might be good at managing the negative aspects of romantic life yet fail to appreciate the positive aspects. In chapter 8, I consider how we can grasp these good things and become less comparative by exploring contentment and the idea of compersion, the emotion of feeling good for a partner's flourishing with someone else.

I conclude by considering how we cultivate romantic agency. This is partly the personal task of working on ourselves, but also the social task of encouraging exploration and working to minimize domination. Some of these personal changes are best served through building nurturing environments, not just introspection.

Method

Writing about romantic life can be difficult. When we generalize, we risk neglecting the particularities of love and relationships, but if we fixate on detail, we risk having limited relevance. It is also easy to moralize or be uncharitable when writing about intimacy or, to avoid those dangers, to be clinical and overlook its messier aspects.

Hopefully I can avoid these dangers. I want this book to contribute to the wider conversation about romantic life. Many of the themes I examine are being discussed with care in everyday conversations around the world. My contribution is to systematize some aspects of these discussions by approaching them with the resources of modern philosophy.

Occasionally, people have suggested to me that romantic life does not need philosophy; that we should leave alone a fun and intuitive part of life. This seems wrong to me. Intimate life is practically and intellectually challenging. Romantic relationships are shaped by social and political factors, not just personal ones. The ordinary concepts we use in talking with partners, concepts such as commitment, consent, respect, reciprocity, and love, are intricate and subject to different interpretations. The ordinary work of making sense of these ideas, of bringing them into focus and acting on them, is partly philosophical work.

This does not mean we are always theorizing. In practice, we usually think hardest when we disagree or have to make tough choices. We rarely stop to scrutinize our assumptions or core concepts. Occasional reflection is useful, however, and I hope to contribute to those moments and provide new questions to consider. One relevant idea within the book is that we have to create nurturing surroundings because rational reflection is rarely sufficient to change us as we would like.

A note on my choice of language. This book is written from my perspective, and I have biases like anyone. I have intentionally decided to write of what 'we' think or what is good for 'our' romantic lives, for two reasons. I want you to feel included and to consider these ideas from your perspective, but I also know it can be annoying to be attributed a viewpoint you do not hold. My hope is that the occasionally jarring quality of 'we' can be more useful than the neutral 'one' because it helps you to recognize the places where we disagree.

Finally, a note on notes. This book uses endnotes only to provide references to the texts I mention or to relevant readings. All caveats, objections, and asides are in the main body of text.

1
Modern Romance

> ... most approaches to society presume that society equips individuals with the tools to be competent members of it.
> (Eva Illouz)[1]

Depending on who you ask, you will get a characterization of modern love as a time of great decline, a time of exciting possibility, or something halfway between. This chapter offers my perspective. I want to unearth and organize some of the norms and constraints which structure our romantic interactions and ideals. With a good grasp of our romantic situation, we are better able to understand how it can impact us and why we might seek to live differently.

Selves

Our romantic lives are doubly constrained. We are creatures of a particular kind, but we are also receptive to the norms and structures of our society. To understand our romantic situation, we must appreciate both sources of constraint.

So, what are we like? Here are some dimensions of an answer that will prove important as this book develops.

We are *vulnerable*. Irrespective of our self-image, we are creatures who depend on others. This dependency marks our lives from the beginning and is visible in our attachment bonds. In infancy, we form attachments to caregivers. An attachment bond is an orientation to a specific person who serves as a source of security and an anchor around which we strike out and explore the world.[2] This bond takes different forms, depending how we are treated, with 'secure' attachment being prized in connection to later development and even virtue.[3] We form attachments throughout our lives, including in our romantic relationships.[4] These bonds are not easily moulded by our conscious thought. As Monique Wonderly describes attachment, to be attached to someone is to experience them 'as felt needs, such that without them we are not quite alright, but we feel as though we are in some sense unwell, less together, and unable to navigate the world quite as competently'.[5] Our ability to act well, and feel grounded in our abilities, depends on the behaviour of our attachment figures.

Our relationships with attachment figures also illustrate the many ways we are *porous*. We are open to, and absorb, the presence of other people by internalizing their presence. Family, friends, and lovers become figures in our interior conversations; they are perspectives from which we view the world.[6] Our patterns of thinking, storytelling, and even how we move our bodies are marked by the idiolects we form with these people. Sadly, the way a specific person shapes our interior life often only comes into view when things change suddenly, such as after a break-up or bereavement.[7]

Internalization enables us to be *historical* and shaped by our past. New relationships are often seen through the eyes of old relationships, which can be confusing. Specific traumas can reignite in a present moment and shake our sense of place or identity.[8] Past abuse, assault, and betrayal can colour a relationship with someone new. Further back, our character is shaped by our time as children in the home or the classroom. Deeper still is the social impact of poverty or oppression, which shapes our life chances. Significantly, the past does not just impact what we want or think, but also how our bodies behave and what we are prone to feel. Insecurity or jealousy, for example, can overwhelm an open mind.

Conflict and ambivalence, which are common features of romantic life, are exacerbated by our *opacity*. We are not easily known to ourselves, and our peculiarities can evade easy understanding. This is a structural feature of creatures like us – our attention is not broad enough to capture our complex habits and interior lives.[9] Our defensiveness makes this lack of self-knowledge harder to overcome. It can be easier to seek refuge in fantasy, rather than confront unpleasant aspects of ourselves or those around us.

Opacity would not be as challenging as it is if we did not change. But we are *mutable*. We change in ways which can outrun our ability to make sense. Our bodies age and undergo significant shifts through puberty, midlife, parenthood, the menopause, and into later life. Our surfaces and textures change. Sexual desire and even orientation may alter unpredictably.[10] We might transition gender. Illness or injury may require chemical response. Sustained exercise can mould our muscles and mindset. These physical shifts sometimes have psychological shadows which together alter intimacy. Social changes also shape us. When we take on new roles or identities, like becoming a parent or starting a new job, we are acquainted with new values and patterns of action.[11] Even moving to a different built environment can change how we are prone to act around other people.[12]

Finally, we are fiercely *comparative* creatures. We understand ourselves in reference to many standards: social ideals and role models, traits of character, conceptions of what is normal. Our sense of success and failure also relates to social standards of excellence, to the 'regulative ideals' of being a friend, lover, or spouse.[13] Similar forms of comparative evaluation shape our judgements about gender, ability, race, and appearance. This ranking is ongoing, and inflects every aspect of our lives, including our emotional responses. Aaron Ben-Ze'ev goes so far as to say that 'emotional meaning is mainly comparative'.[14] Emotions, such as envy or hope, make sense of our world relative to a baseline. This baseline includes both our sense of how things are for us, or others, and our sense of how things ought to be. In turn, our sense of how things ought to be is informed by our social context, and enlarged by our imagination. Our emotional lives will suffer if the grip of either is too dominant, or inflexible. This will prove important when thinking about contentment, in chapter 8.

I have described some dimensions of our nature. As should be clear, we are vulnerable to being shaped by forces which either predate us or seem external to us. People working within the existential tradition of philosophy would say we are *sedimented* into our context. Jesse Prinz, for example, describes sedimentation as 'the phenomenon of experiencing the world and acting in it through the filter of the past, without necessarily realizing it'.[15] The geological metaphor captures the sense in which the influence of history and our social context norms, ideals, and significant projects is not some 'benign residue that we can bring into the light and then wipe away' but rather 'a pervasive lattice of forces that make deviation difficult or even impossible'.[16] One reason why sedimentation is hard to notice is because it appears natural. Our experiences, the meanings associated with them, and the norms structuring them, can seem 'just how things are'. Actively understanding, let alone freeing ourselves from, this sticky sediment is not easy.[17]

This is not to suppose that sedimentation takes one form or is experienced the same way by everyone. Nor must we think that our actions are rigidly determined by our social world. But recognition of the ways we are open to influence, the ways our social context provides that influence, and the stickiness of that influence, should make us inquire more into the content of our social world. In particular, we can ask: which norms shape our romantic context?

Society

Three norms lie at the heart of our romantic culture: amatonormativity, mononormativity, and sex negativity. They can be given simple definitions, but their reach can be hard to recognize until they are threatened.

Amatonormativity is a term coined by Elizabeth Brake to capture 'the disproportionate focus on marital and amorous love relationships as special sites of value, and the assumption that romantic love is a universal goal'.[18] Amatonormative societies such as my own, the contemporary United Kingdom, privilege romantic love over friendships or other kinds of caring or intimate relationship; they hold that love is more significant than sex; and they are hostile to people who are intentionally single. Amatonormativity can be seen in every restless question about when we will find love, secure a partner, and marry.

Mononormativity expresses the idea that our romantic relationships should be dyadic and exclusive, which means they should involve one and only one person at a time.[19] This exclusivity should ideally be sexual and emotional, and we should also be 'partisan' – that is, closed off to the idea of meeting new people or interacting with them romantically.[20] Talk of 'the one' is evidence of mononormativity, and 'supermonogamy' is the even more extreme idea that we have literally only one soulmate.[21]

Sex negativity, or what Michael Warner calles 'erotophobia', expresses the idea that sexuality, attraction, desire, and sex are fraught, potentially dangerous, and need hiding away or controlling.[22] In sex-negative societies, free expression of sexual desire and delight in sexual pleasure is suppressed, or tightly managed, or is only available to some people.

These three norms form part of the fundamental romantic ideal of our time, where someone is meant to have a life oriented towards one partner, who is the sole focus of their romantic desires and feelings, which deepen over time, and with whom they share a domestic life. In turn, this ideal is fleshed out by other social norms concerning sexuality and gender, race, class, age, and ability. For example, the dominant social conception of a romantic relationship, the picture that comes to mind or which features in literature, film, and adverts, is one involving cisgendered, heterosexual, able-bodied people of a similar racial and class background. Other forms of romantic life are increasingly tolerated, but do not come to mind as easily when people talk about romantic love, and are rarely celebrated.

It is worth noting that the three core norms do not share the same historical trajectory. Amatonormativity is perhaps the most recent in the sense that romantic love has only recently been viewed as central to committed relationships and individual flourishing.[23] These core norms also intersect uneasily. We could embrace one of them without embracing the others. More interestingly, they are in subtle tension with each other. If amorous relationships are so important and central to our flourishing, for example, then the monogamy norm seems restrictive. Why not have several amorous relationships? If sexuality is dangerous and needs careful management, then why are relationships where sexuality is typically absent, like friendships, valued less in our society than amorous unions?

The practical impact of these core norms is also uneven. Some of us have more 'intimate privilege' than others. This is a term coined by Nathan Rambukkana to capture the fact that if, relative to other people, we have more of an ability to take up social space, to use resources, take action, express opinions, and generally chart the course of our lives as we please, we have more of an ability to shape our romantic relationships as we like and deviate from established romantic norms.[24] Marginalized and oppressed people have this ability to a lesser extent. So, although amatonormativity, mononormativity, and sex negativity are deeply sedimented in many societies, we must resist the temptation to suppose they shape everyone's experiences evenly.

It is tempting to think these core romantic norms are waning due to social change, the impact of the sexual revolution, and the radical activism of feminists and sexual minorities. But look closer and they remain dominant. Local deviations from one norm are often allowed only if accompanied by the vocal explicit endorsement of the others.

Increasing acceptance of homosexual marriages, for example, often involves the explicit attempt to emphasize their monogamous character and distance them from forms of plural intimacy. Philosopher Stephen Macedo, for instance, offered arguments in favour of gay marriage in the United States only to then suggest that 'legitimizing the "poly" option within marriage undermines the good of marital commitment as currently understood because so many married persons would find this a deeply unwelcome option'.[25] Only a few years previously, people were directing the same reasoning towards gay marriage itself.

Nor have the sexual revolution and modern 'hookup culture' replaced the social ideal of exclusive amorous relationships, or the thought that marriage should be to one person at a time. Similarly, sex negativity sits alongside the sexualization in society, as paradoxical as that can seem. As Warner makes clear, an underlying social aversion to eroticism 'can coexist with and even feed on commercialized titillation, desperate fascination, therapeutic celebration and punitive prurience'.[26] Sexual expression is tolerated insofar as it does not fundamentally challenge amatonormativity, or monogamy. In my current political climate, for example, it is hard to imagine people, especially women, being elected to national political office after proclaiming their enthusiasm for uncommitted casual sex and disinterest in long-term loving romantic relationships.

Shifts

Deeply sedimented norms serve as fixed points around which societies change. We can better appreciate our own romantic context by briefly considering some of the ways our romantic practices and intimate ideals have changed.[27]

One broad shift is the move to romantic individualism from relationships embedded in community. There used to be more clarity around romantic life partly due to its underlying contractual structure which left less space for personal inclinations and expression.[28] People understood their individual roles relative to family, wider society, and the state; they had a reasonable sense of how to form, maintain, and possibly end romantic relationships.

The social changes instigated by industrial capitalism brought pressure to bear on the social oversight of courting and marriage and began to muddy romantic expectations. The grip of community and family weakened as industrialization changed how people lived, where they lived, and for how long they lived.[29] As jobs clustered in cities, so did romantic opportunities. Proximity bred passion, and passion bred politics as new people formed new visions of love and marriage and sought greater romantic freedom.

These social changes transformed how we understand romantic life. Love went from being a welcome side-effect of some pragmatic unions, to the core goal of courtship.[30] Relationships became increasingly private and domestic sites of personal romantic happiness, rather than social units of production.

These changes continue into our time. Our use of dating apps and websites helps to further 'privatize' intimacy.[31] Even friends and family might struggle to know who we are attracted to, dating, or have relationships with. Romantic entanglements can become 'public' much later, and in ways we try to control. In countries with a free internet, we can experiment and seek romantic satisfaction with little oversight.

Romantic relationships are now increasingly viewed as what Anthony Giddens called 'pure relationships', which we sustain only as long as they meet our desires.[32] Relationships are viewed as good in their own right, and can be enjoyed without pooling resources, sharing a home, or raising children with someone. We still value commitment, clearly, but we increasingly see ourselves as bound by personalized bundles of rights and responsibilities rather than traditional obligations. Perhaps the limit case of our modern forms of romantic self-definition are 'situationships', where we engage in sexual or romantic activity but 'implicitly or explicitly agree that they are to be non-relationships'.[33]

I do not want to overstate these changes. We may form relationships in new ways, and value them for different reasons, but our romantic ideals would not be alien to someone from the late nineteenth century. Romantic life remains amatonormative, monoganormative, and sex-negative. These norms are points of orientation around which we experiment; we have some flexibility in how we respect these norms, but less freedom to walk away completely.

The psychological dimensions of the shift to romantic modernity are more interesting.

Sociologist Eva Illouz argues that romantic modernity fosters a distinct 'emotional modernity'.[34] This mindset is a consequence of the fragmentation of romantic life into domains of domestic, emotional, and sexual competence. Our conduct in each domain has become a matter of expertise. Keep house. Work on our relationships. Stay attractive. Be good at sex.

As the proliferation of dating shows illustrates, albeit in exaggerated form, modern romantic culture is explicitly comparative. We evaluate our performance and prospects against those of other people, and delight in judging celebrity relationships. Dating apps put the gameshow in the pocket. We can screen potential partners in terms of discrete categories – likes, traits, values, looks – or sift them using an aggregated 'match' score. Opaque algorithms promise to make our comparisons easier and compatibility more tangible.

Disorientation

Although the shift to modern romance generates uncertainty, people disagree about whether this is a bad thing. Eva Illouz, for example, gives voice to uncertainty in pessimistic mode. She argues that modern romantic life is characterized by 'negative' relations in which the shape of our personal desires means that we either shy away from relationships, or struggle to form and maintain them.[35] According to her this happens in several ways.

First, as our romantic relationships become associated with possibilities for self-expression, development, and the exercise of autonomy, we might stop relating to other people as distinct individuals and use them instead as instruments for our fulfillment. Our striving to be romantic experts, or to compare and judge, hamper our ability to see someone as a messy, particular, individual.

Second, the casualization of romance creates a 'generalized, chronic and structural uncertainty'.[36] Lack of clear dating rituals, for instance, can make it hard to understand and appreciate the feelings of other people. We think that was a friendly drink, but they thought it was a date. These ambiguities often favour privileged people who can exploit them while denying they are doing so. Another example concerns our increased romantic choices. When we are trying to evaluate ourselves and stand out relative to the 'shifting reference points' of romantic worth, such as our beauty, humour, or sexual experience, it is easy to feel our confidence fade. We risk becoming defensive and braced for rejection. These doubts about our worth may also hinder our ability to appreciate other people as individuals.[37]

Third, the rising demand for romantic expertise, and the division of romantic life into spheres of competence, including emotional competence, means we are trying increasingly to seem confident and secure rather than 'needy'.[38] Neediness can be viewed as a burden from the perspective of the pure relationship ideal, in which we evaluate each other in terms of what we each contribute to a relationship. Detachment can also appear sensible when we are unsure whether a date will lead to something more, or whether they really like us.

Fourth, we are prone to monitor ourselves. How vulnerable should we be? How much personality is it wise to show? Romantic life involves strategizing and self-awareness as we question how much risk we are prepared to embrace in the pursuit of intimacy.

Curiously, Illouz thinks that these forms of 'negative' relating have 'no moral implications'.[39] To me, however, they sound troubling (not to mention exhausting). We should worry, I think, if modern romantic practices or norms make it harder for us to attend to other people as individuals. This attention is central to plausible accounts of what romantic love involves.[40] It also seems central to good sexual interactions.[41]

Strategies of detachment are also likely to hinder intimacy and alienate us from a valuable aspect of human interaction. Signalling detachment to someone is rarely helpful when we *are* attached to them, and hiding neediness in contexts of genuine need only makes our lives harder, and lonelier. If our attempts to withdraw become habitual, they can morph into what I would call romantic irony, where we hold the joys and disappointments of romantic life at arm's length and resist becoming emotionally invested or vulnerable.

Alternatively, we might get trapped in tiring efforts to stand out from the crowd and make ourselves seem like a good romantic match. It is hard to change our appearance, harder to change our character, harder still to adjust our social position, and impossible to alter our history. These efforts also risk turning our attention away from other people or the positive features of our situation.

The coping strategies which Illouz regards as central to modern romantic life look to me to be examples of what Lisa Tessman calls 'moral damage'.[42] We are morally damaged when we develop traits that help us to cope with an oppressive social context, but in ways which make it harder for us to lead flourishing lives. She notes that we cannot guarantee that 'society equips individuals with the tools to be competent members of it'.[43]

Tessman's work focuses on societies marred by racial or sexual oppression, but her general ideal can be adapted to any context where norms and practices are entrenched. To be clear, this is not to suggest that the personal impact of romantic norms is as severe as that of racial norms, nor to overlook the ways that these norms intersect.[44]

Moral damage takes at least three forms: we can fail to develop a useful trait or virtue, such as compassion; we can manifest a helpful trait too much, or in the wrong contexts, like caution; and we can develop a trait or habit which undermines our wider flourishing, such as jealousy or romantic irony.

Romantic coping strategies, such as vigilance about our appearance, efforts to not appear needy, or attempts to shape our personality to suit our date's interests, look like forms of moral damage, especially as they become habitual. They may be useful strategies aimed at finding and keeping a partner in the messy world of modern love, but they can hinder access to the kinds of good things having a romantic partner is supposed to involve, from good communication in moments of vulnerability, to self-confidence, generous attention, or the absence of competitiveness.

Not everyone is morally damaged in the same way or extent. People with greater romantic privilege can navigate romantic uncertainty more easily; either they have the resources to do so, or they simply face less uncertainty. People with less privilege, due to gender, class, ability, or appearance, will have to work harder to try to stand out, accept greater risk of harm, or become more used to rejection.

Moral damage in romantic life is made worse by the rigidity of the three core romantic norms. Many of us try to respect these norms, and seek exclusive romantic relationships, but find our desires or character do not align easily with contemporary romantic practices and the self-management strategies required to navigate them.

Democracy

Illouz paints a gloomy picture of modern romance. But we should evaluate her view with care. On the one hand, she wrongly downplays the negative moral implications of the dynamics she identifies. 'Negative relations' do risk alienating us from important forms of human interaction and intimacy. On the other hand, however, there are also positive aspects to modern love.

For one thing, hindsight will likely show that some of the problems mentioned above are just transitional issues. New technologies and romantic practices are always confusing and raise concerns but we adapt quickly, and new rituals emerge to help us navigate uncertainty. Recent empirical work into online dating, for example, shows it has not eroded committed relationships as previously feared.[45] Neither have these new practices done much to change the core romantic norms we endorse, or to expand the relatively narrow scope of our attractions.

More importantly, we should not ignore why the ideal of the pure relationship seems appealing. One way to do this is to explore the position of Anthony Giddens, who initially gave voice to this conception of romantic life.[46]

Giddens thought there might be a reciprocal connection between democratic social change and romantic change. He adheres to a substantive conception of political democracy which incorporates ideas from moral perfectionism – the idea that certain goods make human lives go well – and from republican political thought, which is concerned with how the ability to interfere in people's lives, called 'domination', restricts our freedom. For him, democracy is a process which helps us to develop our abilities and potential; reduces coercion and domination; helps us to decide how we want to relate to other people; and expands our opportunities.[47] In simple terms, democratic processes can help us direct our lives as we see fit; they are agency enhancing.

Giddens suggests romantic life has the potential to become democratic in an analogous way to social life. The very ideal of the pure relationship involves a sense of us and our partners as autonomous and equal, at least in the sense that we are participating in the relationship because it benefits us personally. Our relationships are also their 'own forum' because decisions about them are made by participants in the relationship, not by family or community.[48] Practically speaking, these discussions range over our goals and use of resources and so require us to consider each other in ways which help to exercise our agency. Giddens is clear that these interactions will not remove domination completely while society is patriarchal or tolerates emotional abuse.[49]

How does romantic life become more democratic for Giddens? Political democracies are organized around constitutions and institutions. These mechanisms set the parameters for people to meet and make decisions, and help to regulate disputes. Unsurprisingly, Giddens' description of the core mechanism in play in romantic life is more fluid than that of the political equivalent. He writes: 'All relationships which approximate to the pure form maintain an implicit "rolling contract" to which appeal may be made by either partner when situations arise felt to be unfair or oppressive. The rolling contract is a constitutional device which underlies, but it is also open to negotiation through, open discussion by partners about the nature of the relationship.'[50] Unlike other contracts, which are formalized in advance and referred to only when people dispute a breach, the rolling contract is its own subject and we can refer to it at any time. This is not to deny that more specific boundaries and rules will give a relationship its shape, or to suggest that we are constantly referring to the arrangement.

Giddens hoped that emotional modernity could be liberating and generate 'social relations formed through mutuality rather than through unequal power'.[51] As we have seen, Illouz doubts this is possible. She critiques Giddens for purportedly overlooking the impact of the pure relationship ideal, and being insufficiently attentive to how destabilizing it might be. She argued his emphasis on the rolling contract neglects the fact that men are typically more powerful than women; cannot accommodate the way modern internet technologies 'undermine or bypass the traditional cultural signposts of the stable will presupposed by contracts'; and is undermined by the 'specific type of entrepreneurial will' required by the romantic agent in a neoliberal society.[52]

Illouz's complaints strike me as uncharitable. Giddens is clear that the idea of the pure relationship as a rolling contract provides us with a minimal framework. As with political processes, actual romantic relationships require extensive practical work to add detail. How, exactly, shall we arrange things? What do we expect of each other? Who is doing the dishes? These are not simply trivial matters, either. Some romantic conversations concern our sense of the good, or our understanding of values such as commitment or respect.

Giddens is also clear that the pure relationship framework can inherit social difficulties. Romantic relationships can be scarred by unequal or oppressive social relations, diminished agency, or conflicting conceptions of the good. Similarly, the actual outcome of any discussion of the relationship framework depends on the abilities of the people involved. Our relationships can falter if we are poor communicators, domineering, or unwilling to be vulnerable.

In all this, romantic life and political democracy are alike: a specific framework is only as good as those operating within it, and the context in which it is situated. But this is not to detract from the value of the framework itself. There is truth in Giddens' optimism. The waning of traditional modes of romantic relating makes possible, even if it does not guarantee, more equal relationships. Similarly, changes to facilitate the pure relationship, and so to erode older laws which hold us in relationships long after we want to leave, help to reduce domination. If the relationship is its own forum, then there are more opportunities for us to voice our needs and desires, and to be recognized by our partners. In turn, the need for these interactions draws people closer and can foster trust and emotional intimacy.

Conclusion

Modern romantic life is complex, and presents us with opportunities for optimism as well as concern. Illouz is right that the shift to romantic modernity can leave us feeling uncertain and insecure. But this is not without moral implications. Moral damage, whereby our coping strategies or insecurity restrict our flourishing, is not good and should be avoided if possible.

Giddens is right that we now think of relationships largely on their own terms. They are frameworks for us, as romantic partners, and we have discretion to modify the framework. Our partners are our primary focus; we must consider them and it is to them we have to justify our position and choices. This is an advance over historical alternatives.

That said, ideology and reality collide here. The social processes which decoupled romance from social and familial relations have not fundamentally changed the fact that the exclusive amorous relationship, which provides a safe and socially acceptable place for sexuality, remains the social ideal.

Practically speaking, the close amorous relationship can feel remote. The ideal of pure relationship places the responsibility on us to make things *work* romantically, but it is easy to be work-shy. Most people know that relationships are open for reconsideration in principle, but want to avoid doing this in practice. Hence the appeal of compatibility: if only we can get it right at the beginning, find a suitable partner, our relationship will unfold nicely from there.

We are perhaps less work-shy as romantic consumers. Although Illouz overstates her criticism that Giddens' view presupposes a certain kind of person – an atomized, neoliberal, consumer-bargainer – it is certainly not hard to see that the ideal of the pure relationship will certainly appeal to, and benefit, someone who is looking for a good deal and who associates romantic satisfaction with ideas of possession or status.

But the ideal of the pure relationship and its democratic potential can be seen in a different way. Sometimes certain processes, like rowdy democratic conversations, create new forms of agency; they help us to acquire skills of justification and respectful disagreement. Romantic life can be viewed in a similar light. The appeal of the pure relationship is not that it offers a new arena in which old interests can be pursued, but that it offers a distinct kind of mutual endeavour which shapes our ability to be intimate. At least, that is a possibility I explore in this book.

Making sense of modern romance is not easy. In this chapter I described our starting point as one shaped by deeply anchored romantic norms and various facts about our nature. The rest of this book considers how we might respond to this starting point. Can we, for example, view romantic life in a way which reflects how other people might shape our agency for the better? Can we challenge the core romantic norms? Even if our desires remain steady, might we adopt a more relaxed posture towards exclusivity, the privileging of love, or the wariness of sexuality?

I think we can. The bulk of what comes next consists of an attempt to sketch out some traits, and a few practices and policy suggestions, which help us to approach romantic life in a constructive agency-focused manner. The rippling impact of romantic modernity, and the tensions visible between Illouz and Giddens, are unlikely to subside anytime soon. There are no workarounds, no definitive '10 rules for success in love'. Instead, I hope to persuade you to set wishful thinking aside. Romantic life will emerge as a domain of activity and the capacity for intimacy, a fragile bundle of skills. We should do all we can to nurture them, and we cannot do that alone.

2
Opening Up

... negative promises become important tools for creating ethical and agency-enhancing possibilities. (Quill Kukla (writing as Rebecca Kukla))[1]

Nonmonogamy

In this chapter I focus on the norm of monogamy. Of the three core romantic norms mentioned in the previous chapter, monogamy is perhaps the most entrenched. The status of monogamy as something 'natural' is less stable these days, but it remains widely held that if someone has a romantic partner in a loving relationship, then that relationship should be exclusive. This is so even if we are increasingly open to periods of sexual experimentation, having several partners throughout life, or people who thrive without any romantic partner.

That said, people who embrace nonmonogamy are often enthusiastic about its transformative possibilities. In addition to the greater opportunities for love, sex, and intimate friendship, advocates of nonmonogamous lifestyles stress the benefits of a more open approach to intimacy, more explicit forms of communication and boundary setting, and creative domestic arrangements.

My discussion is motivated by the gap between the status of monogamy as an entrenched norm, on the one hand, and the growing awareness of valuable alternatives to it, on the other hand. Discussions around nonmonogamy usually do one of two things. Either they starkly oppose these forms of life, suggesting one is morally superior or the other doomed to fail, or they assume the only real difference here is one of personal preference. I find both approaches unhelpful. The first approach keeps alive some dubious arguments and obscures important features common to monogamous and nonmonogamous relationships. The second approach obscures the ways our romantic agency might constrain the romantic lifestyle we are able to pursue.

In this chapter, I want to look beyond these debates in doing several things. First, I will address some criticisms of nonmonogamy which make it seem like some of the more harmful aspects of romantic modernity. I then address the view, expressed more frequently recently, that it is actually monogamous relationships that are morally problematic. What will become clear by the end of this discussion is that we need a better understanding of the ways different kinds of relationships shape our ability to be intimate with each other.

To begin with, a note on practicality. When I first started writing about nonmonogamy, people used to worry it was impractical. Over a decade later, it is increasingly untenable to think we should avoid nonmonogamy for that reason. We have a better sense that practicality is understood relative to the wider circumstances of our lives. If you value multiple relationships, nonmonogamy is no more impractical than having several jobs, niche hobbies, or a large blended family. Most people can cope with competing commitments and ensure their attention is not spread too thin.

Even if nonmonogamy was impractical, that fact would not give us a reason to reject it out of hand. Living a virtuous life, for example, may be impractical if you are surrounded by vicious people, but that does not count against it. Lots of sporting, artistic, or ascetic pursuits are impractical but intrinsically rewarding; indeed, we might value them *because* they are impractical if navigating constraints or dealing with challenges helps us to become better people.

Worries about practicality should always be put in context. Maintaining any relationship is difficult when we are working long hours at precarious jobs with insufficient leisure time, but few people would argue we should not have relationships. Instead, we would critique the social arrangements and political policies which marginalize intimacy.

In chapter 1, I suggested that some aspects of modern romantic life seem individualistic and consumerist. Here, we might worry that the desire for 'more' – whether that is partners, love, intimacy, sex – which underlies nonmonogamy will heighten these approaches to relationships. Specifically, we might be tempted to think wanting more makes us bad people, or prevents us attending to the people we already care about, or is only possible for the privileged and so undermines the democratic potential of modern romantic norms. Together, these are worries about agency: that nonmonogamy makes us individually and socially less able to pursue intimacy. I will now reply to these concerns.

Greed

Some people are greedy, but a nonmonogamous lifestyle is not evidence of greed. To see this, let us think more about what it is to be greedy. There are several different ways of understanding greed. Greed can be characterized in terms of what we *want*, and how we *act*. Greedy people both want more than others, and are often unwilling to share what they have.

This 'wanting more' is central to greed, but what it means needs clarifying, since we can ask: wanting more than what? Two subtly different answers are: 'more than what I need' and 'more than my share'. In turn, the notion of 'my share' is subject to different readings, the most common being in terms of fairness or equality.

Depending on our circumstances, our share of something can diverge from our needs. Mountaineers trapped during a storm might divide their last chocolate bar into equal pieces. Everyone needs more than what they get, but everyone gets the same. Bankers, in contrast, might receive an equal portion of an excessive bonus which far exceeds their needs. Is a mountaineer greedy to want more than one square? Is the banker greedy in accepting an equal cut?

Talk of need and fair shares also misses out another dimension to greed – namely, the desire to have *more than others*. This is a competitive, and not simply comparative, desire.[2] The mountaineer compares his square of chocolate to the idea of the whole bar, or multiple bars, and wants more. The banker looks at her base rate of pay, and wants more. But greed takes on a different character if the banker looks at her colleagues or friends and wants more than them. The latter inclination is social, comparative, and troublingly related to envy and *Schadenfreude*.[3]

Is the practice of nonmonogamy greedy in these senses? It seems implausible that people pursuing a socially stigmatized form of romantic life see themselves as competing with monogamous people. They have rejected the monogamy game altogether. This is not to deny that nonmonogamous people might compete with each other, however – one patriarch might brag to another about his wives, for example. But critics of nonmonogamy do not usually have those scenarios in mind.

What about the idea that nonmonogamous people are greedy in wanting more than they need? Mark Regnerus, for instance, suggests that 'people "need" multiple partners like they need four houses or six automobiles'.[4] We might think people should be satisfied with one romantic partner. (This thought can be especially tempting when we are that partner.) But the assumptions underlying this idea need examining.

First, we should be wary of possessive terminology in which partners, relationships, or intimate experiences are viewed as goods to be possessed. Our relationships and romantic interactions are dissimilar to a square of chocolate, or money in the bank. Relationships are formed *with* other people.

Worries about greed in romantic life also typically rest on a simplistic sense of need, and are marred by sex negativity. Possessive terminology is the legacy of patriarchy, in which some people – slaves, servants, women, children – are considered property. Possessive attitudes had traction in part due to ambivalent thinking about the subjective life of women. On the one hand, they were viewed as lacking something (rationality), but on the other hand, they were viewed as excessive (in emotion). They were objectified in terms of having no inner life,[5] or in terms of requiring others to silence and overlook their inner life.[6] These attitudes helped sustain systematic ignorance of women's actual sexual and romantic desires. It is a short step from being regarded as property, with your inner life denied, downplayed, or denigrated, to the idea that one romantic partner is enough for you. These attitudes persist.

To a lesser extent, worries about male desire also fed into the assumption that people only need one partner. Baron Montesquieu's eighteenth-century critique of polygamy, for example, partly rested on the idea that plural partners, far from satisfying desire, will catalyse it further into unending greed; that, 'it is as with lust as with avarice, where thirst increases by the acquisition of treasure'.[7] These attitudes also persist.

We should also be wary of making assumptions about romantic needs. As with talk of what is 'natural', talk of 'needs' is often an artifact of a particular social context where the interests of the powerful shape our expectations. In reality, our romantic needs vary. Aromantics live happily without any romantic relationships. Some people need more intimate support than others. Our life situation, personal history, and personality all vary.

Even if we did all need the same 'amount' of intimacy, it does not follow that we would best satisfy this need by having one romantic relationship with one person. One person may struggle to be present for us if our life is unsettled or precarious, or if we have many commitments. Even in a settled life, it is arguably harder to have all our needs satisfied by one person than if we were open to other people too. If we have multiple relationships, the satisfaction of our intimate needs is resilient or over-determined. We are also more likely to find different people who excel intimately in different ways, rather than one person excelling in every way. Someone who is emotionally articulate, for example, might not be a good domestic or sexual partner. If our intimate needs are complex, then multiple relationships may be better than one.

To be clear, in suggesting we can accept that romantic needs might vary I am not committing myself to a single view of what these needs are. I think we should be sceptical that such an account exists. For example, I am hesitant to embrace the idea that monogamous culture supresses an underlying 'polymorphous' sexual drive which would be unleashed – and presumably need to be satisfied – if cultural conditions changed.[8] These claims might be right about the repressive character of social norms and institutions, but their conception of human nature seems insufficiently pluralist. The waning of romantic repression would arguably make it easier for some people to lead lives where friendship is more important than sexual intimacy. We might speculate that individual needs for specific forms of intimacy will wane the more society loosens its grip on amatonormativity and nurtures intimacy of all kinds, because we will be less likely to view romantic relationships as refuges from oppressive social relations.

So far, I am suggesting that, before mentioning greed, we need to understand someone's needs and how they might be satisfied within their specific life circumstances. The idea of intimate needs is liable to be shaped by questionable assumptions about gender or human nature, and nonmonogamous lifestyles can help some people to satisfy their needs.

Talk of greed and need might seem to the miss the point, however, because we risk wrongly viewing relationships as containers of discrete goods about which we can ask distributional questions: has everyone got enough, is intimacy spread equally, should we redistribute? Romantic life is one domain where it feels strained to adopt this 'distributive paradigm'.[9]

We might also want to consider greed alongside sexual orientation. A common way of describing and thinking about nonmonogamy is to think of the configuration as enabling 'more' of something or other: more relationships, love, or sex. But nonmonogamy has also been described as a sexual orientation. Ann Tweedy, for example, argues we have good reason to think polyamory is sufficiently 'embedded' psychologically into the personal identity of polyamorous people for it to be akin to other forms of sexual orientation, like being gay or bisexual.[10]

The precise details of Tweedy's view are not relevant here, but what does matter are the implications of her claim for talk about greed. For if nonmonogamy is a sexual orientation – that is, if nonmonogamous people have a settled disposition towards relationships which are not monogamous and this disposition informs their identity – then the choice between a monogamous relationship and nonmonogamous relationships is not that between 'more' or 'less' of some good, and is instead the choice between two radically different outcomes. To be romantically satisfied, the polyamorist needs to be open to having multiple partners at the same time. If polyamory is a sexual orientation, then having a monogamous relationship is *not* satisfying, rather than simply being *less* satisfying. This means we cannot evaluate whether someone is greedy or not by looking at the form of relationship they prefer. Instead, we might have to look internally at their inclinations and behaviour in trying to act on their dispositions.

Put in terms of a crude analogy, nonmonogamy viewed this way is akin to the difference between two people – one who has a settled preference for apples, and the other for pears. An apple-lover might be more satisfied if they had two apples rather than one, and perhaps they would greedily hanker after all the apples on the tree, but they would not be satisfied with a pear. Vice versa for the pear-lover. We cannot establish that someone is greedy because they favour apples over pears, but we might be able to judge that one apple-lover is greedy and another not.

Personally, I am ambivalent about extending orientation-talk to nonmonogamy.[11] But this approach cautions us against simplification or thinking we can isolate distinct goods which are common in different kinds of relationship. Of course, we often talk of love, intimacy, and sex as if they were discrete and quantifiable, but there is also a real sense in which a polyamorous person with two simultaneous relationships differs from someone with two relationships at different times, or a monogamous relationship with double the intimacy (whatever that might mean). I explore some of these differences in chapter 4.

A final aspect of greed is worth mentioning, and that is the reluctance to share. This language obviously risks retaining the idea that romantic partners are possessions. But if we ignore that implication, we see that lots of nonmonogamous romance involves situations in which someone has a relationship with a person who themselves has intimate relationships with others. This can be viewed as a kind of sharing which monogamous norms try to restrict. So, if resisting greed is resisting the impulse to hoard and keep to oneself, then nonmonogamous intimacy fares better than monogamous intimacy.

None of this is to deny that some nonmonogamous people are greedy. But it is mistaken to think nonmonogamy as such requires us to be greedy, to have more than we need or more than we deserve. Talk of greed oversimplifies the complicated and often frustrating situations that we find ourselves in, while masking the undercurrents of possessiveness inherent in some forms of monogamy.

Unfairness

Some concerns about greed in romantic life are better described as worries about fairness which focus on the consequences of our actions, rather than our character. For instance, we might fear that if a growing polyamorous minority have several relationships at the same time, it will be harder for everyone else to have one relationship.

Mark Regnerus, for example, thinks of monogamy that 'no other form of organizing relationships between the sexes does a better job of fostering fair exchange between the distinct interests of men and women'.[12] This system apparently 'allows for more winners' because monogamy 'reduces competition among men for women, which functions to reduce the pool of low-status, risk-oriented, unmarried men'.[13] Regnerus views modern forms of polyamory, in contrast, as presenting a kind of 'free rider problem' where a minority 'flout (but still benefit from the fruits of) the trust, fidelity, and stability exhibited by the vast majority of couples'.[14]

Regnerus' language and assumptions are heteronormative and patriarchal. Queer women might wonder where they fit in his worldview. We should also resist the reduction of romantic life to a domain of resource, risk, and reward. But, since it is quite common, I will examine his underlying worry.

Regnerus thinks that monogamy, with its one-to-one pairings in exclusive romantic relationships, gives all of us the best chance of finding a romantic partner. We might term this way of thinking the 'dance-hall model' of romantic life. On this view, societies are better to the extent that fewer people are excluded from romantic relationships. We can motivate this idea in different ways; perhaps we are concerned about the lives of those people who fail to find partners, or perhaps, as in Regnerus' case, we have more general concerns about social stability.

Versions of the latter argument are often directed at polygamy, where one person is married to several other people.[15] But the concern applies to any settled romantic relationship, whether it involves marriage or not. The general thought centres on status and stability: the rich and powerful have more partners, the poor and weak have fewer partners, and this will destabilize society and perhaps even impede democracy as the latter resent and struggle against the former.[16] Andrew March calls this reasoning the 'Lockean Proviso' argument, after John Locke's argument that we can come to have ownership of things, in a situation before governments existed, as long as we leave a sufficient amount of them left over for others to enjoy.[17] The worry is that nonmonogamous people violate this proviso in having several partners at the same time. They are like settlers who take all the food or water, leaving none for others.

It is not hard to see that this is a shaky line of reasoning. For starters, these arguments assume we live in a homogeneous heterosexual society. Talk of polygamy, for example, is usually actually talk of poly*gyny*, in which one man has several wives, and not poly*andry*, where one woman marries several men, or other marital dynamics as might exist between lesbians or polyamorous bisexuals. (Although I suspect many critics of plural marriage would not be happy with those unions either.)

Still, we could modify the argument to be more inclusive. We might worry that lesbian women who want monogamous relationships, for example, are more likely to be left out if other lesbians embrace polyamory or open relationships. Indeed, we might think the underlying issue here, visible in the dance-hall way of thinking, is more pressing in queer communities, which are smaller than heterosexual communities. So it is important to tackle the concern directly.

It is helpful first to consider some of March's points aimed at polygamy even though my main focus here is on the ethical nature of different relationships, not on legal questions surrounding the recognition and regulation of marriages.

One way of considering what the state should permit and support is to think about what rights we have. We can distinguish loosely between negative and positive rights. The former leave us free from interference. For example, I have a negative right against you stealing my water bottle. The latter, however, are rights to certain kinds of aid or provision. If we think there is a right to water, say, then you have a right to access water and I might have a duty to provide you with some.

Let us assume for the sake of argument that we have negative rights when in romantic relationships with consenting adults: that other people should not interfere. (Historically, this has not been upheld, as gays and lesbians can attest.) March asks: do we have a *positive* right to a romantic relationship, such that some entity like the state has a duty to provide one or to protect us against the actions of others which might frustrate our chances?[18] He observes that we typically do not think we have a positive right to marriage; the state does not have to provide us with a partner. Nor is it easy to see how this right would be enforced without invasiveness or violating basic freedoms.

Still, we might be tempted to think that state intervention is justified if a social practice makes it difficult for us to arrange our lives in valuable ways. This is not a contentious idea; we often think the state should support us in our search for flourishing. But March points out that intervention seems justified only when a social practice, such as nonmonogamy, makes it difficult to a point of an 'extreme level of deprivation' for other people to find a romantic partner.[19] Writing of polygamy, March thinks it is implausible to suggest that its legalization will have this extreme social impact. For one thing, few people currently want polygamous marriages. For another, it would be equally available to women who want to marry multiple men, and to people who are not heterosexual, and so its overall impact is unlikely to be disproportionate.

These points apply to romantic relationships other than marriages. If there is no positive right to those relationships, it seems that intervention is justified only if a social arrangement significantly disadvantages a minority. March points out that this kind of worry is not like other concerns around the fair distribution of resources. Instead, he suggests that the concern about the social impact of us being able to have multiple relationships is akin to saying: 'if many people acted at the same time on this right *which we don't think most will actually find desirable* then this could be *frustrating for an unspecified number of left-out people*'.[20] It seems wrong to prevent us from doing something conducive to our flourishing by appealing to the as-yet-unclear impact our intimate choice might have on an unknown number of other people. An analogy: if thousands of people exercised their right to walk on a remote mountain trail, their collective actions might frustrate those people who wanted to hike the trail in solitude, or together they might degrade the environment. But awareness of this remote possibility is not sufficient to stop me from walking on the trail now. Restrictions are justified when they are relevant.

I will offer two more general considerations about the potential role of the state in addition to March's points about the existence of a positive right to a romantic relationship, and the uncertain outcome surrounding the impact of allowing plural relationships. Then I will add some further considerations about unfairness and access to intimacy.

People who argue that nonmonogamy has unfair social implications typically assume that monogamous norms are neutral in terms of their impact on other people – that deviations from monogamy need justifying. This is a mistake. Single people, asexuals, aromantics, and all forms of the nonmonogamous could just as well point out that the social favouring of monogamous amorous relationships makes it harder for them to live as they want. Those who embrace the dance-hall approach to romantic life fixate on the hypothetical worry that monogamous people will miss out, while ignoring the fact that single people, or people with unconventional romantic and sexual preferences, are *already* missing out. If fairness in romantic life is important, then the perspective of these people needs to be given the same weight as the perspective of monogamous people. (And this is before we consider whether being subject to historical injustice means we should give greater weight to the interests of some over others – a view we might think applies to the plight of those whose romantic flourishing has been restricted by monogamous norms.)

How might we consider everyone's romantic flourishing fairly? One approach might be to apply John Rawls' 'veil of ignorance' to romantic life.[21] To do this, we engage in a thought experiment and ask ourselves: how would we organize society if we did not know what our sexual orientation, preferences, or identity would be, nor which forms of life would help us flourish romantically? To me it seems clear we would be less inclined to adopt restrictive romantic norms or have the state inhibit certain forms of romantic relationships if we could not assume we would be relatively privileged monogamous heterosexuals.

This is not the place for an extended discussion of this thought experiment and its implications. Instead, let us consider two responses Regnerus could make. He might argue that the impediments faced by single people and the nonmonogamous are insignificant, or he might try to balance them against the social benefits of restrictions.

Both options weaken the initial worry about fairness in romantic life. The first option, downplaying the impediments, commits us to the view that we need only worry about the social impact of a form of romantic life when it has a big impact on a group. To be consistent, we would have to apply this reasoning to the impact of permitting nonmonogamous relationships. We could only restrict them if allowing them would have a big impact on the monogamous. At the moment, we have reason to doubt this.

The second option, trying to balance the benefits and harms arising from enabling some forms of romantic life and not others also moves the debate into the empirical realm. We would have to look carefully at the wider impact of promoting monogamous norms at the expense of other kinds of intimacy, and take seriously the place of single people, asexuals, aromantics, and the nonmonogamous. These considerations should not be merely quantitative, i.e., solely a question of how many people of each social group would be impacted, because we are already approaching this discussion from a position where certain relationships are favoured and others are supressed. We would also have to consider how many more people *would be* identifying as aromantic, say, if our society was not so amatonormative, mononormative, and sex-negative.

Another way to notice the ways monogamy is presupposed in discussions of fairness and romantic life is to entertain again, for argument's sake, the idea that we have a positive right to a relationship. Stated in this general way, this right is left unspecified. It could be fulfilled in different ways: by having a relationship with a couple, or someone of the same sex, or with a polyamorous person. Without additional argument to fix the content of the right to a relationship, why assume it is a right to a traditional monogamous relationship?

Suppose we went further, however, to say that the right of a relationship is understood as a right to a relationship with one person – this still falls short of that relationship being *exclusive*. The dance-hall conception of romantic life, which lies beneath worries about scarcity and people being left out, actually helps us to recognize the potential benefits of thinking this right should not be understood in terms of exclusive relationships. There is a big difference between making sure everyone has a dance partner, and saying that everyone has to have one and only one partner. In an actual dance-hall, we might dance with more than one other partner; partners might shift and change; some might sit out a song; groups can dance together.

Someone like Regnerus might finally protest that the right we are considering is to have a romantic relationship of the kind we desire. Aside from the difficulties of making sense of how the corresponding duties would be upheld, and by whom, notice this is a view that nonmonogamous people should happily agree with, and one that dissolves the force of the initial objection.

All this talk of rights and the state can make it hard to focus on the underlying issue: namely, worries about the social impact of enabling people to have unconventional relationships. Most of the discussion so far has centred on a worry about scarcity; nonmonogamous people are viewed as intimacy hoarders who will destabilize society. I have suggested that for this worry to have force, we often have to presuppose a monogamous outlook. But concerns about the social impact of nonmonogamy on the availability of partners are not the only issue. We can also consider the impact of social change on our attitudes or ideals.

Some social changes which make it harder for some groups to find a romantic partner might be good. As I first wrote this chapter, for example, I stumbled across an article in the popular *Psychology Today* titled 'The Rise of Lonely, Single Men'.[22] Rising loneliness is bad, but the author suggests one reason for this is that women are raising their relationship standards to 'prefer men who are emotionally available, who are good communicators, and who share their values'. Against a historical context in which women's desires and interests have been overlooked, these social changes are surely positive. It is hard to lament male loneliness if it arises because women are no longer settling for unsatisfying lives of their own, just as we are unlikely to shed a tear for slum landlords who find it hard to find tenants when building standards rise and regulations change. A full understanding of male loneliness needs to be formed in the context of loneliness in general, which would include the loneliness of many women trapped in unfulfilling relationships with emotionally distant male partners.

There is another important dimension to fairness in romantic life. Worries about supply of partners, and the implicit dance-hall model of romantic life, neglect the separate but important matter of what our relationships are actually like once they are under way. Finding a partner is only a small part of romantic life; arguably, the most important question concerns the nature of our relationships and how we are treated by other people. To return to the dance-hall analogy again, there is no point patterning people up if some people do not like dancing, or dance in different ways, or end up with harmful partners. If this is right, and if the state does have some role in facilitating romantic life, then this role is not unqualified. The quality of our relationships must be considered alongside the question of how easy it is to find a partner. Most people, I suspect, would rather it were harder to find a partner but easier to have a good relationship with a partner they do find, than it being easy to find a partner with whom they will have a bad relationship. This seems especially likely when people are monogamous and so want to find only one partner for an exclusive relationship.

So far, I have been responding to worries about the social impact of nonmonogamy, but there are positive dimensions to this change too. I will highlight two of these dimensions: one about the ease of finding partners, the other about the nature of relationships with the partners we find.

First, finding partners. If more people embraced nonmonogamy, this would arguably have a positive impact on our ability to have romantic relationships. The more we are open to different forms of romantic intimacy, the less restrictive the 'dating pool' becomes because we do not have to exclude people already in relationships or people who are open to unconventional forms of relationship. If we are able to experience multiple forms of intimacy at the same time, the pressure to find one person who excels in most areas of life would reduce. This means that people who do not want an exclusive relationship, or a domestic relationship, or to raise children, or who are in some other way not regarded as 'marriage material', would be more likely to find romantic partners.

Second, the nature of relationships. Relationship norms would likely change in a society where nonmonogamous romance is more common. We would be more realistic about the ways we can contribute to each other's happiness and less concerned if we are not romantic superstars, or if we do not want domesticity, cohabitation, or a family. Weakening mononormativity helps us to resist the temptation to view partners as scarce resources to be protected, and helps us to focus instead on the quality of our relationships and the individuality of our partners. When, as a society, we are less captivated by romantic ideals of 'the one', and the hopes associated with compatibility culture, we will find it easier to resist dismissive comparisons and rivalrous insecurity.

These social changes would of course be gradual, and their overall social impact remains unclear. But we should be careful not to assume at the outset that only a minority would benefit. Current evidence is patchy, but using the contemporary United States as an indicator, there are clear signs that many people are dissatisfied with monogamous romantic culture as it manifests on dating apps;[23] that a significant minority of people have experimented with nonmonogamy;[24] that nearly a fifth of Americans are bisexual, but only a small minority feel able to be open about that fact;[25] and that more people are single than ever before.[26] When we add to this the number of people who are asexual or aromantic,[27] or who have intimate friendships, or wish casual sex was less stigmatized, or who would want to organize their lives around friends rather than romantic partners,[28] then it is not hard to see that a large number of people stand to benefit from changing social attitudes. And this is before we consider the people who might experience new romantic desires as a result of social change.

We have little reason to fear social changes which make society more accepting of unconventional forms of romantic life. Worries about the ease of finding a partner, or the fairness of society, hold only if we make some dubious assumptions or overlook the benefits of social change. Many hostile arguments around this topic trade on references to polygamy, which is a poorly understood, stigmatized, and anyway marginal practice. These arguments and their advocates overlook the people who stand to benefit greatly from social change right now. Finally, everyone stands to benefit from a society in which mononormativity is less strong as they are better able to choose the relationship form which suits them, free of social pressure.

Monogamy

More people are becoming comfortable with the idea that there is nothing troubling about nonmonogamous relationships. If they help some people to flourish, they should be celebrated. Some want to go further, however, and argue that it is actually monogamy which is not morally permissible.

This idea may seem clearly wrong. After all, what is bad about two people agreeing to be together as long as the other person's affections are exclusive? If their agreement is consensual, and formed freely, it appears to be an exercise of their autonomy and an expression of their intimate preferences. There is value in looking seriously at this more radical claim, however, as it helps us to appreciate some important dimensions of romantic life and will set up my discussion of romantic agency in the next chapter.

Harry Chalmers is one person who has recently argued that monogamy is not morally permissible. His core reason for thinking this is that the monogamy norm is restrictive in a problematic way because it prevents us from accessing valuable goods while offering no corresponding benefits. Chalmers motivates his position with an analogy:

> Imagine that two partners are in a romantic relationship, and that they are also (or perhaps *a fortiori*) friends. Yet theirs is not a typical relationship, for the partners have agreed on a most unusual restriction: Neither is allowed to have additional friends. Should either partner become friends with someone besides the other, the other partner will refuse to support it – indeed, will go so far as to withdraw her love, affection, and willingness to continue the relationship. Many of us, I think, would sense that there's something morally troubling about such a relationship. If asked to explain what's morally troubling about it, we might say something like this: Friendships are an important human good, and when we're in a romantic relationship with someone, we should want our partner to have such goods in her life. Or at least, we should want our partner to be free to pursue such goods as she sees fit.[29]

Clearly, we are meant to be troubled by this restriction on a partner having additional friends. Chalmer's basic thought is that romantic restrictions are no different and should also trouble us. Chalmer's argument can be summarized as follows:

1. Monogamy involves a 'categorical restriction' on someone having more than one amorous relationship at once.
2. Amorous relationships are important human goods, because they contribute to well-being.
3. Restricting someone's access to important human goods is morally impermissible, unless justified in virtue of some further good-making feature.
4. There are no good-making features to monogamous restrictions.
5. So, monogamy is morally impermissible.

By 'categorical restriction', Chalmers has in mind the idea our romantic partners will not support and may actively leave relationships where we want nonexclusivity. The notion of human goods he appeals to is broad, and romantic relationships contain goods like 'sexual pleasure', 'a special kind of emotional support and closeness', forms of self-awareness, and other kinds of intimacy.[30]

Chalmers concludes that we should be nonmonogamous. If you are reading this and worrying about what this means for you and your partner, do not worry, drastic action is not required. Chalmers does not mean that we must have multiple relationships at the same time; instead, we must remain '*open* to having multiple relationships at a time'.[31] This means we should not restrict our partners, or ourselves, from becoming intimate with other people. As Justin Clardy has pointed out, Chalmers' argument also applies with equal force to exclusive nonmonogamous relationships, like some triads or polycules.[32]

Chalmers' argument seems simple, but it can be hard to unpack what is driving our intuitions about his example. Monogamy cannot be bad because in practising it we miss out on some valuable goods or experiences. Most life choices, from choosing dishes at a restaurant, weighing up competing job offers, or even focusing our life around one group of friends rather than another, prevent us from experiencing other good things. Romantic life is no exception.

We also do not want to be beholden to the demanding assumption that we must try to *maximize* the romantic goods we experience. I share the popular intuition that our personal relationships are not subject to those maximizing considerations. I would certainly resent being dumped by someone who thinks their next relationship would yield them a marginal gain. The problem exposed by the friendship analogy is not that we are settling for less.

Finally, we would also seem to miss the point Chalmers is making by offering serial monogamy as a solution. We might be tempted to compromise and suggest that restrictions within relationships are fine as long as we have enough relationships, and so experience enough intimate goods within our lives as a whole. This sly response seems to miss the point Chalmers is really concerned with – namely, that monogamous relationships themselves seem restrictive.

Thankfully, Chalmers clarified his position in a later article. He stressed that his main concern with monogamy is that it shuts us off from goods that are *significantly* important, that these restrictions involve an extensive loss of individual freedom, and not complying with monogamy restrictions is very costly.[33] This emphasis on freedom is crucial for what follows.

Before offering my own evaluation of his argument, I want to highlight an important but obvious feature of Chalmers' analogy, and monogamy generally, which is that the restrictions we face appear to be imposed on us by other people, rather than external factors. We are *withheld* from valued goods, not simply unable to attain them, and this is a significant difference. This distinguishes the frustrations which stem from monogamy from those associated with being single and struggling to find a partner in a small town.

Chalmers adopts a simple argumentative strategy in discussing monogamy. First, he commits to the premise that we are permitted to withhold each other from valued goods only if we somehow benefit each other in doing so. Then he claims that monogamy has no such benefits.

For the sake of argument, I will not contest Chalmers' underlying premise, and focus instead on his suggestion that monogamy has no distinct benefits. This is likely to be news to many monogamous people and is worth considering.

Chalmers arrives at this conclusion after considering some candidate benefits of monogamy. In a wide-ranging discussion he rejects the idea that monogamous relationships are distinctly special, are more sexually healthy, provide the best environment to raise children, are more practical than nonmonogamous relationships, and are the only relationships that can shield us from jealousy.

I find Chalmers convincing on these points, and his arguments resonate with some I have explored in other writing.[34] There is at best a loose relationship between monogamous relationships and these outcomes. I am sure you can think of a monogamous couple whose relationship does not seem particularly special to the people concerned, or sexually healthy, or good for children, or practical, or free of jealousy. Where monogamy does seem to have an advantage, perhaps in terms of practicality or the raising of children, this is attributable to the unjustified stigma and state interference nonmonogamous couples experience.

The obvious question, then, is: are monogamous restrictions good in some other sense? A different strategy is to suggest there are beneficial *indirect* connections between monogamy and various goods. Natasha McKeever offers an influential argument for this view.

Like me, McKeever is sceptical about any privileged connection between romantic exclusivity and love, specialness and intimacy. She does not think monogamous relationships are morally better, and nor does she think they fare well when it comes to avoiding jealousy. She is also clear that people should choose monogamy carefully, after considering alternatives.

That said, she argues that monogamous exclusivity has 'supportive value in a romantic relationship, and can act as a symbol for, and expression of, the exclusive shared identity that is distinctive to romantic love, as well as partly constituting and building it. [Sexual exclusivity] can help lovers to reaffirm the value of their exclusive shared identity and life by marking their relationship out as distinct from other relationships.'[35] McKeever focuses on sexual exclusivity but much of her argument also applies to emotional exclusivity. She concedes that we could do other things to distinguish our romantic life from other relationships, but she thinks the social significance attributed to sex means it is well suited to this function.

To my mind, McKeever captures the fact that we might value exclusivity ourselves while understanding it is not required to thrive romantically. I am not sure, however, that exclusivity *should* have the functions McKeever ascribes to it, so it is hard to appeal to it as a benefit which justifies the other restrictions of monogamy. Here is why I think this.

One concern is whether we should be trying to distinguish our romantic relationships from our friendships. The desire to do so stems from amatonormativity, the idea that amorous relationships are more important than friendships and warrant social recognition. But if we reject that premise, as I think we should, the need to distinguish relationship types is less strong.

A related point concerns the symbolic value of sexual exclusivity on both practical and moral grounds. Practically, there is little social value in affirming a relationship through its most private feature – namely, sex. (I accept this argument applies less to people who have public sex.) More visible markers of specialness, perhaps a shared address or matching surnames or tattoos, would have a greater impact. In fact, the symbolic value of sexual exclusivity is of limited value even to ourselves because we cannot verify that our relationships are exclusive. All we can do is trust our partners and believe what they say. But if we are willing to do that, then we can also believe them when they say, 'this relationship is special to me, and different from my other relationships', without the need for any exclusivity at all.

Morally, it strikes me that we should also be wary of marking relationships through features which have an oppressive history. Sexual exclusivity is a notion linked to male possessiveness and control over female sexuality. If McKeever is right that we are free to stamp our loving shared identities symbolically in different ways, then we should choose ones which lack negative expressive significance. Taken further, we could even try to mark the specialness of our relationship in a way aimed at redressing these injustices – perhaps by supporting a partner in the unrestricted exploration of their sexual identity as a marker of a special emotional bond.

This idea is reinforced by the simple point that exclusive sex, or exclusive relationships, are not good simply *because* they are exclusive. Such a fact is extrinsic: it concerns the connections between the relationship and other people or relationships. What matters is what the relationship itself is like. You would doubt your relationship was special if all your partner could say in favour of it was that it is exclusive. They would be like someone who thinks a painting is good because they are the only person who can look at it.

These points count against the idea that exclusivity might 'partly constitute' the specialness or uniqueness of a relationship, but maybe what McKeever has in mind is the idea that special relationships, ones we already value, are those we can justly make exclusive. Kyle York also holds this view.[36] Approached in this way, however, monogamy does not have distinct benefits of its own which justify these restrictions. Instead, these restrictions are permitted because the relationship is special for other reasons. Finally, and more bluntly, this idea seems strange to me. Special things which we value, revere, or find beautiful are worth sharing, not restricting. Elaine Scarry, for example, thinks that experiences of beauty exert pressure 'towards the distributional', in the sense that they make us want to turn to others, to speak, to share, to show, and to celebrate.[37] We should approach talk of 'sharing' people or relationships with caution, of course, as I have already criticized possessive language and the notion that intimacy is a good to be distributed. That said, there is force in the idea that there is something awry in the desire to hoard or hide the things we find special.

Freedom

So far, this discussion is strengthening Chalmers' claim that there are no distinct benefits of monogamous exclusivity. But I think he might have overlooked something. To appreciate what I have in mind, I propose we change how we think about the restrictions we place on each other in our relationships – instead of barriers to good things, how might they facilitate our romantic agency?

I suspect the restrictions in Chalmers' friendship analogy strikes us as troubling because of how extreme and encompassing they are. I suspect we would be less concerned if the restrictions were more targeted, or had a clear rationale. We can imagine cases where someone asks us not to be friends with a specific person, like our partner's abusive ex-partner, or their overbearing boss; or not to be friends with a specific group of people, such as misogynists or Trump supporters; or to avoid additional relationships for a set period of time, such as until our partner has recovered from their illness.

Limited restrictions like these seem more reasonable for several reasons. First, they leave us with sufficient options to form other friendships, or friendships at other times in our life. If we do miss out, the loss is not extensive. Second, heeding these restrictions looks like a way of showing we care about our friend and we respect their interests. Heeding them might demonstrate our loyalty and affection.

Most significantly, these restrictions help us to maintain and potentially increase our romantic agency. I started seeing romantic restrictions in this way when I was exploring a related exchange between Halle Liberto and Quill Kukla about the nature of sexual promises.

Halle Liberto wants to argue that sexual promises seem impermissible. She first considers cases where someone promises to have sex with us.[38] She thinks these examples are morally problematic. It would be wrong of you to accept the promise as this would give you the power to decide whether they do something potentially burdensome. We might quibble about the best way to analyse these examples, but most people find this thought rather obvious; because sex is involved, we would be wrong to take such a 'promise' seriously. But Liberto also argues, much less obviously, that we would be similarly wrong to promise to a partner to never have sex with other people in a so-called 'monogamy promise' of the kind spouses might make on their wedding day.

Liberto's underlying thought is that some promises are 'over-extensive' and so should not be accepted. Her examples of these include promises to act immorally, promises which are too burdensome to perform, and promises whose 'content is of the wrong kind to be transferred to another person's discretionary control'.[39] She thinks sexual promises are of the third kind: we should not accept them because it would be wrong for us to assume moral authority over someone's sexual life.

In a rich article on sexual negotiation, Quill Kukla offers a brief but interesting response to Liberto's argument. Kukla concedes that some sexual promises, such as monogamy promises, can be over-extensive and so wrongly restrict us. They then observe, however, that 'if we look at more fine-grained sexual negotiations, negative promises become important tools for creating ethical and agency-enhancing possibilities'.[40]

Sexual examples make Kukla's claim seem obvious. If you ask someone to promise not to choke you during sex, or to tie you up, or tickle you, or call you by a nickname you hate, you expect them to take you seriously. You do not expect them to try and negotiate or complain that they are missing out. As Kukla puts it, 'the fact that keeping [these promises] might compromise [their] own bodily pleasure or sexual agency is morally irrelevant'.[41] You want to be taken seriously because these restrictions on others help make intimacy possible for you. They enable you to be open to sexual touch without worry, and so help you feel comfortable about being vulnerable with someone.

Kukla's point is not simply that the limits established by these promises help to protect our existing agency. They also think that 'establishing such limits, constraints, and stopping points actually increases the space of sexual possibilities and enhances sexual agency for everyone concerned'.[42] Again, this seems right from both directions. On the one hand, if we have confidence that our partner will not violate our boundaries, then we feel more secure, which helps us to relax or explore. On the other hand, our partners benefit from the clarity these restrictions provide since they carve out a defined space of permissible action. Finally, the activity of communicating to someone and securing these promises itself helps to generate trust and intimacy.

Kukla is discussing sexual promises in the context of a broader argument about sexual ethics. They make the important point that, in focusing on whether or not we have consented to sex in general, we overlook the important question of what it is we are actually consenting to, and how we want sex to proceed.[43] A similar point could be levelled at some of the disputes between proponents of monogamous or nonmonogamous romantic life: focusing on whether such a lifestyle is restrictive or not detracts from the more important question as to what those restrictions are, how they come about, and how they function.

Crucially, I think Kukla's point about negative sexual promises can be applied to romantic life more generally. Chalmers and Liberto might be right that broad restrictions on our romantic lives are morally problematic (whether or not we understand this in terms of promises), but this should not detract from the significant ways in which more specific, circumscribed, or temporary restrictions help us to protect and build our romantic agency.

We can build on this thought by returning to the idea of freedom in romantic life alluded to in my discussion of Chalmers' friendship analogy. Chalmers worries that monogamy restricts our freedom to access important intimate goods by placing barriers in our way; if we try to access them, perhaps by striking up another relationship with someone, our existing partnership will be strained and our partner may leave us. This chain of events is also socially expected and supported.

Chalmers seems right in his description of what often happens when people voice their desire for less monogamous lifestyles. But, in general terms, freedom is a more complex notion than his approach suggests. Appreciating this complexity has implications for how we think about romantic life. To help explain what I have in mind here, we need a brief detour through contemporary republican thinking about freedom.[44]

First, the name. 'Republican' accounts of freedom have nothing to do with Trump and his followers, and take their name from the conception of civic liberty found in the Roman republic, and those subsequently inspired by that period. I will not be arguing independently for the truth of republicanism as a theory; I reach for it here as a useful framework to organize our thinking about freedom, or kinds of freedom. To my mind, republican theorists do a good job of capturing the complex dimensions of our several different and interlocking ideas of freedom.

Philip Pettit is the main contemporary exponent of republican theory. He argues that to be free: (1) we must have the 'room and resources' to be able to act as we wish; (2) the first condition must apply to different possible actions we might take, not just the one we happen to *want*; and (3) our actions are not constrained by what others may want us to do.[45] I will explain what he has in mind, before turning to romantic life.

Petitt's first condition captures the idea that freedom has to be 'real freedom'.[46] Real freedom itself consists of two things. First, other people do not meddle with us (this is often called negative freedom); and second, we must actually have the resources to pursue our goals (this is often called positive freedom). We have the real freedom to fish the river, for example, only if others do not restrict us *and* if we have the abilities, time, and resources to do so. Our lack of a licence, or rod, or the surefootedness needed to walk down the uneven banks could all rob us of real freedom, even if no one would physically stop us from fishing.

As it will be important later, it is useful to clarify that Pettit has a broad account of resource which includes *personal* resources such as the 'mental and bodily ability or knowhow' needed to make a choice; the *natural* resources of a receptive environment; and the *social* resources of infrastructure, institutions, norms, and conventions.[47]

The second condition is meant to stop us identifying freedom with simply getting what we want. This matters because one way of making it the case that we nearly always get what we want is to want very little, or to want only what is ready to hand in our present situation. These might be useful coping strategies, but they do not capture what is important about freedom. A prisoner does not become free simply by coming to want to be in prison.[48] We are freer to the extent we could do more, if we wanted to.

The third condition is distinctive of republican accounts of freedom. It captures the idea that to be free we must not be *dominated* by another person or institution. We are dominated when another person or institution has arbitrary power over us, in the sense that they have the ability to interfere in our choices, which is not being sufficiently constrained.[49] This power can be enacted relationally or structurally.[50] In either case, domination is a feature of our situation, not the result of targeted bad treatment. A slave owner still dominates their slave even if they treat them kindly, for example, because their kindness could be revoked and they are legally empowered to be cruel.

It is no accident that traditional marriage is a reoccurring example in discussions of republican freedom.[51] Marriage often involves domination because the law, social institutions, and wider norms and expectations typically afford men greater power and discretion than women. Women often struggle to leave relationships, to dissent, or be recognized, and their happiness is contingent on placating men.

The republican characterization of freedom helps us to focus on several morally relevant dimensions of agency. Hopefully you will agree that, ideally, we want there to be no barriers between us and what we want to do; we want to have the ability and resources to pursue our desires; and we do not want to be subject to others' arbitrary influence.

In thinking about monogamy, Chalmers focuses on the connection between restrictions and the goods of intimacy. He is right that removing the former makes it easier to achieve the latter in a narrow sense; if your partner allows you to date other people, then you are better able to experience new intimacy and remain in your existing relationship than if they did not allow you. But the republican analysis of freedom helps us to see there is more to freedom than the absence of restrictions. Two points are significant.

First, what about real romantic freedom? Republicans resist characterizing freedom as the mere absence of restrictions because they think the absence of barriers is valuable only if we can actually achieve our ends. We are freer to the extent that we can actually do more. This point applies to romantic life. Removing barriers to romantic goods is valuable only if we have the resources to attain them.

Consider a monogamous couple. Let's imagine they read Chalmers' article and decide together to explore nonmonogamy. As a result, both people agree to permit the other to explore new romantic connections and to be open to this themselves; they will not attempt to stop each other and both are confident they will not be annoyed or otherwise pose barriers to this new arrangement.

In communicating this new arrangement to each other, the couple remove some interpersonal barriers which typically prevent people from exploring nonmonogamy. On a republican conception of freedom, however, lack of barriers or interference is only one feature of real freedom. What the couple also need is the resources to act on their new arrangement.

Talk of 'resource' in a romantic context can seem strange but the basic idea is the same as in any other context. Having the permission to explore new intimacy is of little value if you lack the time, money, or other means to do so.

Social resources also matter. It is no use having a supportive partner if we live in a repressive society where social institutions, the state, and community norms all weigh against unconventional romantic lives.

Finally, and most crucially for my argument, personal resources also matter. Pettit stressed that freedom can be compromised if we lack the 'mental and bodily ability or knowhow' to act as we wish. This idea applies to relationships. There is little value in being permitted to pursue multiple forms of intimacy if our body or mind is not sufficiently resourced. Our freedom to be nonmonogamous can be compromised if we do not know how to meet people, or struggle to communicate openly, or if we are shaken by insecurity, jealousy, or resentment.

I develop this point in later chapters. Here it suffices to highlight several ideas. First, we cannot presuppose everyone has these personal resources; indeed, they might be rare in the disorienting romantic context described in chapter 1. Second, many of these abilities are relational. They are developed and sustained alongside other people, especially those with whom we are intimate. Third, these abilities are fragile. The traits and practices required to sustain flourishing intimacy can be undermined by cruelty, abuse, indifference, or an unsupportive society.

We might be tempted to reply to my discussion so far by suggesting that both an absence of barriers to intimacy and personal resources are important, but that these factors are unrelated. This would be a mistake for the reason I gestured towards in mentioning Kukla's idea that some sexual promises can support agency – namely, restrictions on what we are prepared to do, or want others to do, are precisely what help us to develop the resources which constitute our romantic agency.

Again, the republican literature is instructive. As Pettit puts it, the republican conception of freedom is one 'of the city ... not the freedom of the heath'.[52] This means that we experience extensive liberties in our society only because there are structures which delineate and maintain them. Laws, institutions, and public norms ensure we have basic liberties and can relate as equals. Without this framework, domination would prevail. But the presence of a legal framework restricts our negative freedoms. Property rights are protected; businesses are regulated; the political process is subject to checks and balances, and so on. Republicans do not lament these limitations, because they *constitute* the broader freedoms we enjoy in our community. Similarly, some restrictions on what we are able to do as romantic partners work to constitute the abilities required to experience real freedom.

This brings me nicely to my second point: what of non-domination? The republican conception of freedom shows us that we might have great latitude in which to act, have the resources to act, but remain unfree because we are subject to arbitrary power. This point applies forcefully in romantic contexts. We can imagine a situation where we are 'permitted' to pursue intimacy beyond our relationship with someone, are not hampered by lack of time or other resources (perhaps because our partner provides these), but are nonetheless subject to our partner's capricious will. The term 'permission' itself is telling since permission can be rescinded. Perhaps our partner is more privileged, and so better placed to complain about, modify, or exit our relationship without social repercussions. They might own property, or control a bank account, or be viewed more favourably by legal institutions in matters of significance such as child custody. These situations are not hard to imagine. They are situations of domination, irrespective of the behaviour of our partner and irrespective of how we view our relationship.[53] Domination is bad and something we want to be rid of, even if our partner is kind and our relationship thriving. Attention to these structural threats is also central to much feminist writing about romantic life. Discussions of romantic freedom are impoverished to the extent they proceed in terms of restrictions or resources alone.

We can always ask: will changing our relationship framework increase domination? This question matters because we might worry the openness to nonmonogamy that Chalmers favours could increase the domination experienced by someone within a relationship. This can happen if nonmonogamy is not sufficiently socially recognized or protected. Unequal romantic privilege may mean that the open pursuit of nonconventional romantic relationships is more fragile for some people because they lack power or are dependent on others. Women, even those with enthusiastic male partners, for example, may find their pursuit of nonmonogamy is subject to stigma and socially dependent on the 'support' of men, and so they remain at a structural disadvantage.

This suggestion is tentative, and I return to domination in the conclusion. Here I only hope to convince you that discussions of romantic freedom should consider domination. My core point is that romantic restrictions can facilitate real romantic freedom and reduce domination, just as some barriers to action in a civic society are required if we are all to be treated fairly in a secure environment. Put in terms of Pettit's phrase, romantic restrictions provide us the love of the city, not the heath.

Before discussing some implications of this approach, you might press the question put to me by Tom O'Shea, about the comparison between republican freedom and romantic freedom. Does this comparison fail in an important respect? In discussing republican freedom, I described the familiar idea that some restrictions constitute a social context in which we can enjoy basic liberties. Laws are established and upheld for the benefit of all, even if they limit some of our actions. But what is the analogous 'restriction' in the case of romantic relationships? We do not subject each other to laws with their accompanying costs in any plausible sense, so what might this mean?

The restriction that Chalmers has in mind, and that is visible in his friendship analogy, is that we might withdraw 'our love, affection, or willingness to continue the relationship' with someone if they want intimacy with others.[54] Such restrictions are unlike the legal frameworks that facilitate our freedom as citizens.

Two critical points need considering here. First, we can ask: does the possibility that someone might leave a relationship when it develops as they do not like constitute restrictive interference? This seems implausible if the relationship is formed in a society where we are free to choose our partners and able to leave relationships. All romantic relationships are marked by the possibility that someone might leave.

Second, love and affection, and the absence of insecurity, anger, or resentment, are not always under our direct control. We could find Chalmers' argument intellectually persuasive but struggle to support our partner as they explore nonmonogamy. We might find ourselves withdrawing affection unwittingly due to feelings of insecurity or jealousy. This 'restriction' on our partner experiencing the affection they desire is unlike legal penalties because it is unintentional.

The best response to O'Shea's concern is to remember that not all domination is agential. Social norms and ideals can render us subject to arbitrary power even if many people have positive attitudes about relationships. Entrenched norms shape how we interact with each other by shaping our states of mind. Patterns of aversion and esteem make certain forms of life easier than others, and play a role in sustaining oppression.[55] If we grow up in a society that is hostile to unconventional relationships, or seeks to control desire, then our insecurity and aversion manifests social domination. Put another way, some restrictions on us are not imposed through the will of a partner, but through the will of society which *works through* people who have been socialized within it.

Finally, I need to address an issue which might have been on your mind since I introduced Chalmers' friendship analogy at the start of the chapter. Surely it makes a difference *how* romantic restrictions are imposed. The couple in Chalmers' example, we can imagine, deliberate together and decide to impose their restriction on their relationship. Does it matter whether this choice was mutual and not imposed on one partner by the other? We might think this fact makes a moral difference. Both parties miss out on additional friends, and this is certainly an odd restriction to make, but it seems significant that their choice is mutual and unforced.[56] Indeed, their situation resembles the democratic ideal of the relationship as its own forum envisaged by Giddens.

Conclusion

In practice, the different dimensions of romantic freedom must be balanced against each other. Some restrictions on each other can help to secure our real romantic freedom because they enable us to develop the resources to act on the other freedoms we have. These limitations may also help to create relationships with less domination.

Since we have to balance different dimensions of freedom, we can ask which dimension should take priority. As my discussion of romantic agency will show, I am most concerned with relationship dynamics which shape our ability to be intimate with other people. There is little value in being permitted to explore, romantically, if we are unable to do so in the first place, or if the process of doing so will undermine our ability to enjoy the products of our exploration. My concern with real romantic freedom stems from my suggestion that modern romantic culture can be morally damaging. Our social context can mean we grow up without the psychological resources we might need to pursue the romantic lifestyle we desire. Important questions remain, however. Is there more to say about romantic agency? How, exactly, do forms of romantic exclusivity help us to maintain the ability to have the intimacy we desire? What of the impact of nonmonogamy on our agency? I discuss these questions in chapter 4.

Here are some implications of the view of romantic freedom I favour. The possibility of trade-offs between freedom to pursue romantic goods and the ability to enjoy them brings pressure to bear on a binary view of monogamy and nonmonogamy. Defences of monogamy over-estimate the extent to which restrictions make possible the enjoyment of intimacy, *and* defences of nonmonogamy underestimate the extent to which restrictions help us to be intimate. We need instead to consider relationships in context and look at their internal workings, the specific arrangements people adopt.

We should also look at our social position and the norms shaping our agency. The relational character of romantic agency and its fragility also mean the absence of all restrictions, or total restrictions, is unlikely to be a viable practical option in romantic life, so there may be no common 'good-making' property shared by all relationships of a certain kind.

It's time to summarize my argument in this chapter. One way to reduce friction between changing romantic practices and lingering norms is to ditch the norms. I explored this idea by focusing on nonmonogamy, which can seem to offer us an alternative to restrictive romantic lifestyles.

Talk of fairness or greed does little to undermine the appeal of nonmonogamy. I argued that not only do these common criticisms fail, but they obscure the ways in which wider acceptance of nonmonogamous ideals might help to create a society in which fewer people are excluded from romantic flourishing.

That said, I also rejected attempts to argue that monogamous lifestyles are morally wrong. This conclusion will seem strained if you accept, as I do, that we should respect free agreements between people, even if their results are limiting or strange. Chalmers' argument was useful to consider, however, because it focused our attention onto the tensions between different aspects of freedom, social constraints, and our agency. There are many layers to this issue, but the core idea presented in this chapter is that we often restrict each other's freedom to act because doing so helps to nurture our underlying ability to sustain intimacy with each other. I develop this thought in the next chapter.

3
Romantic Agency

The lover stands ready to interpret the beloved's words and actions as signposts towards further discoveries about what it is good to be or to do. (Talbot Brewer)[1]

Abilities

Relationships shape us. You may have met someone who makes you feel able to do things that before seemed impossible. Your confidence grows, your insecurities weaken, you are less defensive. They help you to see familiar situations in new ways and you begin to act differently. You used to be averse and ironic. Now you are interested and assertive.

Not all relationships are so wonderful. Some are stifling, where people feed your doubts and insecurities. Romantic partners can be controlling, arrogant, or emotionally unavailable. Over time they make it harder for you to be yourself, or to act as you would like. Distance can replace intimacy, suspicion replace spontaneity, anxiety replace joy.

Who we are and who we will become is always at stake in romantic life. But at the time this is often hard to notice. Relationships are contexts which stratify our experiences until they harden into shape. We become stronger, or we crack. These changes manifest in different ways, ranging as they do over our emotions, our beliefs, and our desires. We also experience changes in our ability to be intimate with others, in our romantic agency.

In the previous chapter, romantic agency emerged as a useful way to think about the impact of restrictions in our relationships. But what is romantic agency, exactly, and how is it shaped? How might different relationship dynamics shape this agency? In this chapter, I turn to these questions to consider romantic agency in general terms, looking at the way in which it is relational and therefore fragile. In the next chapter, I explore how specific romantic configurations shape romantic agency.

An assumption underpinning my argument is that our understanding of what relationships are like should constrain the way we date, choose partners, have sex, and build relationships. Embracing this constraint is not easy. On the one hand, we are easily seduced by unrealistic romantic fantasies, the products of our intimate culture. On the other hand, we might feel the need to explore unconventional forms of intimacy as a way of trying to move beyond the limitations of the status quo. How we navigate a path through these two concerns is a topic for later chapters. Before we get there, it helps to have a better grasp on what romantic agency is. This will provide us with an evaluative framework that helps us to make better romantic choices.

What is romantic agency? I have in mind our personal capacities to experience and act upon sexual and romantic attraction and desire; to form and maintain romantic relationships; and to tell our own romantic story. I understand action broadly to encompass the control we exercise over our thoughts, imagination, and feelings, and also over any technology which mediates our intimacy.

My formulation of 'romantic agency' is adapted from Quill Kukla's discussion of 'spatial agency' in their book on city life.[2] Both phrases help to direct our attention to a specific dimension of human agency. Nor is the juxtaposition of spatial and romantic agency unwarranted. Spatial metaphors are common in thinking about love and relationships. We see it in the epigraph to my introduction, for example, where Berlant's description of love as 'a space to which people can return' gestures towards the homeliness of intimacy, and we will encounter similar ideas in later chapters when exploring the connections between nurturing environments and difficult emotions.

Kukla describes some of the ways city spaces either enclose or expand what we can do. We often 'tinker' with space in urban settings to adapt it to our needs. Relationships can be viewed in a similar light. They are normative spaces, structured by rules and expectations, and often overlain on specific places, from the domestic home to bars and clubs. As in a city, our movement within relationships is shaped by what preceded us, the social norms and familial expectations which underpin our developmental journey. Unlike city planners and urban tinkerers, however, we have greater discretion to amend, adjust, and adapt our relationships to suit us; to try and build new intimacies in the shell of the old (to co-opt the anarchist slogan).

This activity has limits. Structural ghosts, the grip of old norms and habits, hold our ambitions in check. Our psychological geography also limits us; it can be hard to find the mental space to make sense of new ideas, feelings, and forms of living. Our intimate imagination is often more agile than our ability to process difficult feelings or have hard conversations. The desire to demolish and build radical and expansive forms of life can also have unexpected consequences which prove ultimately unlivable.[3]

We differ in how we exercise our romantic agency, so it is useful to think in terms of different *agential styles*. Some people are comfortable exploring, for example – others less so; some like to plan, others to be spontaneous; some like to practise and then apply their learning, others to learn as they go, and so on. Romantic agency also comes in degrees. We can be more or less able to articulate our desires, build relationships, or tell our romantic story. Some people may excel in some areas but not others, for example finding it easy to relate sexually to a partner while struggling to be emotionally vulnerable. When discussing romantic agency in general, I do not mean to elide these differences.

Two dimensions of romantic agency are significant. First, romantic agency is relational and largely developed and maintained within romantic contexts. We acquire it 'on the job' rather than in other areas of life. Clearly, our relationships with family, friends, and role models shape our personality. We learn how to communicate and interact with people. But we can be good siblings or friends while struggling romantically. This is partly because the kinds of intimate activity often differ, as does the extent of our proximity to others and the complexity of our entwined interests and projects. But it is also because we are subject to different social expectations and sources of community pressure, and come to view our actions through the lens of distinctly romantic narrative frameworks.

Second, romantic agency is fragile. We cannot assume that everyone has romantic agency to the same extent. Nor is romantic agency static or stable over a lifetime. Two people entering into a new relationship will differ in terms of the extent and style of their romantic agency. Crucially, our agency can expand and contract once in relationships due to the influence of other people. We can get better at being vulnerable, or become reticent and defensive.

To be clear, romantic agency is not our only concern when thinking about intimacy. Most of the time, our satisfaction and flourishing are more salient. My suggestion is simply that attention to romantic agency should constrain this thinking. The matter of our thriving cannot be divorced from the matter of what we are able to do. Misunderstanding our romantic agency, through either timidity or hubris, limits us in ways which can be hard to repair.

Romantic agency is conducive to, but does not guarantee, flourishing. Competent lovers may struggle to find a partner, or be undone by life circumstance. The people we love might have radically different desires to us. Our social circle might reject our attempts to be unconventional. Much has to go right for us to experience thriving intimacy, and much of this is outside our control.

Nor is romantic flourishing contingent on having romantic agency of a certain kind. Talk of 'expanded' or 'developed' romantic agency might be taken to imply that there is one set of good romantic capacities underpinning all flourishing relationships. This is not quite right. What having sufficient romantic agency will involve depends on the specific person, context, and relationship. The general ability to be intimate romantically can take different forms, and be shaped by our varying agential styles and practices.

Relationality

We can best understand the idea that romantic agency is relational by considering the difference between two broad attitudes towards romantic life.

On the *individual* attitude, romantic life is a domain in which we seek to fulfil our existing desires. Compatibility is our driving concept; our relationship is shaped by rules we specify in advance; we have written our romantic script and just need to cast the leading role.

On the *relational* attitude, romantic life is something we are always working out. Discovery is our driving concept; our relationship is shaped by our hunches about what might work, but we are open-minded; we have no romantic script, but look forward to telling our story together with our partner.

In practice, these attitudes are not mutually exclusive; they describe points of emphasis on a spectrum of approaches to romantic life. Clear desires can coexist with openness to new ways of living; talk of compatibility can be a useful way of ensuring we are respected; rules can help us to avoid the insecurity stemming from ambiguity. That said, I think the relational attitude better describes what romantic life is like – aspects which can be overlooked or masked by the romantic scripts and passionate stories we like to tell.

Romantic relationships move into us as much as we move into them. Relationships are not simply contexts in which we acquire objects of desire. Intimate interactions unfold in ways we cannot predict and can relate us to ourselves in ways we dislike. Confident people can experience new vulnerabilities; vulnerable people, new confidence. Relationships force us to discover, clarify, and refine our lives. These shifts are scary because they can make us feel out of control, or that we are unsure where our story is heading. As a result, we might be tempted to pretend intimacy is simpler than it really is. Most romantic films and novels encourage this temptation in ending just as the hard work of relating to someone begins.

Here are some further dimensions of romantic relationality. First, relationships shape us as knowers. Close interaction with others helps us to understand more about human motivation, but also offers opportunities for increased self-knowledge. Knowledge often becomes concrete in experience, and so our ability to develop intimate self-understanding requires us to have intimate experiences. When we have these encounters – whether sexual, emotional, or practical – we get to experience our abilities in action. If this goes well, we are able to align our practical understanding with our imagined grasp of what we would be like, defuse our anxiety, and develop confidence in our skills.

Our partners also shape our desires. Relationships are contexts of exploration. Other people help us to focus our existing interests into something concrete, or initiate us into new desires altogether. Relationships are not just contexts in which existing desires are enacted. Indeed, they are perhaps rarely this; instead, our relationships help us to find out what we want.

Some aspects of romantic life are also arguably 'transformative experiences' in the technical sense described by L. A. Paul.[4] A first romance, exploring same-sex intimacy, or plunging into polyamory are candidates for this kind of experience. Because they will radically change who we are, we cannot understand in advance the ways these aspects will shape our lives and so decide in a rational way whether to endorse those changes. Instead, we take a leap of faith grounded on hunch.

Our romantic partners also shape how we value. We can acknowledge many things are valuable, but we are more limited in the things which we personally value. To personally value something is to be vulnerable to it, emotionally; to feel good when it thrives and bad when it falters.[5] When we care about someone, we often take an interest in what they value and may come to value those things personally ourselves. Our partner loves the environment; we come to love it too. Not just believe that it matters, but feel it matters. This process is complex, but part of what goes on here is that our affections for someone motivate us to look harder at parts of the world we had previously overlooked. Notice that this process is not always harmonious. We should not accept, as some are tempted to do, that romantic love or affection *requires* us to share our partner's values. We might be motivated to look harder, but this does not guarantee that we will like what we see. In fact, romantic closeness can shape our values through tension and conflict. Our partner's concern for the Conservative Party, for example, might turn our prior political indifference into a sharpened sense of disdain. Our partner shapes our values, but in ways they might regret.

Of greater interest are the ways our intimate partners hone the values we already had. We usually share broad concerns with the people we are drawn towards. But broad concerns are a thin basis for any relationship. Perhaps we agree that education, or care, are central human goods, but what that means practically is unspecified. Together, how might we act on those values? What forms of life open up, or close down, when we value in certain ways?

In a discussion of romantic love, Benjamin Bagley argues that our lovers shape us through 'deep improvisation'.[6] Together, over time, we give our shared values a determinate shape, just as a loose musical theme morphs into something specific during musical improvisation. This process can surprise. A partner can cast unexpected light on an established value we have, or add detail to our vague intimations. We might value caring, for example, and associate this with raising children, only for our partner to show us another way this value could shape a life. Our readiness to be receptive to this process feels central to experiences of love – as Talbot Brewer puts it in the epigraph to this chapter, 'The lover stands ready to interpret the beloved's words and actions as signposts towards further discoveries about what it is good to be or to do.'

The unpredictable nature of deep improvisation is partly what makes romantic life intoxicating. Anyone we meet could shape our values in ways we cannot imagine; they are the point of departure of a new life. Bagley also thinks deep improvisation is what makes romantic love the love of a specific person. We can share general values with lots of people, but we cannot swap out one partner for another without loss, because of the unique way they shape the values we share. Because our values partly constitute our identity, such a loss would also impact who we are.[7] The disorientation after bereavement or break-up is partly the unravelling of these processes of improvisation.

Even if we were unconvinced by some of Bagley's stronger claims about deep improvisation and love – perhaps analysing love in a different way, or thinking that deep improvisation can be found in contexts where love is absent or platonic – it seems clear to me that deep improvisation and the shaping of ourselves that follows is a substantive and common feature of romantic life. This matters because it brings pressure to bear on individualistic compatibility culture. Our relationships are a context in which our values assume a clear and determinate shape, rather than being the *product* of clear and determinate values. To insist that we want a partner with the same values as us is to neglect the important and unavoidable ways we will improvise together, and the sense in which what we come to value will depend on their input.

You might point to your previous relationships, and ask about the value improvisation that took place there: hasn't that given shape to your life already? It has, but improvisation is ongoing. Each context is different. We arrive at no fixed 'score' from which to play out the music of our remaining life. Romantic experience does help us to understand ourselves and seek partners who are receptive to our outlook. But each relationship moulds our agency in new ways, no matter how old or stubborn we are.

Romantic life also shapes and is shaped by the narratives which make sense of who we are and what we are doing. These narratives are often quite minimal, from 'fooling around' to 'going steady'. They might be negative, too, as in cases where we focus more on saying what a relationship is not, rather than what it is (like the 'situationships' mentioned in chapter 1). Even schematic narratives, however, organize our actions into a trajectory, and impose some order on the messiness of our lives.[8] Over time, our romantic stories become more detailed and accommodating as they cover different phases of life.

Romantic relationships are understood in terms of co-authored narratives. Our separate senses of what the relationship is, how it started, where it is going, and what it means are influenced by and must live alongside a shared sense of the relationship as something built with another person. This process of joint authorship need not be simple: a couple might disagree about their story, or hold conflicting views, but as narratives become joint, how we think of ourselves in terms of them changes. Other people have a say when it comes to describing our relationship, who we are within it, and where it is going. This process can creep up on us. Suddenly, we start thinking of situations in terms and perspectives which make sense only because we are relating to a specific person. Relationships also yield idiolects, habits of speech which are unique to the people concerned, such as little pet names, complex jokes, and context-specific references.

Relationships shape us as knowers, desirers, valuers, and sense-makers. These shifts, in turn, alter our romantic agency. This is a broad process of mutual self-fashioning.[9] This fashioning is not always conscious. We can also distinguish between its more or less active forms.

The active forms involve conversation, criticism, guidance, and providing examples for each other. Other people can help us to develop and sustain the ability to be intimate, to accept vulnerability, communicate, and act on desire. These activities are often the subject of relationship manuals and community advice.

Our agency is also shaped passively. The way we resonate emotionally to other people, for example, is scaffolded by our environment.[10] Unsafe or chaotic spaces can make it hard to communicate or be vulnerable. Calm and nurturing spaces can foster romantic agency, or enable people to experience clearly the capacities they already possess. Similarly, different kinds of interpersonal *dynamic* – that is, broad patterns of interaction – can shape our abilities. As Diana Meyers puts it, in talking about autonomy: 'constellations of companionship can in themselves constitute individual resolve, and they need not be set up deliberately. As with the collaborative insights of consciousness-raising groups, volitional structures can arise through the dynamic of interaction.'[11] These dynamics often escape our notice at the time, and it is only once we have left a certain home or workplace that the contrast becomes apparent. That said, immersion into a new 'constellation of companionship' can be transformative.

The active and passive ways that we are shaped by others are intertwined. They can also conflict in ways that shape us as romantic agents. Our partner might give us good advice, but create a chaotic home; or we might slowly sense the gaps between the stories they tell, 'we're such a great couple', and the undercurrent of tension in our relationship.

We are not only shaped by our current relationships. Past ones can exert influence. Joy, trauma, and previous idiolects can stay with us as we meet new people. This can have its benefits – we might continue to value the environment for example, or benefit from the calmer style of communication we experienced in the past. But we can also experience conflict and disorientation as different perspectives collide.

We are not simply shaped by long or committed romantic relationships. A short encounter with a receptive partner can be transformative, especially if our previous relationships were stifling. Informal relationships, like sexual friendships or casual dating, can be contexts where we experience respect and esteem. Indeed, these encounters can give us radically fresh experiences of our own agency if we communicate clearly, articulate our desires, and pursue pleasure intentionally.

Similarly, it would be a mistake to think talk of romantic agency is irrelevant for single people. 'Single' often means that someone is not currently in a committed relationship, but their romantic agency can still be shaped by flings and flirtations. Single people also grapple with the lingering impacts of past relationships. We can also shape ourselves. A single person who is looking for a committed loving relationship can consider and mould their character and shape their environment to support their ability to experience intimacy.

You might wonder whether our romantic agency is shaped only in situations where we have *agreed* to be influenced by someone else. Do we have to commit to this? I think not. All romantic interactions shape who we are and can support or undermine romantic agency. This is so whatever we think about our situation, and even in cases where we try to resist someone's influence.

A critic, perhaps someone inspired by Giddens and the idea that modern romantic life empowers us and helps us to resist domination, might worry that all this talk of relationality and shaping gives too much power to other people. In response, I distinguish between the fact that relationships shape agency and the separate issue as to whether other people should have authority over this process, especially the narrative authority to settle which developments are good, and which are bad. To accept that relationships shape us in ways which often outrun our understanding is not to cede control to other people. There is room, here, to think that our romantic narratives should be co-authored as equals or, to take a slightly different view, to think that our partners have more authority over how we are to view them, and we have authority over how they are to view us, because giving each other such power is what love requires.[12]

There are advantages to thinking in terms of agency, and the ways romantic agency is relational. First, it captures the ways our relationships and other romantic interactions are productive. They generate knowledge, desire, and values, and do so in ways that are difficult to anticipate. If they did not, it is hard to see how relationships would last. We know little about ourselves, and we would be bored quickly if our relationships were contexts only for the desires we know about. Second, this approach foregrounds individuals, and our interactions with them, rather than grappling with *kinds* of relationship, or kinds of romantic good. Third, this view helps us to understand why changes in romantic life can be liberating or constraining: because they shape our abilities to enjoy intimacy. Finally, this emphasis has us looking at individuals within their specific social context, as their social world plays a role in shaping their romantic agency.

Fragility

I have already hinted that our romantic agency is fragile. Our ability to experience intimacy can be built up and broken down. This fragility is a consequence of several factors, some of which I described in chapter 1. We find ourselves in a world of romantic norms and ideals which impact us deeply. These norms often conflict with how we would like to pursue our relationships, or would have us adopt forms of life which we lack the resources to thrive within. Our interactions with others also make us vulnerable. We might care about, or love, people who hurt us, or fail to nurture our agency.

In trying to navigate modern romantic norms and practices, we can become evasive or focused on self-preservation. Our desire to avoid loss, humiliation, or insecurity can mean we form habits which are not conducive to experiences of intimacy. At the same time, we might embrace stories or a sense of identity which valorize our habits – stressing, for example, the 'importance of not getting played'[13] or taking pride in our hardened emotions. Although these behaviours are often understandable in the modern context, they are self-imposed threats to romantic agency.

Other people can pose direct threats to our romantic agency. Our vulnerability, propensity to form attachments, and to compare ourselves to other people mean we look to others for care and validation, particularly when we are developing capacities which require support over time as we struggle and backslide. We are especially vulnerable in romantic life because we might be involved in activities which encompass facets of our identity or body which are seen rarely, or because we have had comparably little time to come to know ourselves as romantic beings, or because we have been subject to restrictive social norms. These forms of exposure mean other people can more easily harm our romantic agency. A partner might be unreceptive, fail to acknowledge the care we require, trigger traumatic memories or hinder our ability to process past experiences, play into our insecurities, gaslight us and undermine our confidence, or be coercive or violent. These experiences set back the ability to be intimate with others or to take joy in romantic life, or prevent these aspects of our agency from developing altogether.

Our romantic agency is shaped also by the kind of relationship we build. Choosing to be nonmonogamous, for example, gives romantic life a certain structure. Selecting a specific form of nonmonogamy structures it further still. Within the purview of a specific relationship, the choice of particular boundaries and guidelines also shapes our romantic agency in giving our daily life a specific practical form. These structural decisions, whether general or specific, can help or hinder our ability to be intimate.

Conclusion

Romantic agency lies at the heart of this chapter, and the wider book. Our abilities to sustain intimacy with each other cannot be taken for granted. They are complex, formed on the job, require the support of other people, and can be diminished. Our relationships shape who we are, which, in turn, shapes our relationships. This shaping can spiral in both positive and negative directions. If we can look beyond some of the more attractive simplifications of romantic culture, and if we are lucky enough to relate to good people, our ability to be intimate will improve. If we overvalue compatibility, fixate on romantic ideals, are unlucky in how our personality developed, or have an uncaring partner, then our romantic agency can be threatened. These possibilities should inform our choices. Attention to romantic agency is a useful vantage point when thinking about our desires. We might find ourselves unable to do what we want to do. Often these tensions are tragic; the kind of romantic life we are drawn to, or which resonates with our values, might lie beyond our current reach due to no fault of our own.

4

Shaping Intimacy

There must be eyes on the street. (Jane Jacobs)[1]

The kind of romantic life we pursue will shape our romantic agency in different ways. An exclusive domestic relationship is clearly different from being part of a queer polyamorous network, or a romantically exclusive but sexually open triad.

We might want to know, in advance, how our romantic choices will impact our agency. Will they make us more, or less, able to pursue the kind of intimacy we want? Answering this question is not easy. We have different personal histories, different agential styles, and, most obviously, form relationships with different people. Attention to these particularities should make us resist rigid generalizations. In practice, our exploration of romantic life and choice of direction always involve uncertainty.

My goal in this chapter is to explore some reasons why different styles of romantic intimacy seem attractive from an agential perspective, and to describe some of their associated pitfalls. I consider reasons of specialization, continued romantic appreciation, increased oversight and corroboration, and an emphasis on relational practices.

Although the latter three discussions focus on nonmonogamous relationships, it is important to remember that nonmonogamies vary dramatically. Exclusive polyamory, for example, can be very different from relationship anarchy. More generally, we need to resist the temptation to draw a rigid binary between monogamous romantic life on the one hand, and nonmonogamous romantic life on the other. My discussion of intimate specialization, for example, can apply to smaller nonmonogamous relationships, and aspects of my discussion of relationship anarchy can apply to exclusive couples.

In practice, our romantic choices will be influenced by our personality, agential style, and romantic privilege. Are we someone who favours efforts to protect our agential capacities over efforts to develop them? What do we value more: the effortlessness of being guided by romantic defaults, guidelines or social expectations, or the investment involved in actively constructing our own relationship frameworks? My goal here is just to offer additional perspectives to consider alongside our inclinations. It is not my intention to explore moral reasons for favouring one kind of relationship dynamic over another.

Specialization

Not everyone chooses to be monogamous simply because it is conventional or because they cannot imagine an alternative. Monogamous relationships have a distinct appeal. Many couples are aware of how other people organize their relationships. Perhaps they have nonmonogamous friends, or friends whose sexual identity has meant they have had to forge unconventional ways of loving. They will also have single friends, friends who are dating, and perhaps friends who do not want a romantic life.

The appeal of exclusive monogamous relationship can be explained in different ways. One thought is that monogamy can seem easier than some alternatives. A big attraction is precisely the desire to stop having to engage with other people as potential partners – to leave the dating arena. We might find looking for a partner to be a frustrating and unnerving process – an activity which we engage in begrudgingly, but in which we take little enjoyment.

Finding monogamy to be easy is compatible with different attitudes towards romantic life. For some, intimacy forms a big part of their identity, and relationships a big part of their life. But this is not the case for everyone. Most people have some other concerns and some would prioritize their other activities over the goods of human intimacy. For such people, an exclusive monogamous relationship allows them to be intimate with someone without occupying much time or effort, as would be the case if they remained alive to additional partners, kept dating, or embraced nonmonogamous styles of interaction.

But the appeal of exclusivity is not limited to people who are uninterested in romance. We could also be drawn to monogamous life precisely because we value romantic intimacy and want to make it central to what we do. Although romantic life can clearly admit of various kinds of plural intimacy, we might be attracted to the idea that there is something distinct about trying to develop a romantic connection with just one person. Monogamy can be viewed as a form of romantic specialization: the process of developing and deepening the ability to be intimate with someone. A monogamous person might explain the appeal of their relationship by highlighting how rare these opportunities for specialization are. As friends, family members, colleagues, we are used to relating to other people in group contexts. Modern monogamous life, especially in its domestic variants, offers up a unique kind of agential engagement that we may not experience in other areas of our life.

What might be distinct about this specialized focus on another person? One answer might be the ideal of effortlessness and familiarity. We could hope that we can come to understand our partner and communicate in ways which do not require our relationship to become an issue at hand. In a sense, we want an exclusive relationship precisely because we want no 'relationship' – none of the uncertainty, talking, conflict and *activity* of interacting with others as romantic persons. This desire is visible in union theories of romantic love, where lovers are said to fuse or form some new entity.[2] This approach to romantic life can be attractive, I think, because it seems to require little reckoning with the separateness of persons – with what Iris Murdoch called 'the extremely difficult realisation that something other than oneself is real'.[3] It is the relational equivalent of individualism. In lives where so much else is fraught, or contested, or requires constant and careful reflection, effortless intimacy with someone can seem appealing.

Monogamous relationships might also seem to have some advantages when it comes to the kind of value improvisation I discussed above. Bagley argued that 'deep improvisation' is central to our loving romantic relationships. Our lovers make our values concrete, they give them direction in unique and unfolding ways. In turn, these values help to structure our relationships as they develop. If Bagley is right, then exclusive romantic relationships might help us to avoid improvisational conflicts, since we are less likely to be shaped in different directions by different lovers. Constraint and conflict are unavoidable features of all relationships but there is unique value in not experiencing tensions around the things we care about most, especially if we are conflict-averse.

Some caveats. Not all romantic entanglements involve love or deep improvisation. Nor is improvisation inherently between two people only. Members of a romantic triad can improvise together like members of a band, so this concern with value improvisation is better put as a point about exclusive relationships, not necessarily dyadic relationships. Nor should we assume that value conflicts are always bad. Conflict can be evidence we are sensitive to what matters.[4] My claim is just that monogamous life might help some people to avoid a specific kind of value tension.

Exclusive relationships can help us to protect what romantic agency we have by limiting the pressures that come with attempts to be intimate with multiple people. Exclusivity can help us to focus on someone with fewer distractions, get to know ourselves better, help us to address a specific problem in our relationship, or make it easier to care for someone when they are uniquely vulnerable. Our needs can wax, our abilities wane when ill, pregnant, grieving, or disoriented as we are vulnerable, exposed to difficult feelings, and struggle to think and communicate clearly. When we are less able to relate well to others, nonmonogamy can seem unachievable in the ways that other complex activities seem unachievable. Exclusivity, monogamy, perhaps even periods of no romantic engagement at all, can be practical responses to these situations.

Some of these exclusions might be open-ended but with a clear sense of when they would end (when our partner is better, or the child starts nursery); others might be more limited ('Let's have that conversation when we get back from the trip'). Similarly, sometimes exclusions respond to unexpected life-shocks like illness and bereavement, but other times they are a conscious response to our choices, like the desire to focus on a holiday romance, or raising children. In all cases, however, exclusivity helps us to be intimate with an existing person, given our specific circumstances. This discussion builds on Kukla's insight about the connection between restrictions and agency: we are better able to be intimate when free of certain pressures or triggers, or if we do not have to rely on our faltering vigilance alone when navigating situations.

So far, talk of exclusions has been specific. I have presented situations where we decide to focus on our exclusive relationship (dyadic or not) or where we exclude certain kinds of people for instrumental reasons: to grieve, raise children, or to avoid being reminded of a past assault or oppression. These exclusions are aimed squarely at protecting existing intimacy. In some cases, this is because the intimacy is just starting – for example, we might want to get to know someone well, or make sure we can communicate clearly, before exploring an open relationship. In other cases, this is because the intimacy is established – for example, we want to nurture and care for someone who is grieving and who knows they will be more vulnerable. In all these cases, the exclusivity in question is compatible with an intellectual commitment to nonmonogamy and with the desire to explore intimacy beyond the couple in other contexts or stages of life.

But many people have no desire to explore alternative forms of romance. Considering this helps us to broaden the link between exclusivity and the fragility of our intimate agency. It is relatively easy to appreciate how temporary or circumscribed forms of exclusivity help us to protect the intimacy we already have. But that discussion made it seem as if the pressures to which we respond are mostly external: traumatic events, life choices, temporary forms of dependency.

We might feel, however, that monogamy is preferable even in the absence of those external shocks because our romantic agency is fragile *in general*. This fragility is internal: a consequence of how our character developed in our social world. In an individualistic and competitive society, with much romantic choice, we manage risk, emotionally withdraw, and develop strategies to manage loss. These practices are morally damaging in Tessman's sense: they help us cope, but they can also inhibit our romantic agency and leave us ill equipped for navigating the emotional landscape of unconventional intimacy.

I am not suggesting that romantic norms are fully rigid. Some people respond creatively to the social world they inherit. But the appetite and ability for this are not shared equally; to some, exclusive relationships seem like the only practical way of maintaining their ability to relate romantically to anyone. Anything else would induce too much anxiety, insecurity, and disorientation.

People who feel this way about monogamy need not endorse their situation. Indeed, they might think nonmonogamy would make for a great life and find themselves frustrated with their averse emotional response. In these situations, exclusive relationships are a response to an imperfect predicament; they reflect our agential constitution, not necessarily our desires or values.

In practice, of course, we can worry that we are driven by fear. Distinguishing our personal limitations from what is socially expected of us can be difficult. Sometimes we fail to know ourselves, are pessimistic, or cowardly. Some experiences of jealousy or anxiety can be so intense that we cannot imagine a way around them. Or perhaps we just have poor imaginations. In later chapters, I consider how we might explore romantic relationships in spite of these challenges.

If you are drawn to the radical potential of unconventional romance, these remarks about exclusivity and agency may seem disappointing, even tragic. I can only respond that we cannot assume life is not tragic. We have to recognize that our agency could be constrained in ways we do not like. Some people are luckier than others in being better suited to experiment and do things differently. These are not personal failings.

Appreciation

Monogamy might offer opportunities for intimate specialization and could favour people who value the opportunity to focus their attention on one person, or who like to separate the dynamics of dating from relationships.

Nonmonogamy, in contrast, may appeal precisely because we want to resist distinguishing sharply between the abilities which help us to date people and find partners, and the abilities which help us to sustain relationships with the people we find. Nonmonogamy can help us to keep active our capacities of romantic appreciation, and this may have a positive impact on our wider romantic agency.

Romantic appreciation is more than simply being able to find other people attractive, but also includes the active attention to others as potential intimates, a desire to know them, emotional responsiveness, and an openness to act on our desires.

Why is ongoing romantic appreciation valuable? Practically speaking, trying to remain open to other people may help us resist 'dyadic withdrawal', where couples retreat into romantic relationships at the expense of their other relationships, particularly in middle life.[5] Openness to romantic interactions with new people may also help to guard against the 'closeness–communication bias', in which we wrongly think that we communicate better with intimates, rather than with strangers.[6]

Meeting new people, especially in contexts of potential intimacy, also encourages us to occupy different points of view and remain alive to their experiences and values. We can see one aspect of our romantic life from the perspective of another aspect, a bit like an art critic whose ability to appreciate one painting is informed by their encounters with other paintings, as opposed to the art critic who focuses narrowly on one subject.

Like art criticism, romantic appreciation is a skilled activity. Skills are maintained by practice over time, in different situations, in response to feedback. Since romantic skills cannot be easily acquired in non-romantic contexts, limiting our romantic appreciation once in a relationship could impact our overall ability, especially if we are young or have little experience. Although individual relationships, especially long ones, are full of novel situations, repeated intimacy with one person has a different character from staying romantically open to people.

We should also resist presupposing a rigid model of how we relate to each other. It is tempting to think that attraction is a precursor to romantic intimacy but not everyone experiences attraction in that way. For demisexual people, for example, sexual attraction arises within relationships, not prior to them, so they might not want to shut down attentiveness once a relationship begins. Friendships are also relationships which require us to remain broadly attentive over time. We do not typically find a friend, like we might a romantic partner, and then settle down into a relationship of a different kind with them. Friendship is a dynamic process of attending to and appreciating someone over time. If we were to lose that ability, our friendships would wane.

Ongoing romantic appreciation can also shape our identity. Although some people embrace 'union' conceptions of romantic love, for example, in which lovers are understood to form a 'we' or new self, there are also people who find this idea claustrophobic and alienating. We might want a relationship without 'losing ourselves' in someone or having our identity defined by the relationship. Retaining our romantic attention could help us to do this. Our attractions, romantic inclinations, desires, and interactions are deeply expressive of our individuality.

So far, I have considered how we might romantically appreciate others. But we might want our partners to retain this ability too. Over time, we will change dramatically. As we age, get ill, or have children, we will look different. As we adapt to unforeseen situations, we may behave differently. In wanting our partners to lose the ability to be sensitive to what makes other people attractive, we might find they struggle to be attracted to us as we change.[7] We might want to avoid a situation in which fondness makes the heart grow absent.

This concern with romantic appreciation is not just self-interested. Graham Bex-Priestley helped me to realize this is an ability we can want *for* our partners. To love someone is to want them to flourish in different situations. If we were to die, fall into a coma, or break up, it is good for our partner to be able to be romantically attentive to other people – to experience attraction, desire, and have new romantic relationships. Therefore, we might encourage these aspects of their romantic agency while we are with them.

A similar thought applies to attachment. In chapter 1, I briefly mentioned the ways we can form attachment bonds with romantic partners. Those bonds are often sources of security, but they also leave us feeling like we need someone. We are disoriented when an attachment-figure is absent. Given the potential for attachment bonds to disrupt agency, we ought to help our lovers to manage their attachments to us and other people. This need not involve attempts to avoid attachment, but rather attempts to correct against the excesses of attachment. Open romantic attentiveness can play a role in this process if it makes romantic need less brittle.[8]

Not all romantic relationships involve attachment, however, and we are attached in different ways. Similarly, the open romantic appreciation I have in mind here can be arrived at by different routes. Some people will find nonmonogamy just removes some of the guardrails they placed around their existing desires and romantic appreciation. Other people might find romantic appreciation requires active effort.

In both cases, the ideal of ongoing romantic appreciation has to be viewed with care. It is less a matter of rushing into multiple romantic entanglements and more a matter of not shutting down the forms of romantic appreciation which animate romantic life. In many cases, this appreciation is in the head: our thoughts, fantasies, and feelings remain sensitive to others as romantic subjects. But this is challenge enough to monogamy norms which encourage partisan focus on one person and the taming of rogue desires, or which make space for the mental appreciation of someone's beauty but want us to remain unmoved by it. Monogamous people can embrace some of the agential potential of nonmonogamous life in weakening their attempts to subdue attraction and desire.

Open romantic appreciation can keep alive valued forms of romantic agency. But it is possible to want a partner both to have the ability to appreciate other people yet to only focus on us; or to recognize that appreciation is a skill, but only want them to practise it on us. We might also think that open appreciation has its place in exploratory phases of life but can be set aside within relationships, especially in cases where we are forming romantic engagements in later life when we are more experienced.

Certainly, these scenarios are better than the alternatives, where we altogether lack these skills of appreciation. But we might wonder if they miss the spirit of the ideas explored here. One worry is about the timidity inherent in wanting to have a certain capacity yet restrict the contexts in which we manifest it. As Edna St Vincent Millay famously expressed this idea in a letter to her lover: 'If you loved me, I should not want you to love only me. I should think less highly of you if you did. For surely, one must be either undiscerning, or frightened, to love only one person, when the world is so full of gracious and noble spirits.'[9]

Oversight

For some, the main appeal of nonmonogamy lies in the possibility of forming new romantic 'constitutions', to use Giddens' metaphor from chapter 1. We might positively shape our intimate agency by setting up relationships in different ways, with new rules and expectations.

We should be wary of generalizing, because nonmonogamous relationships vary widely, but some themes are common between cases of group relationships, open relationships or polyamory, where we have several partners at once, and forms of networked intimacy where we might be casually dating or part of a larger group of intimate friends. In all these situations, our efforts to include more people or to remain open to others might shape our interpersonal dynamics for the better. Two benefits stand out: the corroboration of intimate identity, and increased checks and balances.

Nonmonogamous lifestyles can help us to understand and corroborate our intimate identity. Our intimate identity is our grasp of who we are as a romantic person: what we desire, our habits and quirks, and how other people appreciate our actions. When we are intimate with more people, it is easier to arrive at an accurate and realistic understanding of these things. It is hard to maintain an inflated or inaccurate sense of oneself as a romantic person when we have several partners, and harder still if those people talk to each other or even live together. Partly, this is a matter of having different contexts in which to act and react to other people, and partly it is a matter of being able to cross-check our sense of self against the interpretations of several people.

Nonmonogamous relationships also shape our romantic behaviour. When several people are involved, there is the potential for greater oversight and accountability. Poor behaviour is more likely to be exposed; a divergent story or explanation is less likely to take hold; our insecurities are more likely to be addressed. Conversation will often be joint conversation, which is informed by different points of view.

The exact nature of this increased oversight depends on the kind of relationships we have. Someone pursuing 'solo polyamory' and dating within a wider community of like-minded people will benefit from increased 'eyes on the street', to co-opt the urbanist metaphor popularized by Jane Jacobs.[10] Members of their community provide information and scrutiny which helps to regulate individual behaviour. A rich network of friends, exes, acquaintances, and event organizers or bartenders creates a web of accountability.

A polyamorous group might function in a different way. Imagine four people who are in a relationship and practise kitchen-table polyamory together.[11] They openly discuss their feelings and relationship dynamic regularly, and their conversations sometimes include the other people they are dating. Their structural dynamic can be compared to the separation and dispersal of power within some governments, which is designed to ensure one branch of government does not dominate the others.[12] Each person in the group benefits from a degree of intimate oversight that is often lacking in monogamous relationships. They will be less able to neglect or dominate another member of the house without consequence, and more able to receive feedback and support. Clearly this is not a dynamic for everyone, but if we take seriously Giddens' idea that a relationship can be its 'own forum', the kind of forum in this situation is expanded and more boisterous in ways which might help us to act better.

To some extent, we can benefit from related dynamics in other kinds of polyamorous or open relationships where we have several separate relationships at the same time. As long as some information is shared between partners, we can benefit from the perspective of one partner in considering the behaviour of another, and vice versa. In a sense, each partner serves as a public for the others, because their behaviour and account of the relationship are visible to other people who are also intimately invested in us.

Two obvious objections need considering at this point. The first concedes the value of oversight and accountability, but asks whether this can be provided in the same way by friends or family. The second concerns the possibility of uniquely harmful dynamics within groups.

We can be supported by family and friends, and they often provide a valuable check on the actions of lovers and partners. In many situations, an outsider's perspective is hugely beneficial. But our understanding of ourselves as romantic agents, people trying to sustain intimacy with others, is shaped and deepened in the romantic and sexual interactions we have. Advice from a friend is only as useful as the accuracy of the stories we tell them, and so of our understanding of our experiences. If we are mistaken, prone to exaggeration, ashamed or deluded, our friends and family will inadvertently reinforce our perspective. A wider intimate forum makes this harder because there are more people to whom we stand as an intimate partner. Our behaviour, emotional responses, and self-understanding are more widely known in relevant detail.

We are also right to worry about the potentially harmful side of group dynamics. A natural riposte to the promise of increased accountability and oversight in the kitchen table polyamory example is to imagine situations where two people dominate a third. At first glance, these situations seem worse than in a monogamous relationship where we are dominated by one person since our domination is overdetermined: if Jack stopped dominating us, Jill would still do so. There may be some situations where this kind of dynamic exists.

Cases of sustained manipulation, abuse, and gaslighting are possible, and the group is arguably better able to sustain an environment of subordination. But I suspect these cases are less prevalent than our fear of them.

First, they are possible only in tighter group forms of nonmonogamy, especially those isolated from wider communities. These are rarer than other kinds of nonmonogamy. Second, the structure of these cases is complicated as group dynamics shift. In the group context, someone who is being pressured by two other people has double the chances of changing the dynamic of the group in their favour than in the monogamous case. Similarly, power in the group is still dispersed and separate even if contingently wielded against a minority. This introduces some structural instability into the dynamic which makes resistance and accountability a bit more likely.

In practice, much depends on the specific arrangements, relationship practices, and personalities involved. Group dynamics are often fraught in less dramatic ways, which can nevertheless cloud our individual agency. Emerging group idiolects can be inflexible; discursive practices can privilege articulate people; exiting the group might be easier for some but not others. And this is before we have considered the issue of explicit *hierarchy*.

Many nonmonogamous people find it quite natural to embrace intimate hierarchies. They might date alongside a core relationship, or have sex outside their marriage. In some cases, the hierarchy is explicit; in others, it emerges in practice. It is tempting to argue that hierarchy is inherently problematic: a form of intimate inegalitarianism which can only be dominating. But this view neglects my point about the ways various boundaries, exclusions, and commitments help us to construct our agency. Some people, for example, want and appreciate being a 'second' or 'unicorn' or in a 'comet relationship' where they are involved only intermittently in the intimate life of other people. Others will find their primacy over certain aspects of intimate life – for example, a domestic space – helps them to support their partner's romantic life outside the home.

The issue of hierarchy is a complex one which requires more discussion than I can provide here. It suffices to note both the promise and pitfalls of nonmonogamous configurations which extend oversight and accountability beyond one person. Some of us will find these changes are agency-enhancing because they make it easier to form and sustain a variety of romantic intimacies in a supportive context. But, as with political life, a shift of romantic 'constitution' towards nonmonogamous arrangements offers no guarantee that conflict, instability, even domination, will be absent. There is no such guarantee. We should be careful not to think about relationships from the perspective of the confident and articulate.

Anarchization

Another way that nonmonogamy might appeal to us is because it offers us relational *practices* that help us to appreciate each other, to be caring and intimate. Whether we are excited by this may be down to our personal agential style. Some of us embrace the uncertainty of life-long learning on the job, as it were, whereas others want clear boundaries and guidelines before acting.

Let us first consider the change of agential mindset that can be associated with nonmonogamy. This has parallels with anarchist thinking about freedom and social institutions, and some nonmonogamous people explicitly pursue the parallel with anarchy, or call themselves relationship anarchists.[13] Writing on this topic is in short supply, however, and often underplays the lessons we can draw from extant anarchist work. (I address this in more detail elsewhere.[14])

Relationship anarchists differ from other nonmonogamous people in several ways. First, they explicitly reject amatonormativity. Loving romantic sexual relationships need not be thought of as primary – every relationship has value, and relationships do not have to take expected or typical forms to have meaning within a life.[15] Second, relationship anarchists are wary of hierarchical arrangements, such as calling one partner 'primary' and another 'secondary'.[16] Third, they are wary of state-based solutions to contemporary romantic limitations, even radical ones such as attempts to redesign marriage[17] or use complex intimate contracts.[18] These views help to distinguish romantic anarchism from some forms of polyamory.

You might be wary of the label 'relationship anarchist'. But there is value in thinking about nonmonogamy from an anarchist perspective. Valuable themes come to light when we look at intimacy with what James C. Scott calls the 'anarchist squint'.[19] In particular, we can ask what themes are latent in the actual practices of many nonmonogamous people. Why can nonmonogamy seem like a dynamic form of life? In the rest of this section, I provide my answer, drawing on the relationship anarchist mindset.

Fundamentally, romantic freedom is *presupposed*, not granted. Instead of thinking about rules and permissions to act in romantic life as if we stand as lawgivers to each other, we think instead about what our partners need from us in being able to act as they would like. Our relationships, and their sustaining commitments, are designed consciously to promote what we need, and are able to do, not to meet social expectations.

This focus on needs and abilities foregrounds agency and the activity of relating to other people. This involves a shift of *perspective*; we view relationships as processes of relating to another, rather than as contexts in which we are trying to achieve goals.[20] We regard each other as fellow participants in a mutual endeavour, rather than viewing relationships as 'maximum security institutions' which need protecting from external threats.[21] This shift of perspective, and efforts to acknowledge that relating to people is a process, helps us to build our agency, especially if our abilities to be intimate are precarious.

Emphasis on process is inherently *exploratory*. Our sense of our needs and capabilities is often unclear, as is our sense of which relationship arrangement might help us to relate well to the people we care about. We are prepared to try things out and be open-minded about the arrangements which will suit us. Our agreements can be revisable or provisional – we do not privilege open-ended or long-term agreements.

Being active in our relations to others, and open to exploration beyond familiar routines and norms, means *communication* becomes especially significant. Nonmonogamous life encourages a shift of emphasis towards the significance of clear and open communication. This takes time to learn, requires trust, and increases our vulnerability as we let go of the desire to control our interactions.

This agential focus is not narrow. The anarchist squint reveals great emphasis on the sharing of ideas, skills, and practices within broader nonmonogamous communities. Being attentive to these external influences and advice helps us to relate intimately to each other and softens our arrogance. *Education* and the sharing of skills is the central counterpart to processes of individual attention and activity. Although relationships are unique, many relationship situations or dynamics are common and can be discussed within the community.

The possibility of learning from others rests on the more general faith in *mutuality* common to many forms of nonmonogamous life. Another shift of perspective concerns human nature and how we stand towards each other. The anarchist squint reveals communities of cooperation, non-rivalry, mutual aid, and care. Mutual aid, a central notion in anarchist thought, has wide resonance in nonmonogamous life.[22] We might embrace nonmonogamous relationships because we want to draw upon a broader pool of resources, especially if we share domestic life or raise children together.[23] These resources can also help us to devote time to relationship building – something which is often under pressure if we have busy working lives.

But the notion of resource also has a psychological dimension. With more partners, or the possibility of additional intimacy, we can access greater intimate care and affection, which may benefit our self-esteem. Some forms of nonmonogamy can also offer people the degree of attachment support they require.[24] This is contrary to the idea that nonmonogamy prevents us from having secure attachments. If we find ourselves struggling to feel secure, or benefit from additional corroboration and reassurance, then having several partners can be comforting. Since attachment is connected to our confidence in our agency, additional attachments can help us to act.

Relationship anarchists try to think differently about romantic life. They help us to shift perspective towards the activities and practices which sustain intimacy, and away from frameworks, rules, goals and institutions. Clearly, our relationships will evolve in different ways depending on the kind of nonmonogamy we pursue, and the quirks of our personality and social context, but we can embrace the underlying emphasis on the development of agency rather than the desire to protect agency.

Moreover, we can adopt these shifts in mindset without hostility towards existing institutions. Practically speaking, many nonmonogamous people are engaged in what Ruth Kinna calls 'anarchization'.[25] Anarchization is the attempt to forge new social practices, and develop valuable character traits, within imperfect situations or with people who do not share our broader political views. Anarchization can take many forms, but is often successful to the extent that we can highlight the ways in which we have common values or face shared constraints, and can illustrate our values in action. Although monogamous and nonmonogamous relationships have their distinct challenges, the practical emphasis on process, trust, mutuality, and so on can be shared.

Of course, there are pitfalls when attempting to implement a relationship anarchist emphasis on agency and process. Domination can be a feature of situations where we are inarticulate or lack power, but have to communicate difficult feelings or establish boundaries. Some people will be more able to influence the choices of others in these situations.

Romantic change can also be disorientating. A couple who considers opening their relationship, for example, might experience insecurity or distress that can be debilitating for one or both of them. They might feel their attachment needs are going unmet. This disorientation can expose other tensions in their relationship.

Similarly, hasty shifts of perspective inspired by ideals of 'radical honesty' or clear communication can be harmful if not anchored in sustainable practices. Everyone is familiar with cruelty served under the guise of honesty, or situations where we are forced to ignore our ambivalence in order to be heard. If implemented crudely, nonmonogamous rhetoric of discussion amplifies the precarity of shy and inarticulate people. Similarly, the emphasis on honesty and openness can hamper people who do not know what they want, or who have a newly emerging sense of their romantic personality or sexual identity.

All of this is another way of saying that nonmonogamous practices, as with other forms of political and social change, risk enshrining 'polynormative discourse' which helps to sustain uneven romantic privilege.[26] It is as easy to manipulate, browbeat, and bamboozle someone using the slang of nonmonogamy as it is any other kind of romantic language (perhaps easier, given current cultural associations of nonmonogamy and consent). Nonmonogamous intimacy can be individualist too, and overlook the ways in which our romantic agency is fragile.

Conclusion

Romantic agency is our ability to pursue intimacy. This ability is shaped by other people. We want to both maintain and deepen this ability, but progress is neither guaranteed nor linear. Our intimate abilities might also lag behind our romantic desires; the relationship we want, or are expected to have, is not always one we can make work.

Different kinds of romantic life will shape our agency in different ways. As we have seen, these varying arrangements have their own advantages and pitfalls. Exclusivity can be a form of intimate specialization, whereas nonexclusivity can help us to sustain practices of appreciation, oversight and corroboration, and radical approaches to romantic norms and hierarchy. Whether these benefits are accessible to us will depend on our personality, partners, and the people around us.

What should be clear by now is that we can learn from other ways of organizing intimate life, whatever relationship dynamic we prefer. In doing so, we might reduce some of the anxiety and disorientation that stems from clinging rigidly to romantic norms in a world of changing practices. Even if we remain in conventional relationships, the ways we do so can draw upon other experiments in intimacy.

The first half of this book worked towards a conception of romantic agency. The second half will now ask how we are to nurture this agency. I will describe some traits and practices which help us to protect the ability to be intimate with each other, even in contexts of uncertainty or challenging feelings.

5
Realistic Conversation

... a genuine conversation is never the one that we wanted to conduct. (Hans-Georg Gadamer)[1]

What can we do to nurture our romantic agency?

A short answer might be: we can choose a form of romantic relationship that works for us and our partners. But these choices are hard to make. For one thing, romantic life is often happening around us. Rarely do we sit back, think, decide, and then implement a plan. We often stumble into intimate connections with people, and find ourselves thinking hard only in moments of uncertainty or conflict when we are already invested.

Our romantic thinking is not linear, either. The possibility of change accompanies all intimacy, and we can shift between different romantic dynamics as our relationships develop – at one time favouring experimentation and openness, at another time exclusivity, and so on. Our desires might change dramatically as we grapple with an unexpected infatuation; a new job might mean a relationship becomes long-distance; expecting a child might shift our perspective.

Practically, these factors mean it can be hard to think about romantic life. We can be so invested in someone, gripped by strong feelings, or blindsided by circumstance that reflection seems impossible. We are also prone to being defensive, and may rather think about our situation in terms of popular romantic narratives, not on its own terms.

The best we can do is keep talking to each other. But for those conversations to help us nurture our romantic agency, and inform our decisions about how to organize our relationships, they must be realistic.

Conversation

It can seem trite to suggest that we should talk about the relationships we might want, but many of us resist these conversations. Fear of rejection or loss can nudge us towards familiar relationship patterns without exploring alternatives. A new couple might stumble into being exclusive, for example, because they do not want to consider other options and risk disagreement at a time when they feel especially vulnerable. Even if we are not defensive, we might unreflectively copy the relationships of our family or friends. We should instead talk about the kind of romantic life which aligns with our particular romantic agency. These conversations are valuable irrespective of what we decide to do.

Conversation, as I understand it here, should be distinguished from attempts to exchange information and from negotiation. To converse with someone is to talk with, not at, them, to be open to discovery, and not to have a rigid sense of what we are trying to achieve. Hans-Georg Gadamer captures some of what I have in mind by noting that 'the first condition of the art of conversation is making sure the other person is with us', and that 'to conduct a conversation means to allow oneself to be conducted by the subject matter'.[2] For Gadamer, 'the more genuine a conversation is, the less its conduct lies within the will of either partner'.[3]

There are many layers to this process. Daniela Dover, for example, developed a rich account of what they call 'taking one another seriously', which lies at the heart of a conversational attitude towards another person.[4] To take someone seriously in this sense is to engage with them in a process of open talk in which we seek their input, let them shape our self-understanding, and want them to adopt the same attitude towards us. Conversation is not simply an exchange of information, or the swapping of separate stories. Instead, we are open to our understanding of a topic, or of ourselves, being shaped by the other person's perspective. As Dover puts it, 'I have to see *your* answers to *my* questions.'[5] Taking someone seriously also extends to how we are prepared to view ourselves. Conversation can be one process through which we allow someone's interpretation of us to shape our self-interpretation. Dover calls this a process of 'abdicating our interpretive sovereignty', and it happens when we bring 'our respective self-, other-, and world-interpretations into a sort of discursive and imaginative contact that has the potential to alter them'.[6]

Not all conversations can roam widely, of course. Sometimes we just need to reach a decision. But we need to decide with another person. Andrea Westlund names this process 'joint deliberation'.[7] We can view joint deliberation as the practical version of taking someone seriously in conversation.

Crucially, joint deliberation differs from negotiation. Negotiation is oriented towards our existing goals or desires. When we are negotiating, we might listen closely to our partners, we might compromise and make concessions, but we do so only to pursue our prior ends. It does not matter whether the other person is 'with' us in these situations. We do not seek their input and care little about how they view us. We care about their perspective only insofar as it can be exploited. Negotiation reveals more about our will than it does about the topic at hand.

Negotiation is unlike joint deliberation because we do not need to occupy a shared perspective with someone. When we deliberate jointly, we are *thinking together* about what to do, not simply combining our pre-established intentions or weighing our separate interests. We must be open about our reasons and remain sensitive to the other person. As Westlund puts it, we want our deliberations to 'support and express a conception of our relationship as one between individuals who are mutually concerned for each other'.[8] We take something as a reason for us both – our desire to experiment, say – only if the other person views it in the same way. This involvement of the other means joint deliberation is a dialogical process which unfolds in a series of mutually involved interactions. Openness to someone is a finely balanced attitude. On the one hand, we cannot stand too rigidly behind our reasons for action, because this shows we do not care about trying to occupy a shared practical standpoint. On the other hand, we cannot be too quick to defer to someone, as this shows we are unwilling to engage in mutual activity.[9]

In joint deliberation it matters to us, and our partners, that each of us has a reason to accept the outcome. Negotiation is not like this because we might not care about how the other person views our reasons, nor worry about how they view their position. Indeed, in negotiation we might be pleased to notice someone lacks a good reason for their view, or is overcome by emotion, as this gives us an advantage.[10]

Westlund argues that, although the norms of joint deliberation are similar to general conversational norms, they go further in requiring that the people involved have a 'mutual, non-instrumental concern *for one another*'.[11] For example, we could have a conversation with a stranger about literature in Gadamer's sense of being open to them and guided by the subject, without sharing mutual concern for that person.

Joint deliberation is typically practical and concerned with what to do, as shown by Westlund's illustrative example of people asking whether they should still go for a run even though it is raining. Romantic conversation is sometimes practical in this sense. A couple might think together about what they will do to remain intimate during a long-distance relationship, or decide upon the boundaries which will enable them to have an open relationship.

But romantic conversation is not just concerned with action. We often deliberate about matters of understanding. These conversations require us to take each other seriously in Dover's sense, but they might also be aimed at a certain resolution. 'What is this?', a couple might ask: 'Should we say we are together?', 'Are we exclusive?'

Some romantic conversation is even less practical, and so further removed from deliberation in the classic sense. Together, lovers might be trying to understand a situation; a shared acquaintance; a feeling; their relationship; an ideal, fantasy, or distant possibility. Conversation in this sense blends into story-telling. In romantic conversation, we often ask 'What does this mean to us?', 'Why does this matter?', 'Where do we see this going?', 'Why do you feel like that?' Different interpretations jostle within our shared standpoint.

Romantic conversation has to be carefully distinguished from romantic negotiation. We can talk to people without trying to share their standpoint, seek their input into us, or without showing any mutual concern. In romantic negotiation, we are led by our desires, or ideal of a relationship, and seek to work out whether someone can give us what we want. We are concerned more with what they offer us, and may not think much about whether they have a good reason to agree to what we propose.

You might think this perspective is unavoidable when we have just met someone. Daniela Dover, for example, suggests that, although one-off interactions can be deep and change how we view ourselves or the world, the ability to take each other seriously in rich conversation is most likely to arise and thrive in relationships 'when interlocutors can draw on a deep enough reservoir of mutual trust, goodwill, and interest in one another to be willing to enter into difficult (emotionally fraught, intellectually taxing, or otherwise uncomfortable) interactions and to accept the vulnerability this entails'.[12] This has the implication, for example, that it is near impossible to take someone seriously on a first date.

I am less sure about this. Even when getting to know someone, romantic conversation seems attainable and valuable. We can take someone seriously in proleptic mode – i.e., by acting *as if* we shared mutual concern with them in the hope that doing so will bring it about that we do as our interactions unfold. We can try to talk with a first date, not at them, and remain open from the offset to the possibility that they can influence how we think about ourselves, our interpretation of our interactions, and the hopes we have for any shared future.

Nor is romantic negotiation a risk only when getting to know people. It might be more common if we are dating or looking for a compatible partner, and so prone to reject people quickly, but this attitude can arise within relationships too. We can fall into negotiating mode when we stop looking for someone's input, fail to take seriously their perspective, become rigid in how we view ourselves, or if we no longer care about mutuality. Arrogance, strong desires, or inflexibility can see people fail to take each other seriously.

The importance of romantic conversation goes beyond its practical outcomes. As a rich and perplexing thoughtful activity, romantic conversation is an *exercise* of romantic agency. It is something we do with other people. Through conversation, we can actively feel our ability, or lack of ability, to take people seriously and think with our intimate partners. If we are lucky, and they are able, they can corroborate our efforts and support us when we are confused, ambivalent, or unsure.

Romantic conversation is ongoing in the sense that a current conversation relates to past discussions, and may be developed in future. But ongoing thought is not necessarily frequent thought. We do not need to spend all our time talking. Much of the time our interactions are habitual, and run on default. With this in mind, we want a systematic account of *when* we should start romantic conversations, because sometimes it will be cowardly or unreasonable to evade them. I do not have such an account, but a preliminary answer would refer back to romantic agency: we need to talk especially in contexts which threaten our ability to sustain intimacy.

You might think that this kind of conversation seems aimless, academic, or requires us to have special insights. But this strikes me as mistaken. Romantic conversation is the activity through which we come to have insight – insight is not a prerequisite for romantic conversation. That said, I am sympathetic to the idea that the value of romantic conversation only becomes clear over time. Conversation is a good candidate for what Talbot Brewer calls a 'dialectical activity'. Dialectical activities have:

> A self-unveiling character, in the sense that each successive engagement yields a further stretch of understanding of the goods internal to the activity, hence of what would count as a proper engagement in it. If the activity's constitutive goods are complex and elusive enough, this dialectical process can be reiterated indefinitely, with each successive engagement yielding a clearer grasp of the activity's proper form and preparing the way for a still more adequate and hence more revealing engagement in it.[13]

This means that the practice of continued conversation with other people is required if we are to arrive at a richer sense of why, and in what ways, such conversation has value for us. But all we need to start talking is the hunch there is value in doing so.

Realism

Romantic conversation can be undermined in several ways. All conversation is vulnerable to the influence of domineering people, and our general ability to converse intimately can be shaken by insecurity and fear.

We are better at romantic conversation if we have supportive virtues. Courage, for example, helps us to face hard truths, voice unpleasant feelings without knowing how others will react, and follow a conversation into uncharted territory. Kindness helps us to criticize people without wounding their self-esteem.

My understanding of virtue is shaped by the work of Julia Annas, who regards virtues as settled dispositions to act reliably in commitment to values. These dispositions are best understood as similar to practical skills.[14] As with other skills, we exhibit practical intelligence when we exercise the virtues. This practical intelligence is developed as we are habituated into specific contexts, and deepens with experience as we become sensitive to the relevant features of our situation. We may have to work to develop these dispositions to help correct against tendencies we have to be swayed or distracted from what we value. Beginners might need to reflect explicitly about what they are doing; specialists, in contrast, find their skills manifest more directly, and corrective reflection is less frequent. If we are kind towards our partners, for example, we may find that we rarely need to think about how best to form a criticism, because we have learned how to be sensitive to the demands of different contexts in a way which enables us to act well.

Realism is a crucial virtue in romantic life. In being realistic, we are better able to align our romantic deliberations with a good sense of what romantic life is actually like. For example, realism helps us to see that our romantic culture is shaped around stories and ideals which are hard for ordinary people to attain, or which do not capture all forms of thriving romantic intimacy. In being realistic, we may also appreciate that our ability to be intimate does not arrive out of nowhere, and may depend on how we have been treated in the past.

Realistic conversations are not just shaped by our romantic preferences. Our preferences might diverge from those of our partners. More importantly, our wants have a history, are shaped by our social context, and may diverge from our abilities. We might want an expansive nonmonogamous life, only to struggle with insecurity. Or we might want to settle down with 'the one', only to find ourselves yearning for more lovers. Realism helps us to view these desires in the context of a relationship, if we have one, and of our romantic agency.

This view of realism can resemble historical accounts of autonomy. John Christman, for example, argues that we are autonomous when we act on the basis of desires which we would still endorse once we understand their historical origins.[15] I am not committing to a specific conception of autonomy here, but I should note that we can endorse desires which we would struggle to enact, and we can act on desires which we do not (yet) endorse. It is rare, also, to scrutinize desires before action – rough intimations are quite common when setting out on new relationships. In addition, endorsement need not be a straightforward cognitive task. The process of exploring a form of intimacy with someone, by interacting with them, can itself be a process of scrutinizing desire. We might be aware that our desire for an exclusive partnership, for example, has its historical roots in our social context and upbringing but remain unsure about whether we endorse this desire, and hope that our relationship will make this clearer. This exposes us to some risks, and I consider whether and how we might bear them well in the next chapter.

There are two layers to realism, which I will call *particular* realism and *general* realism. Particular realism requires us to consider how things are. What are we like as romantic individuals? What are our partners or prospective partners like? How do we behave when we are together?

Being realistic in this way requires us to try to understand ourselves, our partners, and our social context. We need to grapple with our immediate social environment, with its norms, ideals, and rituals, but also appreciate our romantic history and its impact. We are not prisoners of the past, but we are permeable beings and susceptible to acting and being attached without awareness of what we are doing.

Particular realism requires us to resist the temptation towards overly simple or complete assessments of ourselves or our situation. Sometimes we know less than we would like. We are ambivalent, or see that one situation can be interpreted in different ways. Or we appreciate that our actions can fall into patterns which only become clear over time. Realism makes space for this unknowing.

General realism, in contrast, has us asking: what are romantic relationships like? To be realistic in this way is to appreciate the broader facts about romantic life and the impact of social context. It is to understand that visions of love and intimacy, and the practices in which those visions come to life, have a history and are shaped by social norms and institutions. General realism also requires us to appreciate truisms about romantic life: that many relationships end; that desires, bodies, and values change over time; that people struggle with insecurity or jealousy, and so on. These can seem like hackneyed observations, but they are easily ignored when they clash with our favoured ideals.

We do not need a sociology degree to be realistic. We just need to try to resist being seduced by romantic simplifications or popular ideals, and look outwards to learn from the experiences of our family, friends, and community to understand the different forms intimacy can take.

Realism is important because it helps us to settle on romantic arrangements which protect, or even improve, our romantic agency. Often realism functions negatively by enabling us to avoid distortions and fantasies, even if we are currently unsure about ourselves or what underpins our ability to be intimate. Alongside this, realism shows we are oriented towards the truth. In being realistic, we are open to evidence and allow this evidence to constrain our attitudes.

Optimism

Talk of realism will raise several concerns. Three stand out: that calls for realism are inherently conservative; that realism prevents us from benefiting from idealizations; and that realism can lead to practical disagreements.

Realism can appear limiting. If we have to be realistic, attend to our romantic agency, and be wary of how our desires can be shaped by our social world, are we not imprisoned within the limits of what we can do? Is this not the life of an oyster? As F. H. Bradley suggested, 'it is no human ideal to lead "the life of an oyster". We have no right first to find out just what we happen to be and to have, and then to contract our wants to that limit.'[16] Might it be good for our desires to outrun our abilities? More troublingly, if we must be sensitive to 'what romantic life is like' are we not tethered to the status quo?

These concerns are important and need handling carefully. The worry about realism and the status quo is perhaps easiest to answer. Our realism can actually upend familiar ideals. General realism about romantic life, for instance, will lead us to appreciate that romantic relationships end, that sexual desire is often fluid, and that many people flourish within unconventional relationships. Long-lasting love or unwavering desires will be viewed as exceptions rather than the norm, and certainly not states to which we are entitled. A realistic person will not be surprised to hear of a blended family, of bisexual masculinity, of asexual romance. These realizations can have broad implications for our relationships. They shape what we expect, alter our frames of reference, and temper our self-criticism. This is so even if we have traditional relationships. The practical attitudes of a realistic monogamist, for instance, will differ from those of someone who views monogamy as the only form of romantic flourishing.

More significantly, the particular realism that has us looking carefully at our own desires and personality could help us to realize we are not suited to have just one romantic partner, or that we do not want to share domestic space, or that we value sexual intimacy more than emotional intimacy, or that we do not want any romantic relationships. All of these conclusions pull us away from what is socially conventional. We arrive at them by thinking about what we are like, rather than what society wants. These realizations might be painful. We might desperately want a relationship which our family would celebrate, only to realize we are better suited to something different. Being realistic is deeply unpredictable, not wed to the status quo.

The worry about the connection between realism, desire, and imagination is more pressing. We can be wrong about what we are like, or fixate on some features of human intimacy while neglecting others. Clearly, there must be space for us to be motivated by desires which pull us beyond the horizon of our current abilities. If not, we would never develop new skills or explore unfamiliar affections.

I explore how we can take romantic risks in the next chapter. Here I will just note that our romantic agency can change over time, and the gap between our desires and abilities can play a role in this. These tensions are valuable provided we can appreciate them for what they are. Similarly, it is rare for all our desires to be satisfied. Desire in romantic life can inform and infuse our lives and actions, and the routes taken by our imagination, even if it does not result in action. Put another way: a realistic person gives desire its proper place in life. This will not preclude frustration or disappointment, but they will see that the ability to be intimate is more important than being able to imagine new intimacies, and the latter should not overwhelm the former.

Another forceful objection to my focus on realism is that romantic life benefits from a *lack* of realism. So-called 'positive illusions' about the chances of our relationship lasting, the quality of our relationship, or our partner's personality have all been correlated with relationship success.[17] In summarizing some of these findings, Lisa Bortolotti writes that 'the idealisation of romantic partners helps us continue to value the relationship as something worth working on, and is linked to more satisfying and more stable relationships in both the short and the long term'.[18]

Several mechanisms might account for this. The first is simply that when we idealize our partners or relationships, we insulate ourselves slightly from more mundane realities.

Seeing things as a little better than they actually are can help us derive more satisfaction from our relationship and be more likely to stay in it over time, especially if our partner entertains the similar idealizations.

The second more interesting possibility, for which there is some evidence,[19] is that viewing someone, or a relationship, through idealized eyes changes us for the better; that, 'over time, the idealised evaluations became more realistic ... because the partners rose up to the challenge and exhibited the qualities that were initially attributed to them'.[20] Viewed in this way, illusions help us 'fake it until they make it', romantically speaking. If this is right, and these patterns of relating *as if* the relationship was great actually help to make it so, then have I overstated the importance of realism?

I think not. To simplify, let us assume for the sake of argument that some degree of positive illusion does help relationships persist because it motivates us to change to fit the idealized characterization our partners have of us. The first thing to note is that these illusions arise *within* romantic relationships. We still have to be realistic in thinking about *whether* to have a relationship with someone, and in thinking about the form that relationship will take.

Moreover, even if positive illusions help relationships to persist, it remains an open question whether those relationships are good. The mere persistence of a relationship is not inherently valuable. If it was, a long but strained relationship could be better than a short harmonious one. Good relationships help us to flourish, and one part of romantic conversation is for us to explore whether we are flourishing with others. That process benefits from the realism described above. Positive illusions cannot carry the weight of our practical thinking about how to live, and love.

The objection about idealizations can be given a different form. Might some positive illusions about our abilities to be intimate actually help to *build* our romantic agency? Our upbeat view of ourselves as a good communicator, of our partner as someone who likes experimenting, might play a role in *making* our relationship more communicative, more open to experiment.

These bootstrapping phenomena are compatible with being realistic. If we have a realistic sense of what romantic life is like, we will understand that we can be shaped by these positive illusions and that there is a softening at the edges of our appraisals of others. But in being realistic, we also understand the limits of this generous way of seeing and how to contextualize it. Realistic lovers are like a parent with a 'best parent in the world' card: they feel good in response to how their child sees them, but they know other parents are good too.

Realism is best considered in tandem with optimism. Indeed, Valerie Tiberius has developed an account of what she calls 'realistic optimism'.[21] A realistic optimist is committed to the truth while remaining disposed to having 'a positive or hopeful view about human nature and human potential'.[22] Being realistic about romantic life, but optimistic about how our relationships might go and about the general human capacity for intimacy, helps us to avoid cynicism and irony. I return to this theme in considering how we can strive to see the good in romantic life.

The third objection was that my discussion of realistic conversation is itself too optimistic. After all, romantic partners, or people contemplating a relationship, could disagree about what would support their romantic agency.

Disagreement is possible in any conversation. But realism helps us to ensure our individual attitudes are well founded. When we compare ourselves to romantic ideals, or fret about our compatibility, we can get stuck in superficial arguments. A realistic approach to romantic life, one which grasps what relationships are often like and which understands what *we* are like, helps us to understand whether a conflict is substantial or superficial. When we are realistic, we are better able to see how our ability to be intimate depends on other people; that we can be constrained by our social context; that challenging feelings can cloud our thinking; that focusing on compatibility can detract us from the dynamic features of relationships. Realism is a corrective against the tendency to be shaped by social scripts. Realistic lovers think generously with each other.

Realism will not glue us together. It is unrealistic to think that wildly diverging agential needs can be accommodated within a single relationship. To think with realistic optimism may be just to see that someone heightens our insecurities or frustrates our attempts to overcome a past experience. In those cases, realism might have us end the relationship.

Conclusion

To make good romantic choices and to flourish in our relationships, we need to be realistic. Realism helps us to avoid the excesses of romantic ideology by ensuring our actions are constrained by our grasp of what romantic life is actually like. This understanding is personal as we attend to ourselves, our situation, and our partners, and also general, as we reflect on the pressures shaping all relationships. Realism comes alive in conversations. Conversation is distinct from negotiation because it is open ended, or involves joint deliberation in which we care whether our partner has grounds to accept our reasons and perspective. We can be realistic without being pessimistic. Realistic conversation with someone is itself an exercise of romantic agency – it helps us to develop the ability to be intimate.

6
Romantic Risks

... people are often said to have integrity when they've already muffed things, miscalled outcomes, left damage, and then take such responsibility as ensues. (Margaret Walker)[1]

Competence

Everyone knows that being realistic is difficult. We often feel uncertain, or defensive, or fail to know ourselves well. The desire to experiment with unconventional relationships can make this worse. People are more likely to be unsupportive and we may struggle to find examples of thriving relationships.

A common doubt is whether we will be able to act on our romantic desires. Relationship anarchy, for instance, might align with our political values and would grant us the freedom we want, but will we be able to make it work? Do we communicate well, can we tolerate insecurity or jealousy, will we be able to defend our boundaries rather than just telling people what they want to hear?

The fact we have these doubts shows that we are realistic; that we understand the practice of intimacy can be challenging and that our ability to act is less certain than our ability to imagine. Entertaining these worries also shows we care about other people, and the harm we might cause.

If they are too loud, however, these misgivings can prevent us from exploring lifestyles which may suit us. Some people around us might be pleased with that outcome, masking their social conservatism behind appeals to caution. Restraint can also seem reasonable in cases of doubt. If realism is a virtue of deliberation, then restraint looks like a virtue of action. When we want to take an unfamiliar path, we should proceed with care, or perhaps not proceed at all.

In this chapter, I take seriously our practical doubts but resist the idea that we must be restrained. We can take romantic risks, experiment, and explore new forms of intimacy, even when we remain unsure about how we will react. Integrity and playfulness are traits which help us to overcome doubt while remaining responsible to others.

Plans

Even hardened conservatives are unlikely to think we have to be fully competent lovers before starting a romantic relationship. Skills are often acquired on the job, as it were, and some skills have to be acquired with other people. It is through having romantic relationships that we understand how to navigate vulnerability and treat people well.

That said, it is not only conservatives who think our romantic choices should be considered choices. It always makes sense to consider some of the implications of our affections before committing to someone. Random or reckless romance might work out, but only by accident. What is more likely is that we leave hurt people in our wake.

What would a balance of uncertainty and consideration look like in practice? Raja Halwani has an approach to these issues which I find helpful to consider.[2] Although I ultimately disagree with some features of his view, I am sympathetic to his project of trying to show that unconventional romantic lives, particularly nonmonogamous ones, can be rational and virtuous.

Like me, Halwani worries about the possible gaps between what we want and our ability to act on our desires. One of his examples, which I shall focus on, is of a couple who are considering opening their relationship. Exploring nonmonogamy can be a fraught and uncertain process, with the possibility for many unexpected feelings. Halwani thinks their decision to open the relationship can be a virtuous one, but only if they have 'minimal to non-existent self-deception about their motives and about their ability to handle open relationships'.[3] He also thinks such open relationships are morally acceptable only if 'the sexual impulse that leads to them is part of a rational and virtuous life plan'.[4]

Halwani does not develop these remarks in detail, but I find them helpful to consider. To start with, he seems to set the bar very high when it comes to self-knowledge. We need to know, in advance, what our motives are and that we can handle a specific form of relationship. This view overlooks the ways in which we often acquire self-knowledge in the trying of new things, not prior to trying them. This knowledge barrier gets worse if we think that embracing open relationships, especially from a place of settled monogamy, can be transformative experiences in the sense I mentioned in chapter 3, because then we cannot easily draw informative parallels between our experience of conventional romantic relationships and our imagined experience of an unconventional one.[5]

Even if exploring open relationships is not transformative in that technical sense, we can wonder whether *anyone* would meet Halwani's requirement of self-knowledge in romantic life? Are monogamous people free of deception as to why they want an exclusive relationship and about their ability to handle it? Perhaps not. There is a tradition, from Sigmund Freud via Herbert Marcuse to Laura Kipnis, of social critics trying to unearth the obscured motives and desires of people in monogamous societies.[6] In the absence of an independent defence of the value of a particular social norm, it is not clear that deviations from it should have to meet higher standards of justification than adherences to it. (Halwani could agree with this, of course, and think the bar should be high for everyone.)

Overly restrictive knowledge requirements should worry us because they risk entrenching the romantic status quo. We will never be able to experiment if we need to understand, in advance, what the implications will be or whether we will be able to sustain our actions over time. If experimentation is not possible, or very difficult to justify, we had better hope the status quo is adequate.

We can also ask *why* it might be hard to have self-knowledge about our likely response to unconventional relationships. This is not simply a rational failing, but a consequence of the social context we are trying to challenge. In chapter 1, I described the ways in which our characters are shaped by our social contexts. We grow up surrounded by norms privileging monogamy, for example, or norms repressing sexual exploration. Our habits and traits also take shape in this context. We can internalize patterns of behaviour which help us to navigate compatibility culture, say, or cope with frequent rejection, but which may not help us to thrive long term. These pressures mean the deck is stacked against people who want to explore unconventional lifestyles, and it is not their fault.

An analogy might help to illuminate the dynamic I have in mind. Recall that I drew on Lisa Tessman's idea of 'moral damage'. She was concerned with how oppression shapes character in ways which obstruct people's flourishing, but help them to survive. To make this concrete, let us imagine such a person: Simone, a lesbian in a homophobic and patriarchal society. Simone wants to reject her closeted life, live openly, and try to actively protest against the social attitudes and institutions which sustain the homophobia she experiences.

It strikes me as unreasonably demanding to require Simone to have to know in advance what her motivations are and whether she will be able to sustain a life of resistance. That condition would prevent her from pursuing a path of activism in the first place because there is much she does not know. Because she has been raised in an oppressive society, she will have to push against her habits of self-preservation in order to live openly. She is not sure how she will react to hostility, nor how her protests will shape her personality over time. When the deck has been so heavily stacked against her, through no fault of her own and in support of norms we should reject, the most we can hope for is that she has a rough sense she can sustain the life of protest.

A similar point applies, in a less extreme way, to unconventional romantic lives. In those situations, people who want to explore the unconventional will run up against constraints which make it hard for them to anticipate outcomes, through no fault of their own and due to a web of social norms which should be challenged.

Clearly, there can be more or less reckless ways of making these decisions. All I have shown is that the bar for self-knowledge can be justly lowered in cases where the barriers to that knowledge are systematic and need addressing. If this is right, however, then it may have the consequence that people can be less confident in their ability to handle polyamory, say, than they can in their ability to handle a monogamous relationship, and yet still act reasonably.

Let us now turn to Halwani's remarks about our romantic choices and rational life plans. Those remarks can be given a weak and strong reading. On a weaker reading, we have to try to pursue a course of life that is internally consistent and makes sense relative to some values. On a stronger reading, we have to develop a detailed personal plan of life which has a clear place for the kind of romantic relationships we desire. Other views will lie between these two.

The weak reading seems uninteresting. We can develop an abstract sense of how a life could be organized around the pursuit of polyamorous multi-partner intimacy just as much as we could around the pursuit of a monogamous marriage. This reading also retains the gap between our theoretical sense of which lives *could* be pursued by someone, and the practical matter of which life should be *our* life.

The stronger view, however, seems more controversial because it also seems restrictive. We can agree that the pursuit of romantic openness ought to be 'intentionally part of a deliberate and rational way of leading one's life',[7] but disagree that we have to have a clear rational 'life plan'.

Halwani's appeal to rational plans stems, I think, from worry that we are liable to misunderstand what matters to us. Deep down, we might most value intimacy, care, and companionship, but find ourselves fixated on the sexual novelty which seems accessible in an open relationship. Halwani also seems sceptical about our ability to maintain multiple romantically *loving* relationships at once.

At first glance, it seems plausible that, to be morally acceptable, romantic experimentation should be situated within a rational plan of life. We do not want to review our lives only to see we have derailed ourselves from the pursuits we value. Or see we have been reckless. Or that we have hurt other people. Nor do many people want a life of practical conflicts, which may arise if we try to juggle incompatible ends. With these worries at the forefront of our minds, reflection on our whole lives can seem like a useful reference point which enables us to make good decisions.

We have to appeal to notions of rational plan with care. In romantic contexts, we risk unwittingly supporting the idea of the romantic escalator, which is the assumption that all romantic relationship should take the same deepening course as we move from casual dating to committed relationships, marriage, and domestic life. If we are to appeal to plans at all, we need to make room for unconventional trajectories.

More directly, there are reasons to be wary of planning language altogether. For one thing, planning risks closing us off to unexpected goods.[8] Sometimes, a sensitive and open-minded response to the people who enter our lives in unanticipated ways changes us for the better, even if our resulting actions would conflict with an existing plan.

An emphasis on planning may also obscure the ways in which we depend on others. Romantic life is not a domain for the 'career self' who is focused, goal-oriented, and downplays their indebtedness to other people.[9] If we do form romantic plans, they will concern other people. In general, planning with others is always a bit uncertain, but sometimes we might disagree about how our lives will unfold together. Plans concerning our romantic partners are especially provisional, which means romantic ethics cannot take the form of an 'individualistic planning ethics'.[10]

These interpersonal aspects of our romantic thinking deepen an additional problem. Trying to figure out whether a particular course of action fits within our rational life plan makes sense only if the choice would not radically change the kind of life we would lead. In the cases where it would change things radically, our life plan does not serve as a good reference point to figure out whether we are acting wisely, as our life is what is up for consideration. The choice faced by the couple considering opening their relationship, for example, would arguably change their life dramatically, so talk of how that change might fit with their life is not as helpful as it might seem. This tension is worse if the couple did not agree, or were not settled beforehand, on their life plan.

Halwani is right that we should consider our choices, but I do not share the idea that they have to fit into a broader rational life plan. We must be able to change our romantic situation without being fully sure of the implications. To think otherwise is to ask too much of ourselves, and risks making exploration impossible. Rough plans can be useful, as can imagining various ways a choice might shape our lives, but these sketches are limited and should be highly provisional.

Put another way, placing great emphasis on the centrality of planning is often unrealistic, as it conflicts with our sense of the interpersonal complexity and unpredictability of intimate life. Since I have argued that realism is an important virtue that helps us to nurture our romantic agency, we should be wary of life plans.

You might think, however, that my argument so far in this chapter conflicts with my emphasis on the fragility of romantic agency. I stressed that our ability to maintain intimacy with other people can be set back, and we need to avoid forms of romantic life which undermine our agency. Does acting on intimations alone, or in the absence of clarity about how we might react, pose a threat to our romantic agency? It can do, but this risk can be reasonable. My conclusion so far has been fairly weak. I have suggested we do not need extensive self-knowledge about our abilities. I have also suggested there are some decisions where appealing to the shape of a life is unlikely to be informative, and so plans have limited use.

I do not deny, however, the important differences between perceptive and blind intimations, and realistic and unrealistic approaches to romantic choice. We can reject a demanding life-plan view while reflecting carefully on our situation and acting on the basis of what we know. The shape of this reflection might be related to the restrictiveness of our situation. Resistance to greater oppression arguably licenses greater personal risk.

We cannot minimize risk entirely, and we can be mistaken about the forms of life we are well suited to. So how should we orient ourselves to potential romantic risks? An understanding of what this involves draws us into a discussion of integrity.

Integrity

How can we make choices and act when we are unsure whether we have the abilities to follow our romantic inclinations, and when our failure to do so might hurt other people?

An answer I will explore is that we should strive to act with integrity. The concept of integrity brings to mind ideas of wholeness, steadfastness, and commitment. These ideas are distinct. We often appeal to integrity in times of turbulence or uncertainty – moments of life where our will is challenged or viciousness a risk. But integrity also matters in ordinary moments.

Unsurprisingly, philosophers disagree about what integrity is and why it matters.[11] I am not fond of accounts of integrity which understand it in relation to identity or the wholeness of self.[12] We might have independent reasons to worry about how our desires are organized, whether we value the right things, and how our identity is constituted, but ideals of integration are useful only if the world is unified, and we cannot assume that things are so neatly ordered. If values are plural, for example, and able to conflict, then it could be important to enable ourselves to be pulled in different directions.[13] Sometimes striving for wholeness can be to impoverish our lives like Bradley's oyster, or fail to be sensitive to what matters. To be loyal to one idea, value, or conception of self is also to live a fragile and undiversified life which can be rattled by external shocks or the discovery that we have been wrong about what matters all along.[14]

Accounts of integrity which understand the virtue in relation to notions of wholeness of the self also seem self-indulgent – of value primarily for us. There seems something awry, however, with the unified selves of deceitful or corrupt people, or the singular drive of someone with an immoral goal. More generally, do we not want other people to have integrity *for us*? Whatever integrity is, it must have some wider social value.

Cheshire Calhoun is one philosopher who has argued for a social conception of integrity.[15] She thinks integrity is a matter of 'standing for something before fellow deliberators'.[16] To have integrity is to arrive at our sense of what matters while remaining responsive to the fact that we have to live alongside and reason with other people. Integrity is therefore not a matter of blind conviction, and nor does it drive a wedge between what we hold to be true ourselves and what we are prepared to present to other people. In a sense, integrity enables us to access the value of our viewpoints and convictions precisely because we persist in sustaining them even when wider society is not receptive.

This social view of integrity helps us to see how integrity could be a response to uncertainty. We have two tasks in those situations: to make sense of what we are doing, and to remain receptive to other people as we act. In relationships, the latter task is especially important. Having integrity is not simply a matter of standing for something, but also of remaining standing *towards* someone by considering them and explaining ourselves to them. If we have integrity, we do not refer to our past decisions as a way of shutting down conversation or overlooking the people around us. We remain accountable over time.

Thinking about integrity in this way helps us to avoid being seduced by what Margaret Walker calls the ideal of the 'pure agent'.[17] This is a caricature of agency which seeks to downplay the grip of social constraints, trauma, and oppression, as well as human vulnerability and dependency. Our agency actually overspills the horizon of what we care about or agree to, and we can be called to respond to people in unexpected ways. In her vision of ethical life, Walker develops an 'ethics of responsibility' which resists caricature and accommodates dependency.

Walker builds on Calhoun's social approach to integrity.[18] Her main idea is that we need to recognize 'liveable flexibility in tandem with reasonable reliability'.[19] I will describe

Walker's account of integrity before showing how it applies productively to romantic life.

For Walker, integrity requires us to remain responsive and accountable towards others. She offers less a set of necessary and sufficient conditions of when we count as having integrity, and more of a rich and provocative account of what integrity might involve. Consider the following description from her book *Moral Understandings*:

> [Integrity's] point is not for us to will one thing nor to be it, but to maintain – or reestablish – our reliability in matters involving important commitments and goods. This view exchanges global wholeness for more local dependability, and inexorable consistency for responsiveness to the moral costs of error and change. It trades inward solidity for flexible resiliency at those points where lives, fortune, and several kinds of histories meet. This view of integrity takes utterly seriously to what and to whom a person is true, but looks with suspicion upon true selves. It features the role of stories in making sense of lives, but is skeptical about certain overly ambitious or monopolistic narrative demands on selves. It links our senses of meaning and responsibility to the stories we can tell, but notices that 'we' are not all in the same discursive positions any more than we are all in the same social ones, and that these are importantly linked.[20]

It is hard to write about Walker's work without wanting to quote extensively, so rich are her ways of exploring this topic. There is a lot to unpack here, and several productive contrasts. Underpinning Walker's depiction of integrity is her scepticism about the need to appeal to wholeness. I agree with her that 'lives are usually of many pieces, not always stably processing in unconflicting parallel lines'.[21]

Walker's main contrast is between our striving for wholeness, of person or life, and our striving to be dependable to others. To have integrity in the latter sense is to be committed to our projects and the people in our lives while remaining alive to the inevitable tensions between them. Having commitments exposes us to forms of contingency and dependency we cannot anticipate. Navigating this contingency is not a matter of being better organized, but of remaining vigilant and ready to engage in shared practices of justification. Integrity understood in terms of self-unity or organization can be private – something we get right and then act on. Integrity understood as 'flexible resiliency', however, is public, subject to correction, and visible in action.

Similar to familiar interpretations of integrity as not wavering, the notion of reliability is also central to Walker's view.[22] But we must not confuse reliability with predictability. Walker has in mind reliability of reflection, response, and repair. If we are reliable in this sense, it may remain an open question what we will do in a given situation. But we will recognize our limitations, explain to others why we acted as we did, repair the damage we cause, and work to restore our relationships. Over time, we might act differently – perhaps we even surprise and hurt some people as our desires and values shift, or we are subject to unanticipated demands – but we keep talking and try to make things work. If we have integrity, people know we can be called upon to do this.

Before considering the place of integrity in romantic life, it is helpful to clarify how Walker's conception of integrity differs from other conceptions of integrity.

First, we assess integrity partly in terms of how we respond *after* we act, and not just whether our actions match a prefixed sense of who we are or the life we lead. A mistake, change of course, or clash of desires is not sufficient evidence that we fail to have integrity.

Second, we can be 'differently reliable' depending on the role or context we occupy, or the concern at stake.[23] This is not just a matter of recognising that different roles have different responsibilities. Instead, the idea is that, over time, the ways we are reliable within the horizon of one role – such as parent, teacher, spouse – might also change due to our unfolding lives. Since these changes can outwit our comprehension and control, we can be pulled in different directions, suffer conflict, even breakdown. In extremes, integrity just involves the attempt to 'start over when everything's gone to hell'.[24]

Third, integrity is not understood in reference to our whole lives. We are typically responding within narrower frames of reference, to the fragmented commitments, relationships, and situations we encounter. We can better focus on the particularities of an individual context by not thinking about our whole lives.

Fourth, to talk of integrity we do not need to presuppose that we are unified moral selves. Walker instead embraces a picture of 'ensemble subjectivity', in which our selves are grasped in terms of a 'history of relationships among [their] various temporally distant and concurrent aspects'.[25]

This is not to deny that a kind of unity has an important place in Walker's conception of integrity. We can try to organize our lives. But Walker has *narrative* organization in mind. This is a complex task which requires us to weave connections between different kinds of story. Our sense of a life is formed out of our identity, our relationships and their history, and our personal and community values.

Talk of narrative alongside integrity can bring to mind grand stories. Although tales of struggle, journey, redemption do shape how we think about integrity, they are misleading. Most obviously, the majority of our narrative efforts are less ambitious. Instead, we make sense of things by reaching for 'motifs, tropes, emblematic patterns, archetypes, styles, rhythms, or themes'.[26] Seldom do we step back and try to tie *everything* together, or relate our actions to a single motive.

Striving for narrative unity can also introduce pressures towards stories which are either 'desperately simple or intolerably suffocating'.[27] As I have suggested, realism requires us to resist overly simple stories. This is important because many of our life narratives are both complex, and co-authored, so we must remain accountable to the input of other people.

The desire for simplification also exposes us to outside influence. It is tempting to fall foul of 'fictionalising tendencies' whereby we view our lives through the lens of established fictional stories or genres.[28] We are troubled by people who insist on seeing themselves as characters in some unfolding story.[29] Their sense of their agency or values risks disconnecting them from reality. More significantly, if we only understand ourselves through common narrative themes, we might overlook unconventional forms of integrity.[30]

I have dwelt on Walker's conception of integrity because it applies especially well to romantic life. Her goal was to describe how integrity could suit the messy aspects of life, have social value, and not caricature our agency. Romantic life requires us to have integrity in this sense, for the following reasons.

In romantic life we are dependent on other people, and they depend on us. At times this is a consequence of our explicit commitments, but often people look to us for care, support, and explanations which arise as a result of the relationships or activities we share. Our vulnerabilities might be more extensive still, especially when we become attached to someone.

Friction can arise in the spaces between our romantic interests and other concerns. Sometimes it can be difficult to make adequate space for romantic relationships within the web of our existing commitments, especially if we have dependents or family. New love, or sexual excitement, can also generate strong desires and feelings which disrupt our existing life path. We are therefore prone to make mistakes and hurt people. We might break a promise, but more often our empathy will fail and we will fail to attend to someone as we should.

Romantic life is also unpredictable. We throw ourselves into practices of dating, and form relationships, in ways which also change us as individuals. If we are lucky, these changes are positive: we learn about ourselves, experience our abilities in action, can benefit when others help us to deepen our values. But we can also be harmed. Unkind, unreceptive, and abusive partners can drain our confidence and leave us grappling with diminished self-esteem.

Walker's integrity is precisely the trait we need to navigate these contexts of dependency where we are prone to make mistakes, hurt people, and change. As romantic agents, we are engaged in the process of finding out who we are, what we want, and what we value – i.e., what it is we stand for. But this process is inherently relational and opens outwards to other people. Ideally, it is not something imposed on others. We are always required 'simultaneously to stand behind our convictions and take seriously others' doubts about them'.[31]

Integrity is necessary if we embrace my concerns about the limits of compatibility, or rational life plans. Romantic life sees us rarely implement a plan, enforce a contract, or align perfectly with our partners. Integrity is necessary precisely because we are unable to prevent difficulties in advance or get all deliberation out of the way before acting. Our interactions with people are instead *both* forward- and backward-looking. We refer to our past inclinations and assertions, but also look forward to our unfolding life path. Somewhere in the middle, we engage in the active process of remaining responsive to others. This process is as much reparative as it is assertive.

Walker's emphasis on being differently reliable also has significance in romantic life. We often occupy multiple intimate roles, standing to others as romantic partners, friends, and family. These roles, and their internal obligations, develop unpredictably. Integrity as a form of flexible reliability helps us to navigate these changes. This trait is particularly necessary if we want to resist existing social scripts about which relationships are more important or should take priority. If we want to challenge amatonormativity, for example, we need to figure out our own ways of making space for our friendships, romantic connections, and other relationships of care and affection. This process is unlikely to be easy, and may hurt other people, so integrity is crucial.

Integrity is a vital trait in nonmonogamous lifestyles. There, we try to remain reliable towards different romantic partners who may themselves stand in complex shifting relationships. Integrity might require different attitudes to different people. On a conception of integrity as steadfastness, these differences may seem problematic. On Walker's conception of integrity, in contrast, we should be wary of the desire to treat everyone in the same way. To do so could mean we are not attending to the particularities of different commitments or the uniqueness of a specific interpersonal dynamic. In trying to treat people in the same way, we might also be tempted towards overly simple forms of narrative explanation. Nonmonogamous lifestyles actually help us to appreciate the value of balancing awareness of change and difference, on the one hand, with the need to remain accountable to others, on the other. Integrity is not the enactment of a personal plan but the practice of remaining open towards other people.

Having integrity helps us to resist narrative pressures which disrupt intimacy. Our romantic culture makes it easy to think of ourselves in simple ways. Many of our stories, in literature and film, are motivationally thin, life-encompassing, and linear: boy meets girl, they date, fall in love, marry, and are happy. These stories have little place for mixed motivations, emotional turbulence, and the weirdness of relationships. Shorter entanglements and meandering intimacies are left off-screen.

This is a point as much about plot as it is about narrative form. We experience a general narrative pressure to subsume *this, whatever this is* under a romantic story that others will recognize. People want labels, 'how did you meet' stories, and clarity about our relationships with other people. But the range of acceptable stories is limited. Nonstandard plots of asexual love, aromantic intimacy, or nonmonogamous plurality struggle for acceptance. If they feature at all, it is either as departures from established plots which help to maintain relationship norms, or they are squeezed into existing narrative shapes. Intimacy is between couples, relationships escalate over time, romantic love surpasses friendship, and so on.

Integrity is a useful companion of realism when it comes to resisting these narrative pressures. Realism helps us to appreciate what romantic relationships are typically like and to avoid being seduced by simple stories. Integrity is the practical trait which helps us to decide to *act* realistically, and respond constructively to people when we mess up.

This is not to deny that integrity and realism can be in tension. A romantic realist could be aware of the limitations of our social norms and scripts and understand that intimacy is often messy, while failing to be responsive to their partner. Integrity as responsiveness requires us not to cling too hard to our understanding of romantic life or our relationship. We can get it wrong; the input of other people is important; we might need to make amends. In its best forms, integrity, understood as our responsiveness to other people, binds dynamically the general and particular dimensions of realism. Romantic life might be complex, but *this* situation might be simple.

Having integrity might also require us to be disruptive. We might have to ditch tired stories and look for new ways to make sense of our intimate commitments. Or we might have to get creative, and continue old stories in unexpected ways. Sometimes boy meets girl, meets boy, meets boy, and they move in together. Our efforts may even morph into what Hilde Lindemann calls 'counter stories', which enable us to reappropriate the components of existing narratives to make sense of our unique experiences.[32] A polygamous family, for example, might deploy familiar ideas of love, commitment, and care, in a radically new way.

As I see it, integrity orients us to what matters in the presence of other people. I am concerned less with whether this is a distinctive trait, than that we recognize its value and distinguish it from preoccupation with unified selves or steadfastness to plans. Integrity is best understood socially, as something we want others to have in virtue of the relations in which they stand to us and our community.

Although we typically talk of individuals having integrity, viewing it as a personal trait of character, there is a sense in which relationships have integrity too. Are we, as a couple, for example, able to remain flexibly attentive to our community, justify our actions together, recognize our mistakes, and make amends?

I have applied Walker's account of integrity to romantic life. Walker builds on Calhoun's insight that integrity is a social trait. Integrity is visible in our efforts to honour our values, and lead a distant life, while remaining oriented to other people. These efforts are forward- and backward-looking at the same time. We reflect, act, explain, adjust, listen, respond, apologize, and make amends.

The idea of commitment is never far away when we discuss integrity. Perhaps you share the worry, put to me by Natasha McKeever, that Walker's conception of integrity seems in tension with how we typically understand romantic commitments. In theory, I might be right that some accounts of integrity are rigid or self-indulgent, and perhaps it is interesting to discuss our flexible reliability or resistance of simple stories, but in practice do we not want our partners to do what they say, keep their promises, and be there for us when we need them? This is especially so in relationships where we have complex responsibilities.

My response has two parts. First, a reminder. Not everyone views commitment in this way, and long-term relationships are not all that matters when we think about romantic life. Some people are happier with episodic or networked forms of intimacy. Others may not require commitments of their partners in the same way, and might shy away from relationships built on promises or rules.[33]

More substantially, is commitment really as important as we might think? Anca Gheaus grapples with this question in a way I find enlightening.[34] She views commitment as a species of intention. Our intentions are practical attitudes which enable us to act because they are rarely open to reconsideration. Commitments have similar instrumental value in helping us to achieve our long-term goals in contexts where we might be distracted or face adversity. Being open about our commitments may also help people to anticipate how we are likely to act. But Gheaus rejects the idea that commitment has intrinsic value. She examines the claims that commitment manifests our agency in determining who we are, or in providing our life with meaning, and concludes that self-governed and meaningful lives are possible without many commitments.

The main thrust of Gheaus' argument concerns the value of commitment in marriages and similar open-ended, entangled, relationships. Those relationships are valuable in part because of the romantic love and care we experience, and the actions which flow from those attitudes. Recognizing this, she makes two points.

The first simple observation is that we do not *want* our romantic relationships to be sustained by explicit commitments. We want all the goods of intimacy and love to flow from our partner's concern for us, not a commitment they made. (To this, I might make the familiar point that it also seems unlikely that we could commit to sustain these things. This is because the ability to intend to do something requires we have control over that thing, and we have limited control, direct or indirect, over our ability to sustain love and care.)

Gheaus' second observation is that talk of commitments in connection to relationships seems to rest on a mistake. The instrumental value of commitments stemmed from their intention-like way of helping us to achieve our goals by not revising our actions. But unlike specific projects, such as finding a house, setting up a business, or even raising a child, relationships themselves are not goal-oriented. Commitments therefore cannot have instrumental value in sustaining relationships directly.

Commitments do have value, but it is local and specific – not the foundation of our intimate relationships. At best, we can make specific commitments to try and nurture our intimacy, perhaps by making time for regular conversations with a partner. These observations help us to realize that, far from being in tension, integrity is vital if we are to give commitments their proper place within our romantic lives. The person with integrity faces the task of trying to juggle and fit together a range of commitments. This requires them to be flexible, attentive to the specific demands of particular roles and projects, and able to make amends when commitments clash. Integrity is perhaps most important in the moments when commitments persist as relationships change or loving motivations wane.

To see this, consider a situation where we have a child with someone who no longer loves us. If we are realistic, we will appreciate that we cannot appeal to any prior commitment, if we made one, to get this person to keep loving us. Talk of commitment in connection with affection and inclination is largely misplaced, especially if they did make efforts to nurture our intimacy.

Instead, what we need in situations like this is for them to remain responsive to us as we figure out what their changing feelings mean for our relationship and our specific projects, most importantly that of raising our child. We want them to try to repair damage that may arise, and attend to the gaps between our wish for continuing love and how things are turning out. We want them to attend to the specific features of our situation, rather than just parroting social scripts. They need to translate into specific forms of action the general commitment to raise a child. 'Being there for the kids' could involve preserving a shared domestic home, but it might involve them moving away, or moving between spaces, or some other creative option. These are difficult questions, but they are practical questions within the purview of integrity, rather than questions which challenge the need for integrity.

This example also helps us to remember that integrity as staying responsive to someone does not mean we capitulate to them. Our responsiveness, the ability to listen, to offer reasons, and to repair our mistakes is not the same as adopting someone else's desires as our own. The person whose love fades, and who wants to move on, is making sense of their life on their own terms and stands for what they believe in. Crucially, they can do this without being narrowly focused on their identity or self. Sometimes life changes, or emotions fade, and people have to adapt. Break-ups are often so challenging because our attempts at self-definition jostle with our efforts to remain responsive to someone we care about.

Having integrity is not about being inflexible or single-minded. Walker and Calhoun help us to see integrity as a trait indispensable within the rich context of our social relationships and roles, and the changing circumstances of our lives. Our romantic lives are often especially messy. We are navigating a heady mix of desires, fantasies, strong feelings, and everyday realities, alongside other people, in a social context with quite rigid norms and ideals. Taking these factors together, it is inevitable we will make poor decisions, be unrealistic, hurt other people, and generally learn as we go. No amount of planning or deliberation will prevent this, so integrity – flexible resiliency – is vital.

Playfulness

I started this book with a quotation from Lauren Berlant which is worth repeating:

> love approximates a space to which people can return, becoming as different as they can be from themselves without being traumatically shattered.

We could replace 'love' with 'play' here, with no loss of meaning. Indeed, the reason why we experience our love relationships as elastic and transformative is precisely because we are often our most playful within them.

Mention realism and integrity and people seldom imagine a playful person. In the rest of this chapter, however, I want to show how playfulness can reinforce our realism and integrity. If we can, we should try to be playful, and to view our relationships in a playful way. My underlying thought is that playfulness helps us to navigate the inevitable challenges in romantic life, and being playful with others is often itself an exercise of romantic agency.

Philosophers have explored games insightfully,[35] but playfulness is surprisingly understudied. (I suspect this is because playfulness, as a trait, impedes the playing of many games.) In a recent attempt to place playfulness on a surer footing, however, Glenn Trujillo characterizes playfulness as a virtue.[36] Trujillo's central claim is that playfulness regulates how we use our leisure time, that is, time not devoted to survival, 'by encouraging us to rest, develop ourselves, and engage our communities via intrinsically pleasing activities that lead us toward better lives'.[37] This understanding of leisure time would include romantic pursuits.

Trujillo's approach to playfulness is a significant study of leisure and virtue, but it does not capture the qualities of playfulness which concern me and which we might seek in our intimate lives. He conceives of playfulness as a regulative virtue governing our free time. We might take this idea seriously, however, allocate sufficient time for play and yet fail to be *playful*. Conversely, we can also be playful while working or trying to survive.

The attitudes and emotions of the playful person are not central to Trujillo's account. He only discusses them insofar as they help people to regulate their leisure time in a virtuous way. I will take a different approach. To better understand the nature of playfulness, we can consider its contrary vices. Plausible candidates might be excessive seriousness or solemnity on one side, and flippancy on the other. Playfulness sits in the middle as a flexible orientation to situations which corrects against these extremes.

My thinking is shaped by Maria Lugones' supple discussion of play.[38] She describes playfulness as 'in part, an openness to being a fool, which is a combination of not worrying about competence, not being self-important, not taking norms as sacred, and finding ambiguity and double edges a source of wisdom and delight'.[39] Understood in this way, playfulness is an inflection of agency – an attitude towards constraint. These constraints might be personal, such as our abilities and emotional tendencies; social, such as the norms and ideals we find imposed on ourselves; or situational, such as the practical difficulties of balancing competing commitments. Playful people are resilient and lack an inflated sense of self-importance. They are not dispassionate or detached.

In only a few pages, Lugones teases out a useful distinction between two ways we can think about play, which she labels agonistic play and loving play.

Agonistic play is play understood as a distinct kind of *activity* which we engage in as competitors, striving for competence at the activity, with the serious intention to dominate and win. Play of this sort is aligned with a kind of imperialist attitude; it offers a field of combat for us to assert ourselves.

Loving play is play understood as a broader 'metaphysical *attitude*' towards situations and other people.[40] By metaphysical, she means playfulness in this sense is a mode of orienting ourselves to the world; it is an attitude which 'turns activity into play'.[41] The playful person is open to surprises, does not think rules are sacred, is creative, and does not worry about their competence. Loving play is not preoccupied with competition or domination.

We can develop the idea that playfulness is a broad attitude. As I understand it, playful people resist at least three dangers: excessive seriousness, hostility to mistakes, and resistance to exploration. We arrive at a richer understanding of playfulness in our intimate relationships by considering the opposite of each of these three dangers and applying them to romantic life.

Playfulness first requires what I will call perspectival seriousness. This is our ability to see something as rightly valuable within a specific context while also being able to view it from the perspective of other dimensions of life. A project at work might be important given the goals of our institution, but our job is less important than the needs of our family or community. Winning the match might be crucial, but playing the tournament might be insignificant in the scheme of things. Perspectival seriousness prevents us from getting locked into the value of one pursuit at the expense of others.

Crucially, perspectival seriousness is not a generalized ironic distance. The project, or match, do matter and we would be wrong to think otherwise, but other things also matter and some matter more. Being serious in this way is a matter of good control over our attention and absorption.[42] We are able to shift our focus as necessary, view situations through the lens of our values, and avoid being captured by the social pressures brought to bear on us.

Ironic distance is a particular risk within modern romantic culture. Think here of the jaded dater frustrated with their inability to meet someone who sparks their interest. They might be tempted towards the view that 'All men are useless', or that 'Dating is impossible here.' These remarks may indicate broader detachment from what they are doing. A playful dater, in contrast, views yet another date under the aspect of their dire romantic record without losing sight of the fact that everyone is unique and has potential. They temper their hope, but remain open to surprise.

Error-friendliness is the second dimension to playfulness. To the best of my knowledge, I am borrowing the term from a talk given by Anna Mense, who used it to describe attitudes to consent violations in sex parties, but it can be used more broadly. If we are error-friendly, we recognize that people can make mistakes or even harm us, but we do not take these mistakes as necessarily ending our interactions. This attitude is common when we are learning new skills, or encountering new ideas, but it is also central to a playful attitude in other contexts. When we are error-friendly, we focus more on what binds us to the other person, whether personal, community, social, or moral relationships, rather than the ways their actions might create distance. Attention to these connections helps us to accept their mistakes constructively.

Crucially, error-friendliness does not mean we are impervious to harm. To be friendly towards errors, we must first recognize them as errors. Error-friendliness is better thought of as combining a certain view of human nature with a nuanced approach to blame. Error-friendly people accept that humans make mistakes and cause harm. This is not to embrace a pessimistic vision of people as morally flawed, but simply to acknowledge that not everything we do best expresses our character, and to appreciate this fact from the other person's point of view as well as our own.[43] Error-friendly people wield blame with care. Sometimes we might let go of blame because we have confidence in the underlying relationship with someone.[44] In other situations, we might reach instead for 'proleptic blame', which means we blame people as kindly and constructively as possible with the goal of helping them to be better members of the community they already value.[45]

Error-friendliness helps activities and communities to persist. Playing children exemplify this attitude. They are attentive to rules and roles, but their games rarely end outright when rules are broken, someone makes a mistake, or cheats. Romantically, error-friendliness helps us to be vulnerable. We are not on guard as much if we know our relationship will withstand mistakes or disagreements. Error-friendliness also foregrounds our bond with someone. It is a commitment to a view of relationships as unfolding processes, rather than discrete episodes.

A playful approach to missteps is crucial when exploring unconventional intimacy. We are more likely to hurt others when there are fewer examples, less clarity, and more baggage. Tolerance of mistakes also helps us to develop new practices and guidelines when relationships are in their infancy. Error-friendliness is therefore not limited to situations where we already have relationships – it can help to create relationships.

The third dimension of playfulness is openness to exploration. We could be perspectivally serious and error-friendly but be closed-minded in how we approach situations. Playful people, however, take pleasure in exploration. They investigate situations from different perspectives, resist hasty binary thinking, and scout around constraints. They look for unexpected solutions and compromises. Openness to exploration is compatible with a realistic acceptance of constraints. Playful people are not deluded about obstacles to action; instead, they are able to find constraints a source of creativity. Sexual contexts are one example of this. Acceptance of each other's limits or preferences opens up a domain of creative play.

This exploratory dimension of playfulness is not simply about action. It also involves the ability to think about situations from different perspectives or to imagine new ways of engaging with people. We can be creative in how we think or feel about a situation even if we are limited in how we act, and creative in the stories we tell. Playfulness is often visible in our conversations, as we resist clichés and conventional themes and find personal ways of expressing ourselves. As with Dover's vision of conversation as the attitude of taking another seriously, playful conversations are not simply moments of information exchange but processes of following themes and drawing connections without a clearly specified goal.

Exploration is crucial in romantic life. In any relationship, we will encounter unexpected situations and have to navigate constraints. It can be tempting to embrace socially common options and not consider alternatives. But the playful person is curious. Could we set up our relationship in a different way? Can we accommodate our different interests and desires? Might a creative solution help to blend our lives? We have seen already that relationship anarchists and other critics of modern norms want us to stop assuming relationships all have to look the same, or that certain kinds of activity go together. Accepting this is easy in theory, but playful exploration helps us to put it into practice. Maybe we do not need to share a house with our main sexual partner, or make sure our boyfriends never meet, or distinguish so sharply between our friends and our more-than-friends.

Taken altogether, playfulness is indispensable in romantic life. Relationships thrive when we can be serious but not narrowly so, can maintain relationships even when we misunderstand and hurt each other, and can explore situations. Few of us are as playful as we might be. We could arrange our intimate lives in so many ways, yet remain loyal to a few limited configurations. Even people who challenge romantic norms tinker mostly at the edges, challenging the idea that relationships have to be dyadic, or involve exclusivity, or that we should be sexually circumspect. But these challenges often retain the idea that relationship structures should be stable over time, or deepen; that their normative guiderails do not change; that emotional intimacy is more important than sexual intimacy; that intimacy is private, and so on.

But we could do more to question these assumptions. One largely unchallenged norm, for example, concerns intimacy and time. The notion of the relationship escalator has us thinking of affection as deepening over time, and we associate important relationships with their presumptive permanence. All this could be different: we could play with time. Love or sexual exploration could be seasonal, as we move between spaces or periods of work and leisure. Or our intimacy could become carnivalesque. Existing relationships could be strengthened by moments of misrule in which the free exploration of sexual desire is socially sanctioned. Our relationship guidelines could be changed yearly. There is no reason why even marriages cannot be temporary.[46]

We could also play with the connections between love and domesticity, sex and privacy. Like intimate Human Resources managers, we could draw connections between intimacy and the world of work, and have 'relationship retrospectives' or actively 'love-craft' our ideal unions.[47] More broadly, we might look for the erotic in our work and wider lives.[48] Or we could strive to weaken the grip work has over love altogether, perhaps viewing the former as a sublimated barrier to an expression of the latter.[49]

Some freethinkers have been playful in their exploration of romantic life. From utopian socialists like Charles Fourier, to Marxists like Alexandra Kollontai, critical theorists like Herbert Marcuse, anarchists like Emma Goldman or Émile Armand, and psychoanalysts like Otto Ross or Wilhelm Reich. They all explored alternative intimacies within the limits of their diciplinary and political visions. Sadly, many of their visions were unpleasant or authoritarian (e.g. Fourier's notion of the 'sexual minimum' or 'harmonic polygamy'[50]). Too much change also risks upending our fragile agential abilities or simply overwhelming us. Any exploration needs to be sustainable.

Playfulness is best viewed as an attitude anchored in respect for agency. Playful people appreciate that our abilities are nurtured alongside others, and can wax and wane. They do not impose their energies on others. Playfulness can infuse every corner of romantic life, from the approach we take to finding partners, how we draw our boundaries, down to the details of daily organization. Because playfulness is an attitude, it can coexist with a stable, conventional, romantic framework. We are not obligated to endorse a chaotic vision of romantic flux, or ride a carousel of different norms, ideals, relationship forms, and partners in search of what works. As Lugones realized, to be playful is to adopt a looser stance towards the norms that structure our shared lives. But this is compatible with respect for those norms, and respect for our personal limitations.

Talk of playfulness is not without objections. First off, you might worry that in valuing playfulness, I risk treating romantic life as a kind of game. Playfulness as I envisage it, however, diverges from popular culture on many points, from romantic gameshows, books exposing the 'rules' to find a partner, to the sinister corners of so-called 'pickup artistry' and 'the Game'.[51] Romantic life is not a game. To view intimacy as a game is to take an instrumental approach to a specific goal, such as finding a boyfriend, or having sex. We might think these outcomes are more likely if we follow certain heuristics, or conform to narrow social norms, such as those of typical gender presentation.

If we 'game' romantic life like this, we are not being playful in the sense I have in mind. At best, this is agonistic play where we are resistant to new ways of approaching a situation, or being creative in how we navigate established norms or practical constraints. We risk being unrealistic in neglecting the ways in which intimacy develops unexpectedly in relation to other people. More troublingly, we might be hostile to 'deviations' within the 'game' of seduction. This approach is a natural bedfellow of misogyny and other modes of oppression which punish deviations from gender norms.[52]

Talk of misogyny prompts another objection. In praising playfulness, am I not making it more likely that some will pressure others to accept their domineering behaviour, or to overlook various harms? The idea of error-friendliness might be taken to imply that there are fewer boundaries in romantic life. This notion seems in conflict with my discussion of the agency-enhancing role of constraints in chapter 2. Clare Winnicott, the wife of Donald Winnicott, the psychoanalyst whose work we will encounter in chapter 7 when thinking about difficult emotions, seemed to embody this permissive attitude in writing that 'the question of hurting each other did not arise because we were operating in the play area where everything is permitted'.[53]

The account of playfulness I have developed is a response, not an alternative, to our proneness to hurt each other. Not everything is permitted – even in the play area. Friendliness towards error is not the same as being impervious towards error, and some errors are significant. No amount of playful integrity can guard against all mistreatment. These personal attitudes need to be accompanied by social structures which help to reduce domination. I consider some in the final chapter, but even those cannot erase all risk of harm. Being playful will help us in our responses to harm. The ability to look beyond binaries or think creatively about what could be done better equips us to hold other people to account effectively.

Conclusion

Being realistic about our romantic agency and social context does not stop us from taking romantic risks. We do not need to know in advance whether we can make a relationship work, or how it fits in our life. A realistic person knows that relationships are unpredictable. The best response to this predicament is to try to cultivate integrity and playfulness.

Integrity is best understood in social terms. We have integrity because it enables us to stand as ourselves in relation to the people we are most likely to confuse, frustrate, and hurt. Making amends and retelling our story is more central to integrity than sticking to a plan or trying to be the same person over time. Playfulness is the natural companion of integrity in enabling us to have perspective, be creative, and explore. Our romantic culture is defensive and competitive, but experiences of loving play help us to appreciate that relationships are not games to be won.

7
Jealousy

... jealousy serves to disturb the rival relationship and to (re)gain the attention and affection of a beloved person. (Anna Welpinghus)[1]

Jealousy

After love, jealousy is the emotion most commonly associated with romantic life. It feels horrible, few of us would choose to be jealous, but we have mixed intuitions about its value. Jealousy can be unremarkable, as when a woman feels bad that her husband spends so much time with his football team. But jealousy can seem plainly disturbing, as when a man is jealous and aggressive whenever his girlfriend glances at another man in the street. Jealousy can also be surprising and frustrating, as when jealousy creeps up on a woman one evening as her wife is out on a date with someone else. She agreed to explore nonmonogamy, had no reservations about that decision, knows her wife is caring and kind, but feels jealous all the same.

Our thinking about jealousy is ambivalent. On the one hand, jealousy can seem like an ordinary and understandable response to many situations. If our partner's attention seems to linger elsewhere, or we doubt our worth, jealousy may intervene in ways that express our vulnerability. On the other hand, jealousy can be oppressive. It can make us ruminate, become aggressive, and undercut our ability to think, talk, and act clearly. Jealousy also seems uncomfortably comparative and competitive, and seems to rest on implicit beliefs about our entitlement to other people, their love, and their attention.

How we view jealousy can depend on our choice of example. The aggressive man is gripped by jealousy in a way that seems abusive; the nonmonogamous women feels jealousy despite herself; the wife compares herself adversely to her husband's teammates. Similarly, our intuitions about the nature and value of jealousy encompass the question of whether it is appropriate in a particular situation, and the question of jealousy's wider consequences and value. Often these details and perspectives are blurred, leading to the sense that jealousy might have unpleasant consequences but is often appropriate and understandable.

These different examples can also shape where we place emphasis when defining jealousy. For some theorists, jealousy is primarily a fear of loss, and this notion might lie behind the woman's feelings as her partner dates another person.[2] For others, jealousy is primarily anger or indignation at being overlooked, disrespected, or failing to get what we think we deserve, and this notion might be visible in the angry man, or neglected wife.[3] Jealousy is usually distinguished from anger and fear by noting it has a complex structure which encompasses the actions of another person and a perceived rival. We fear loss, or feel indignation, *because* of what this rival X does to our relationship with Y.

In previous work, I defined jealousy broadly as 'the emotion of being pained by a perceived threat from a third party to the attention of someone one cares about, and to which one feels entitled'.[4] I argued that we should strive to remove jealousy if we can. Instead, we aim to feel good when our loved ones thrive with other people. I worried that although jealousy might have occasional instrumental value, it was connected to aggression in ways which damage our romantic agency. Since we could achieve the same 'goals' of the emotion – such as seeking reassurance or highlighting how we feel neglected – in other ways, jealousy has no distinct value. I argued that we work to remove it through a two-pronged attack on our vulnerabilities and the beliefs which often work to justify our possessive behaviour to ourselves.

Jealousy now strikes me as more complicated. In this chapter, I will ask whether jealousy can function in different ways in romantic life; whether the value of jealousy might depend on our broader social context; and whether the vision of a life beyond jealousy can reinforce subtle injustices. My aim is to consider the practical stance we should take towards jealousy, and perhaps other challenging feelings. Jealousy needs managing, not removing, and some of us have more responsibility to take up this work than others. In the later sections of the chapter, I will consider two related features of this management: holding, and emotional compression.

Since jealousy feels bad, and has a negative impact on relationships, it is natural to think we would be better off without it. Trying to become someone who is less jealous, or ultimately free of jealousy, is a process of emotion cultivation. This process takes aim at patterns of feeling and what we are disposed to feel, rather than individual episodes of emotion.

The impulse to rid ourselves of a feeling is not isolated to jealousy. Philosophers have long been tempted to offer 'prescriptions for reform' when it comes to emotional life, and feelings like anger have also been marked for removal.[5] Other candidates might include envy, pity, or anxiety.

Specific programmes of emotion cultivation can be justified in different ways. Justin D'Arms and Daniel Jacobson pointed out that we evaluate emotions in at least three different senses.[6] We can evaluate them in terms of their appropriateness or *fittingness*, in terms of how *useful* they are, and in terms of how *moral* they seem.

Fittingness concerns the relationship between an emotion and the world. Some situations seem to merit emotional responses of certain kind. Tigers merit fear; sunsets, awe; kittens, joy. We are sensitive to the fit between feelings and the world in two ways: *how* someone reacts to a situation, and *how much* they react. My jokes, for example, usually merit wry smiles, not hysterical laughter.

We can also evaluate how helpful it can be to feel an emotion. In some scary situations, like being behind enemy lines in a warzone, it is advantageous to not feel fear, or not feel it intensely. Although fear would be fitting in the face of an enemy patrol, the absence of fear helps us to think clearly and evade capture. Similarly, it might be worth your while, prudentially, to feel amused at your boss' jokes even if they are not funny. More broadly, being disposed to feel anger may impact our health by raising our blood pressure.

Alongside questions of fittingness and usefulness, we can also ask whether it is moral to feel certain emotions, or be disposed to feel them. Perhaps it is fitting to feel *Schadenfreude* when the arrogant humiliate themselves, but we can ask whether it is good to feel *Schadenfreude*. Feeling *Schadenfreude* may seem incompatible with compassion or humility. We might also think we can be morally justified in feeling unfitting emotions. Our love for our child seems to warrant a kind of generosity which decouples our feelings from what is fitting. For example, we might feel joy and pride at their dismal performance in the school play.

These ways of evaluating emotions can be conceptually and practically separated but, anecdotally at least, most interpersonal critiques of emotion centre on fittingness. Consider how we talk with loved ones. Sometimes we are frustrated that they are not reacting to a situation. They might be insensitive to our employer's pointless new initiative, for example, and stare blankly as we explain, rather than reacting with indignation. Or we get frustrated as they overreact to something trivial. Relationships are full of these judgements, and our response to jealousy is no different. We can imagine the people in our initial examples reacting to their partner's jealousy with claims that it is an 'overreaction' or 'out of place'.

This sense of fittingness is usually understood in terms of whether an emotion accurately represents a situation. This requires us to assume that emotions have some kind of representational content, which is usually understood in terms of some cognitive or thought-like content.[7] On this view, an emotion is fitting when its cognitive content accurately represents the world. Our fear, for example, will be fitting if its content, 'This politician is odious, avoid!', represents the politician correctly as odious. Discussions of emotions will then hinge on how they track the world.

Seen like this, the central feature of emotion *cultivation* would be to evaluate emotions for fittingness and working to become more sensitive at tracking the world through our feelings. We want to remove unfitting emotions because they rest on a mistaken grasp of our situation.

This approach to emotion cultivation resonates with my discussion of realism, because the underlying idea is that we try to remove the false beliefs and unrealistic ideals underpinning our feelings. The approach also reflects the hope that we are able to think our way out of difficult emotions. Philosophers are not the only ones who might like this idea. Some therapies like Cognitive Behavioural Therapy are attractive because they rest on the idea that we can improve our lives by identifying, considering, and changing the erroneous thoughts which shape our feelings.

There is also a political dimension to this form of emotion cultivation. Some of our emotions have a content which is shaped by socially dominant, but mistaken, beliefs. So, if we can work together to identify the way these emotions rest on mistaken beliefs, we can work to systematically change how we feel and, in changing how we feel, change how society is structured.

Disgust, for example, might rest on implicit beliefs about appearance, disability, race, purity, or health. In turn, experiences of disgust might play a causal role in sustaining the social hierarchies which help to entrench those beliefs.[8] But if those beliefs are unjustified, and if our emotions rest on them, it seems like we can cultivate new forms of feeling by working to interrogate our thoughts about social groups. In turn, we can cultivate new forms of social solidarity by cultivating our emotions.

The idea that we should remove jealousy can be rephrased in terms of fittingness. And we might be motivated to do this for the reasons above: it would be nice to think our way beyond jealousy, and perhaps jealousy is connected to harmful beliefs circulating in our society. The injunction to remove jealousy involves a general premise and a specific claim about jealousy. The general premise is that we should try to not feel emotions which are unfitting. The specific claim is that jealousy, in particular, is usually unfitting and so we should try to remove it. To evaluate the specific claim, we need to specify jealousy's cognitive content so we can appreciate why the feeling typically fails to represent the world correctly.

Later, I will take aim at the general premise. But to motivate a broader view of jealousy, and to think about what jealous feelings might be doing, I will first introduce a particular account of what jealousy is which serves as a good example of how we might motivate the idea that we should remove jealousy.

In a series of books, Kristján Kristjánsson argues for an account of jealousy as an emotional response to situations where someone 'undeservedly favours' another person over us.[9] Like many theorists, Kristjánsson thinks jealousy focuses on three people: ourselves, someone we care about, and a potential rival. His specific analysis involves thinking of jealousy as a 'unique composite of envy, anger, and righteous indignation'.[10] The basic idea is that jealousy is a kind of deserved angry envy. We feel the indignation of jealousy when we see someone favouring a third party, want that favour for ourselves, and think we deserve it as much, or more than, the other person.

Kristjánsson's broad position is that it is important that we have the ability to be jealous. The failure to feel jealousy, he thinks, can indicate 'a lack of self-assertiveness and self-respect … not to mention insensitivity to injustice' because it shows we are not appreciating what we deserve.[11] Some of the details of Kristjánsson's view are distinctive, such as his specific analysis of jealousy's components, but his idea that jealousy arises when we feel we are being disrespected, or not getting what we deserve, is common. His analysis of jealousy aligns it closer to anger than to fear of loss.

Building on this idea that jealousy involves sensitivity to deservingness and respect, Kristjánsson ultimately thinks the emotional trait can be a virtue – that is, it can be morally good to feel. That said, he argues that jealousy is a morally 'unexciting case' in *romantic* life.[12] The reason for this is simple: there, jealousy is rarely rational. He has a broad notion of rationality, suggesting that 'if a case of jealousy involves none of the irrational missteps of disregard for facts, negligent and hasty judgements, or purposeful self-deceptions, and the more "basic" emotions of envy, anger, and indignation are intelligible in the given case individually and collectively, the jealousy can be deemed rational'.[13] The underlying thought, however, is that romantic jealousy is rarely fitting because we make systematic mistakes in how we think about other people.

So why does Kristjánsson think romantic jealousy is rarely fitting? This is his answer: 'The sexually jealous person overlooks the fact that love is not a matter of will and no one deserves to be sexually attractive to another. We cannot decide to love someone (romantically/sexually) because we think the person deserves or owes our love.'[14] Several thoughts coalesce here. First, love and affection are not under our control, and so cannot be directed or misdirected. Second, love and affection are not subject to considerations of deservingness.

Kristjánsson embraces the premise that an emotion must be fitting before we can consider whether it is moral, and so, because he thinks romantic jealousy is rarely fitting, he concludes it is rarely moral in romantic life.[15] (To be clear, Kristjánsson would think we should cultivate jealousy in other areas of our life, where they are more typically fitting.) Kristjánsson's view helps us to see how a specific account of jealousy's content and nature would inform a specific vision of emotion cultivation.

We could critique Kristjánsson's position in several ways. First, we could argue that his analysis of jealousy as an indignation-like emotion focused on deserved favouring does not capture the heart of jealousy. If another analysis of jealousy is better, we might have additional reasons to retain the feeling – at least sometimes. Second, we could accept his analysis, but argue that jealousy is more fitting in romantic life than he suggests. Finally, we might contest his premise that to be moral an emotion has to be fully rational in the sense he described. As it happens, I am sympathetic to all of these critiques.

Before considering turning to a general analysis of jealousy and the question of whether there are moral reasons to cultivate it, we can ask whether romantic jealousy might be more fitting on Kristjánsson's analysis than he thinks?

Catherine Wesselinoff adopts a similar analysis of jealousy understood as a form of sensitivity about entitlement. Her view differs from Kristjánsson's because she thinks some romantic relationships, such as marriage, involve promises or commitments within a socially and legally defined framework of expectations.[16] These commitments can establish legitimate expectations of the people within the relationship. Although she thinks jealousy is often unfitting in romantic life, especially in more loosely defined, casual, or unestablished contexts, she would dispute Kristjánsson's position by shifting focus away from love and deservingness, and towards *relationships* and deservingness – the thought being that our relationships generate legitimate expectations of attention and concern.

We can also contest Kristjánsson's suggestion that love is not a matter of the will. Some aspects of loving interaction, such as attention, concern, communication, etc., are under partial volitional control. Within an existing loving relationship, where we are less likely to question whether we are loved or found attractive, jealousy can be sensitive to the various ways in which the loved one fails to attend as much as we would like or as we might think we deserve.

The bigger issue, however, is whether we should think of jealousy in terms of deservingness and respect at all. I turn to that next.

Pluralism

Jealousy is intrusive. It motivates us to act, to complain, and to lash out. This general idea is visible in Anna Welpinghus' sentence at the head of this chapter, 'jealousy serves to disturb the rival relationship and to (re)gain the attention and affection of a beloved person'. Let's develop this thought and think of jealousy as a kind of emotional nudge. We can ask, why might people nudge each other in this way, and might different people nudge others for different reasons?

Recall that Kristjánsson thinks jealousy is a response to a situation where someone 'undeservedly favours' another person over us. We might also describe jealousy as a response to perceived disrespect. This idea is visible in the examples of the angry husband and neglected wife at the beginning of this chapter.

Respect is a complicated concept, however, and we can distinguish between different forms of respect. Stephen Darwall, for example, usefully separates what he calls 'recognition respect' from 'appraisal respect'.[17] I will explain and then expand his view as it helps us to think about jealousy.

We give appraisal respect to someone when we view them or their actions in positive terms. To respect someone in this way is to esteem or admire them. Kristjánsson's approach to jealousy, and those like it, present jealousy as an emotional response to an absence of sufficient esteem. On this view, we are jealous because someone favours another person when they should be favouring us.

Recognition respect, in contrast, is more rudimentary. Darwall thinks that to respect someone in this sense is to 'take seriously and weight appropriately the fact that they are persons in deliberating about what to do'.[18] When we have recognition respect for someone, we afford them status as a person who matters and might be impacted by our actions. It remains a separate question whether we esteem them. This notion of respect was central to the ideals of conversation and joint deliberation I described in chapter 5.

We can develop Darwall's view. Recognition respect is itself quite sophisticated, and the term 'recognition' is vague. Sometimes the failure to recognize someone is less a matter of not affording them status, and simply a matter of not noticing them. To give someone the appropriate status and to esteem them, we need to first attend to them. Finding space for this kind of response to insufficient attention might also capture what people have in mind when they write of jealousy in relation to loss. Typically, jealousy is connected to fear of loss.[19] But it is perhaps better thought of as a response to an occurrent experience of loss, the moving away of another's presence or attention, rather than a future possibility.

I refer to Darwall's distinction here to highlight the ways in which comparative judgements of esteem rest on the more basic notions of consideration and attention. Appreciating these differences helps us to see that jealousy could be nudging people in different ways. Our jealous reactions can respond to situations where we have not been considered or recognized by someone in the way we would expect. Put simply: as a nudge, jealousy might sometimes be saying 'Value me correctly', but it can also say 'Consider me', or, most basically, 'Notice me!'

This is a pluralist account of jealousy, because it holds that one emotion can have slightly different content and is not only focused on deservingness. This view has two advantages.

First, it aligns our adult experiences of jealousy with infant experiences of jealousy where infants at protest interruptions of attention.[20] These protests arise before infants have an established sense of status. If we can, we want a simple account of emotions, and this view does not explain why our emotional responses change over time. The pluralist view holds that we retain our more basic jealous reactions, like infants, but can also have more sophisticated, concept-dependent, responses too.

Second, this view makes sense of jealousy in situations where appraisal respect is precarious or lacking. When jealousy is portrayed as a response to disfavour in relationships, we presuppose that the people involved are *already* subjects of recognition respect or attention. But sometimes people are not recognized or attended to. In any relationship, there can be moments when we are not really attending to someone as we might. We might even fail to think of someone as worthy of consideration with regard to some matter.

These attitudes can be sustained. People who are subject to social oppression may lack recognition respect within their intimate relationships. Patriarchal attitudes about women, for instance, could coalesce into a man's sustained sense that his female partner is not worthy of consideration, whether in respect to certain areas of life, or in general. She would therefore lack recognition respect.

So far, I have suggested we take a broader look at jealousy and that jealousy might function to interrupt and protest dynamics where we are slipping from consideration or attention, not just cases where we are not being esteemed as we should. One reason for this latter approach is that it accommodates relationships which are shaped by social oppression, and where the emotions of one or more parties reflect their subordinate status.

But our emotions do not just 'punch up'. The emotions of privileged people also work as nudges which enforce their dominance. This general idea is central to the work of Lisa Tessman and others who examine how anger can both perpetuate structures of domination and challenge those structures, depending on who is angry.[21]

Jealousy can be considered in a similar way. Talk of jealousy in terms of misplaced esteem strikes me as talk of an emotion inflected with the perspective of privilege, where we have confidence we will be noticed and considered, but are less sure we will be correctly esteemed in comparison to others. But jealousy can also enforce privilege in relationships where one person has a secure status, the other not. Jealousy can be experienced by other people as hostile, intrusive, and stifling – as demanding acquiescence.

What jealousy is doing in a specific context requires close examination. To be clear, we do not wield emotions like tools. Instead, they are patterns of response to situations, but patterns that unfold within a social context and specific interpersonal dynamics. Since those contexts and dynamics are shaped by subtle inequality, domination, and privilege, then our emotional patterns, and what emotions are best thought of as doing, should be understood in reference to this broader context. For some people, jealous outbursts might connect closely to the worry they have been misesteemed; for others, jealous outbursts reflect a more fundamental worry that they are not being considered or noticed. These patterns are not necessarily easy to identify. And nor will they align neatly onto social groupings so that we can say jealousy always functions in this way for one group, that way for another. Privilege is complex, as are the emotional manifestations of privilege and emotional responses to it. We need a broad notion of jealousy to accommodate this diversity.

Before moving on, it is worth considering an important objection. You might think that *within* romantic relationships we are already considering and noticing each other, and so jealousy is only going to be functioning in something like Kristjánsson's sense – that is, as nudging us to give each other what we are due. Indeed, Welpinghus occasionally writes as if this is the case, saying, for example, that 'jealous approach and protest can serve as moves in negotiation with a beloved person concerning how we ought to treat each other'.[22]

This might be true of good relationships. But even there, jealousy can puncture routine interactions where we fail to consider, perhaps even to notice, someone when we should. Similarly, experiences of jealousy may manifest recognition deficits as intimacy is being developed over time, or in relationships where we are noticed and considered but in a partial or precarious way. In addition to arising in relationships between people of different social backgrounds, these dynamics may also arise within relational contexts where we are struggling to *define* a relationship. A couple might be adamant they are 'not serious', yet experience jealousy as they act on the basis of a belief which their feelings do not share.

My pluralist approach to jealousy covers all of these cases. On this view, jealousy is fitting if we are lacking in terms of esteem, recognition, or attention. This view captures the ways in which one emotion may be a response to different situations, and the fact that feelings can both respond to, and enforce, oppressive dynamics. The pluralist view is also motivated by the difficulties we have in pinning down jealousy, because we do not have to focus on one narrow construal of the emotion's content. I prefer to ask: 'What is going on in jealousy?' This is a wider question which considers the possible range of evaluative notions at stake with respect to a particular emotion.

Removal

You could accept my expanded account of jealousy but still think we should avoid feeling unfitting jealousy. Feeling jealousy when someone is in fact attending to us, for example, would be not fitting and so inappropriate. But why accept this? Some might be tempted to go further and argue that we should remove *all* jealousy, even if it is fitting, because it has a negative impact on our lives. In this section, I shall consider this claim.

I suggested that we typically evaluate emotional episodes in terms of how fitting they are. We worry whether we are reacting to what matters, or overreacting to trivialities. But the way we approach *patterns* of emotion, and emotional dispositions, seems different. There we are more likely to broaden our evaluative horizons. We look at the place of the emotion within a life, rather than viewing a pattern of feeling or disposition as just a series of episodes, each of which can be judged for fittingness. Instead, we judge them in the round in terms of how useful, and how connected to our flourishing, these arcs of feeling are. Aside from considerations of accuracy, we might ask how particular patterns of emotions relate to our health, or whether they make us good people.

I want to motivate this idea further. It is not absurd to wonder whether it would be good to feel only what it is fitting to feel. This question arises in consideration of some forms of mental illness, where a move away from a pattern of over- or under-exaggerated emotional responses can be experienced as a form of loss. Similarly, we might think there is value in the fact that our emotions can occasionally outrun our cognitive grip on a situation – that life is richer and more satisfying because we laugh harder than is warranted, or feel more joyful than is fitting, perhaps even because we despair beyond fittingness too.

Morally, it can also appear good to fail to feel what is fitting to feel. We try to avoid laughing at our children, or being angry with our partners; we might also strive to blame less often or intensely. Clearly, there is room for debate about what would be fitting to feel when it comes to specific situations. There is also the general question whether our fittingness evaluations are made in reference to social norms or some other standard. In either case, however, it seems plausible to think there can be cases where it is right to try to not feel what is fitting. We might explain why this is in terms of our relationship with someone, and the goods and values at stake in that relationship, or by appealing to the links between patterns of feeling and virtues.

This general idea is most easily motivated when we focus on an emotion's *strength*. Examples of a partner *softening* their anger or blame are ones in which they are not oblivious to wrongdoing, they simply feel less angry than is warranted. But since accuracy of fittingness must include an emotion's size, not just its shape, conceding that it might be good for us to feel less intensely, or for less long, is still a significant concession. I also think we embrace an asymmetry in our reactions to unfitting emotions. The call to be rid of unfitting jealousy, for example, is rarely a call to *amplify* the strength of our emotion. But if fittingness is what matters, come what may, we would have to worry equally about someone who is not jealous enough and someone who is too jealous. I suspect most people do not worry equally about jealousy in this way and just focus on situations where people are too jealous (just as we focus on people who are not compassionate enough, and sidestep the question of whether people are too compassionate).

You might object that I am conflating feeling emotions with expressing or communicating them – that we should feel something even if it is good that we do not express our feeling in a particular situation. But I am not making this mistake. The instrumental case for not feeling emotions like anger or resentment often focuses on their personal consequences, such as their impact on our reasoning, sleep, or appetite. The moral case is more complex, because we can have moral reasons to avoid communicating certain emotions. Tact seems to require this sometimes. But other times it seems plausible to say the real goal is to avoid *having* the feeling altogether – that we are still cruel in feeling a certain way about a loved one, even if we do not express our feeling to anyone.

So, should we try to remove jealousy, including fitting jealousy? Here are some of the reasons I offered in past writing to think we should – reasons which have force against the background observation that there are many things it is fitting to feel in life, we are finite beings, and so we can ask general questions about the shape of our emotional dispositions.

First, we can focus on the harmful impact of jealousy. It is easy to write about jealousy in muted terms, but the emotion can be nasty, aggressive, and spiteful. Patterns of jealousy pose a threat to our romantic agency because it can make us ruminate or be suspicious in ways which disrupt intimacy. When we are jealous, other people can retaliate with anger, evasion, and defensiveness.

These considerations provide instrumental reasons to think we should be rid of even fitting jealousy. But we could also cast them as points about the *intrinsic* disvalue of jealousy (a point pressed by Tyler Paytas against anger[23]). In many guises, jealousy is self-centred and fairly comparative, and we might have independent intrinsic reasons to be wary of such feelings. This is so especially if we think about our emotional lives as a whole. We might be limited in our ability to cultivate a complement of fitting emotions because of the practical tensions this might involve. Since we are imperfect, our emotional sensitivity is often misaligned with reality. So in practice, our efforts to, for example, balance fitting jealousy with our efforts to be compassionate can lead to conflict. Mindful of these tensions, we may decide to prioritize the cultivation of some emotions over others. If we have to prioritize, it makes sense, both morally and to help us to have good relationships, to focus on those feelings which benefit other people, such as compassion.

The second reason why I initially thought we should be rid of jealousy is that we have other means of achieving what jealousy seems to be doing which seem more effective in some situations, in the sense that they are less likely to lead to negative outcomes and are more stably connected to good ones. We can *ask* for respect, or consideration, or to be noticed.[24] Focusing on anger, Paytas makes the point that 'there is a general error in the assumption that, since anger is the typical mode of appreciating and responding to wrongdoing, it must be the only effective mode'.[25] Just as we can respond to wrongdoing in other ways, so we can choose other means to secure the same ends towards which jealousy seems aimed.

To this, you could object that the same point can be made for *any* emotion. Why laugh with amusement when we can just *tell* someone their joke is funny? We should reflect on what is gained by having emotions at all, as opposed to other states of mind. An answer, in reference to jealousy, is that it is direct, readies us for action, and is expressively unmissable. Jealous words have a force that calm words do not.

There is some truth to this claim, and below I consider how best to accommodate it. But we need to tread carefully. First, as with anger, what makes jealousy powerful in these respects is also what makes it volatile; it might motivate action, but such action might be impulsive or harmful. The directness of a punch is not always preferable to a slow rebuke.

Second, the volatility in our jealousy and how we express it means jealousy's expressive significance often varies, and much has to go right if someone is to receive it in the way the jealous person might hope in a cooler hour.[26] Jealousy might be a powerful signal, but it is not always a clear signal.

Third, and most significant, we can accept the force of the idea that emotions are preferable forms of interpersonal response only to argue that other kinds of *emotional* response might serve the same ends as jealousy. If that is the case, then we face the question afresh: given the choice, or given our limited ability to cultivate our feelings, which feeling should we prioritize? I developed this argument when writing about compersion: loosely, the emotion of feeling good when a partner flourishes intimately with someone else. I suggested that compersion, like some forms of jealousy, can indicate strength of feeling and concern for a partner or relationship. But compersion is focused on other people, not ourselves, and is not aggressive, and so is preferable to jealousy.[27] A different version of the same thought can be aimed at jealousy's status as a rebuke. Perhaps emotions like frustration or exasperation can serve similar ends without such bad consequences.

These points seem to offer strong reasons to think we should be rid of jealousy, even if it is fitting. So why not just accept that conclusion?

I now think we need to be more cautious. Although jealousy is often harmful, and although there might be other ways we can indicate to each other that we feel disfavoured or overlooked, there can be reasons to stop short of suggesting that everyone ought to try to cultivate away jealousy.

First, a general point. We need to examine the social contexts in which our emotions resonate and assume meaning. Evaluations of fittingness play a large role in emotional criticism, and motivate the idea that we might want to modify or remove certain patterns of feeling. But settling on a characterization of what a fitting emotional response would be is difficult and shaped by social norms. This is especially so if we include evaluations of how 'strong' or 'intense' a feeling is – evaluations which shape our sense of whether someone is emotionally under-reacting or over-reacting. The question of what fitting shame involves, or fitting *Schadenfreude*, for example, evidently draws us into conflict with existing norms. But, in many cases, these are norms we want to challenge. We might be concerned about the pervasiveness of shame, for example, and think shame is less fitting than commonly supposed. The reasons for this are likely varied, and will encompass other social ideals of gender, class, or honour.

Similar questions arise with jealousy. Even if we think jealousy can be fitting, our judgements of fittingness may be shaped by social norms we want to challenge. Mistaken views about entitlement, for example, likely shape our thinking about jealousy as a response to being disfavoured. The gap between our existing thoughts about what is fitting, and the best account, may run in the other direction too. In broadening how we think about jealousy, respect, consideration, and attention, for instance, more episodes of jealousy may turn out to be fitting than seemed previously the case.

These are tentative suggestions. The bigger point, however, is that we should be wary of endorsing a radical view about emotion cultivation while being rightly uncertain about how best to analyse and account for a broad range of emotional responses. It is easy to fixate on certain forms of emotional response – those we are familiar with, or which seem most rational, or which reflect our prejudices, or serve our ends – at the expense of others. The unfolding debate about the nature and value of anger helps to motivate this idea. The more we think about what is going on in anger, the more unreasonable blanket claims that we should be rid of irascibility seem to be.

A second point concerns the idea that we should aim to rid ourselves of jealousy because there are better ways to communicate. I now regard this as simplistic. Previously I wrote that 'the instrumental benefits of jealousy are most readily available to the people who need them least'.[28] I conceded that jealousy can occasionally have instrumental value, but assumed that the people who would be most likely to benefit from jealousy in a relationship were people who were also best placed to communicate their grievances verbally. The idea was that being able to understand why someone is jealous, or enabling jealousy to have a place in a relationship, yet without feeling defensive or aggressive, requires us to have the ability to calmly seek to understand the perspective of another person and process difficult emotions together, and that ability is precisely that which would just allow people to talk to each other directly.

This distinction between good and bad communicators now strikes me as an unhelpful abstraction. Jealousy is better understood in more fine-grained relational contexts. Within relationships, even at different times over the course of one relationship, we differ in our receptivity to emotions and our ability to communicate. Jealousy might also have force precisely because we are prone to reflect on and try to verbalize our states of mind. Emotional outbursts can capture our attention, and surprise us, in ways that can outrun our cognitive capabilities and alert us to what we value. Put another way, there is value in distinctly *emotional* responses to intimate situations, rather than other forms of response. I might be right to suggest that some people are better placed to process and discuss their jealousy, and there may be specific social reasons why this is, but that fact does not always count against the significance of experiencing jealousy.

My main worry, however, is political, and concerns the scope of my previous views about emotion cultivation. Previously, I was concerned about the ties between jealousy and entitlement or possessiveness. I was uneasy with accounts of jealousy which saw virtuous connections between jealousy and notions of deservingness. The comparative, competitive, and rivalrous nature of some jealousy also seems to manifest many of the worst features of our society, as did jealousy's motivational links with aggression and violence.

My unease remains but I have changed my mind about what it entails. Since jealousy might be a nudge that responds to different kinds of neglect, and not everyone occupies the same social stance, we have more to think about when it comes to the question of removing jealousy. Here I have been influenced by recent writing on anger.[29] Fitting anger, like fitting jealousy, feels bad, and can negatively impact life and sustain oppression. Expressions of anger often antagonize people, especially those rightly accused of wrongdoing. As such, it is tempting to argue that anger is counter-productive, harmful, and best avoided.

But some philosophers now resist this conclusion. Amia Srinivasan, for example, thinks the call for oppressed people to remove their fitting anger because it is purportedly counter-productive risks ignoring, or propagating, a subtle form of 'affective injustice'.[30] Srinivasan notes that victims of injustice face a conflict. They can be sensitive to how they are subject to wrongdoing, feel fitting anger, but face potentially harmful consequences from oppressors. Or they can modulate or remove their anger and fail for their emotions to fully reflect what the world is like. Srinivasan thinks this conflict is psychologically painful as people are torn between self-preservation and fitting emotional responses. She also thinks the conflict is normative because it arises between 'competing and significant goods that often feel incomparable', such as personal preservation versus accuracy.[31]

In drawing our attention to affective injustice, Srinivasan helps us to appreciate what is at stake in praising emotional management. Continued calls to temper anger risk marginalizing the people for whom anger is most obviously a legitimate response to their situation.[32] More bluntly, appeals to emotion cultivation can sustain domination, and sit most easily in the mouths of those who themselves seldom have reason to be angry. As a result, she wants us to reserve a place for anger in the public sphere.

Srinivasan's view rests on a premise about the counter-productiveness of anger: that getting angry will not help victims of injustice to resist their oppression. Although plausible as a generalization, two additional strands of recent work on anger help to develop our thinking here.

First, we can ask *why* anger might be counter-productive. One reason seems to be that oppressors are often emotionally fragile – they fail to regulate their emotions, and are not receptive to other people's feelings.[33] If emotions circulate unevenly in society, some groups may be worse than others at being the recipients of other people's feelings. This volatility makes it especially risky for members of oppressed groups to show their feelings as they might like. Attention to these dynamics make calls for anger removal seem worse, since the appeal to the instrumental value of staying calm is necessary partly because the privileged are themselves unable to be calm in the face of ill feeling. Attention to these dynamics also helps us to see that different groups might have diverging responsibilities when it comes to emotion cultivation. The onus is on the privileged to become less fragile.

Anger may also be less counter-productive than some suppose. Myisha Cherry, for example, argues that anger can help people to respond to racial oppression. She carefully distinguishes between different kinds of anger to make room for 'Lordean' anger (inspired by the work of writer and activist Audre Lorde), which aims at social change by motivating people to act together.[34] Similar arguments look to forms of anger which are future oriented, or lack a desire for retaliation, and see them as beneficial tools for social change.[35] These views caution us against unnuanced analyses of anger. Some forms of rage are clearly unhelpful and destructive. But the power and potential of anger has value for oppressed people too. To neglect this is to neglect their agency.[36]

These lessons about anger apply to jealousy. Some people may experience affective injustice if their jealousy is fitting but counter-productive. Their jealousy could be counter-productive due to the failure of other people to regulate their emotional life. The responsibility to address jealousy might fall on some groups more than others. And some forms of jealousy may be productive. These points support the conclusion that we should make some space for jealousy in intimate life.

In making these claims, I have in mind situations of social oppression and uneven romantic privilege. As an example, consider a caricature of a society containing only two groups: Rakes and Saints. The social norms in this society mean that Rakes are better able to make claims on the attention and affection of Saints without reciprocating. Rakes, unlike Saints, can assume they will be noticed and taken into consideration by other people, including Saints; they also know their perspective will be privileged over that of Saints. They are concerned instead with ensuring they get the affection they deserve and preventing rivals from unfairly benefiting at their expense. They are prone to being angry and defensive when disfavoured, or when Saints resist norms concerning affection and attention. Rather than regulating their emotions, Rakes emphasize their reasoning skills. They seldom esteem Saints.

Jealousy functions unevenly in this society. Let us assume that both groups have the same underlying desires for affection, consideration, and esteem. (A stretch in the real world, because we often come to want what is actually available.) Rakes get jealous when they feel disfavoured by other Rakes or by Saints. Their jealousy polices their perceived entitlements – esteem from Rakes, affection and attention from Saints – but their general standing as individuals with entitlements is secure.

Saints are situated more precariously. They also experience jealousy when disfavoured, but are less likely to secure uptake of their feelings from Rakes. Even other Saints tend to favour the perspective of Rakes over their own. But Saints also feel jealous in moments when they become aware they are overlooked, are not noticed, or lack the attention they desire. Saints' jealousy is often fitting – they *are* overlooked and not attended to. But their jealousy is also often counter-productive. Rakes are concerned with status but, since they do not view Saints as equals with similar status, they usually dismiss the jealousy of the latter. When they do register the Saints' jealousy, their engagement can go awry in one of two ways: their fragility makes them aggressive; and their self-image of themselves as astute reasoners leads to dismissive rationalizations. Both dynamics impede intimacy between the groups. As a result, Saints face a kind of affective injustice. They experience a conflict between their fitting jealousy, and the fact that their jealousy is usually unproductive.

But their jealousy is not *always* unproductive. After all, jealousy can be an explosive or persistent emotion. Sometimes, the jealousy of Saints helps to reorient attention and affection from Rakes in ways they want. Perhaps it is targeted, and touches on Rakes' concern with status; perhaps it lingers and just demands a response; perhaps it is shared with other Saints and fosters solidarity.

It seems wrong to suggest that Saints should strive to remove their jealousy. It is not their fault that it is often counter-productive. Their jealousy is also occasionally useful and can be directed, or processed, in helpful ways. Looking at this society, the onus for emotion cultivation clearly falls on the Rakes. They have more power, in the sense that they can expect more, presuppose more, say more, and feel more.

Real societies are more complex than this caricature. We can be members of several social groups at once, and divisions of power, privilege, and standing are rarely as stratified. Still, I hope the example above resonates as a schematic description of some of the interactions between groupings in our society. We can resist crude generalizations about the functioning of jealousy while also noting its power and value are not spread evenly.

The above example also helps us to resist the idea that jealousy is of value only for those who are socially marginalized. Features of the Rakes–Saints *dynamic* can arise within any relationship, even one between relative equals. There is some value in keeping the 'tool' of jealousy in the toolbox. In flourishing relationships, the tool will hopefully stay there. But spikes of jealousy can help to reestablish consideration and attention in contexts where it lapses. Sometimes, we come to appreciate a certain need for support, or understand a specific fear of loss, only when lensed through experiences of jealousy. Other times, we find that our feelings run ahead of us in being sensitive to concerns we assumed did not matter.

Jealousy can also clarify precarious romantic situations. 'Situationships' might arise where our intimacy with someone outruns our ability to make sense of what is going on. Jealousy can orient us to a growing web of care and concern that demands a response despite our protestations that we are 'only casual', or 'just friends'.

Finally, what about jealousy within a lifetime? We interact with different people, not all of whom will be receptive to us, or emotionally articulate, or good at recognizing our needs and vulnerabilities. We might fail to be those things to them, too, some of the time. The unevenness of potential responses to our presence, and the possibility that recognition might not be forthcoming, can make jealousy a useful emotional reaction to retain.

You might accept my conclusion so far, be open to the value of retaining jealousy as a tool, but worry about the scope of this suggestion. Should we try to retain *unfitting* jealousy, too? What if unfitting jealousy helps us to get what we want in a relationship?

This is a complex question. I regard emotions as responses to situations, rather than strategic action-like attempts to achieve goals. Our jealousy might help us to get what we want, but our jealousy is typically not under intentional rational control. Unfitting jealousy might be understandable as part of a patterned emotional response to someone's lack of social or intimate standing, just as unfitting anger might be understandable in contexts of injustice. In those non-ideal contexts, jealousy could prove useful in jolting other people to make them see how they oppress others. Jealousy might play a role in redressing some interpersonal injustice even when specific instances of it are unfitting.

So where have we ended up? I am advocating a more circumspect view of jealousy and emotion cultivation. There are good reasons to be concerned about the nature and impact of jealousy within relationships, but the structural context which shapes relationships is also relevant. Intimate life is shaped by unequal privilege and the impact of oppression as much as any other domain of life; those tensions may even be amplified when masked by love.

I embrace a pluralist view of jealousy's fittingness, but question the connections between fittingness and an emotion's value. I am sympathetic to the view that it can be good to fail to feel what is fitting to feel. Although that view lends support to the idea that we should work to remove jealousy altogether because of its negative effects or the fact that we have other means of interacting, I also resist that conclusion. Analogies with anger help us to see that jealousy can have value in different ways. It is a tool that can stay in the box.

Management

To suggest that some emotions, such as jealousy, do not have to be cultivated away is not to say we have no responsibility for them. In general, we are responsible for the ways in which we nurture, contextualize, and express our feelings. Romantic relationships make people especially vulnerable, and we have the capacity to hurt them, which makes emotion management even more vital.

There is a growing literature exploring the many processes and mechanisms which help us regulate our emotions.[37] The general idea is that we can exercise some control over the situations we place ourselves in, how those situations are structured, the ways we attend to things or divert our attention, the ways we think about our experiences, and the ways we respond to people.[38]

These strategies can be applied to jealousy. We can avoid certain triggers (avoid talking about our partner's ex-relationships), modify the situations we are in (try to be friendly with 'rivals'), redirect our attention (focus on a positive attribute of our partner), reframe our thoughts (stop thinking of ourselves as entitled to affection), and work on the ways we express or communicate our feelings (becoming more tactful). Some of these strategies are quite indirect, such as the desire to avoid triggering situations, whereas others will require forms of self-control, such as the ability to reframe our thoughts, or redirect our attention, in the middle of a jealous episode.

I cannot cover all these forms of emotion management in detail. Instead, I want to focus on two ideas which bear on experiences of jealousy in relationships in different ways: the compression of our emotions, and efforts to 'hold' someone who is in emotional distress. I focus on these aspects of emotion management for several reasons. Together, they focus on both sides of a jealous episode – that of the jealous person and that of a supportive partner – so we reach a richer sense of what emotion management can look like.

Second, emotion compression is superficially similar to problematic ideals of emotional suppression or toxic stoicism. Showing how these ideas differ helps us to appreciate the difference between valuable and troubling attitudes towards our emotions, as well as to appreciate how emotional management can help us to reduce affective injustice or remove emotional burdens on other people.

Finally, my discussion of both helps me to respond to people who worry outright that the very idea of emotional management is calculating and dispassionate, or a form of problematic emotional labour.

Recall my example of the jealous nonmonogamous woman from the beginning of the chapter. I was imagining a situation in which two people have a strong and settled relationship where they love and care for each other. Still, one of them is occasionally jealous, the other is not. This jealousy is particularly annoying because it is recalcitrant. The woman concerned knows she is not threatened by a rival, is not gripped by ideas of entitlement or deservingness, and appreciates her partner's love. Still, she finds her clarity of mind has little practical impact on how she feels.

In common situations like this, we still have some power over how we express our jealousy. We can also try to ensure our jealousy is controlled and contained. We would criticize this woman if she became aggressive, or blamed her partner, or tried to sabotage their relationship in some way.

The attempt to shape how we express our feelings in interpersonal situations is an instance of what Olúfẹ́mi Táíwò calls 'emotional compression'.[39] Táíwò thinks these efforts, which form our 'aesthetics of character', are similar to our attempts to develop other habits and traits.[40] It will take time to nurture these abilities, but we can work on ourselves and become better at how our emotions are expressed.

Táíwò's examples of emotional compression include:

> the boxer who knows and respects his fear, yet not only stands his ground and keeps punching but does so without letting on that he is intimidated; ... the person who fights back tears during a tough conversation with her friend, and speaks in measured terms that communicate her hurt feelings through the verbal content of what she says rather than her tone of voice or her tear ducts; and also ... the soldier who dutifully withholds complaint about an onerous task demanded by his commanding officer.[41]

These examples are constructed with care to help us to distinguish the ability to control how we express our feelings from other phenomena.[42] Controlling emotional expression is not the same as having a reduced *ability to feel* emotions. Nor does it mean we struggle to *understand* what we feel, or that we are *unable to communicate* our feelings. In the examples above, the boxer, friend, and soldier feel various emotions (fear, sadness, frustration), understand what they feel, and could express their emotions if they were minded to do so. Instead, they exercise their agency to shape how they communicate to another person given their specific circumstances.

The jealous woman in my example has these abilities. She feels jealousy and other emotions, she appreciates that she is jealous and does not mistake her feelings for anger or grief, and she is articulate and able to express her feelings. This is an idealization, of course. These abilities come in degrees. In many situations, we might struggle to know what we feel, are poor communicators, or experience few emotions or much emotional depth. These abilities come in degrees. There are many possible reasons for this. We could lack relevant concepts, have had a bad role models growing up, suffer from a mood disorder, or be gripped by shame or awkwardness.

As with other forms of character development, Táíwò thinks we can work to become more skilled at emotional compression. Indeed, because compression has a positive impact on the people we interact with, he thinks of it as a virtue. Even if we disagree with that assessment, the trait shapes our relationships in good ways. I will describe the general positive impact of emotional compression before considering the compression of jealousy.

In difficult situations, emotional compression helps us to 'metabolize' difficult feelings, both positive and negative, and make those feelings available for consideration.[43] Our ability to restrain our shock at a friend's bad news, for instance, can help them to make sense of what happened. It enables them to grapple with their situation, not our reactions. In group situations, emotional compression 'mitigates the dangers of emotional contagion and crossover'.[44] We are gripped by the emotions of other people because we are porous. An intense feeling in a group can disrupt its smooth functioning and prevent the group from pursuing a goal, or respecting a shared value. If we control our fear in the face of danger, or temper our glee after a crushing victory, we can have a positive influence on our group.

I might also add that compression has personal benefits, too. The way we express our emotions can help us to cope with them because we are receptive to our own presence just as we are to the presence of other people. Talking to ourselves slowly when we are afraid, or in a silly voice, or using jokes, for example, are ways of voicing our fear which can calm us in scary situations.

Compressing jealousy helps to reduce the emotional strain within a relationship. Jealous outbursts can be impulsive and tinged with anger, snark, or shame. Being the subject of these outbursts in a relationship can lead quickly to defensiveness or resentment. Few enjoy being the subject of another's jealousy, especially when it is laced with suspicion or seems to negate our care and love. If someone is often jealous, we might unwittingly change our behaviour to try to sidestep their outbursts. These changes can leave us feeling stifled and less than ourselves. These dynamics can be lessened if someone compresses their jealousy and expresses it in a less dramatic way.

Compression is not simply about reducing the impact on the people we care about, it also helps to make our jealousy available to others in a form that can be digested productively, which benefits us. A partner is better placed to consider and respond to our jealousy, fitting or otherwise, if it is measured rather than snide, tempered rather than aggressive. If our jealousy has value as a signal of our insecurity, say, then compression modulates the tone and volume of the signal so it is heard clearly. As a result, jealous emotions are less likely to settle within a relationship into patterns of outburst and frustrated response. Emotion compression helps us to maintain our romantic agency because it makes it easier for us to engage with difficult feelings.

Our emotional compression of jealousy also helps us to respect a partner, especially someone we might not know well. We have different emotional constitutions, visions of romantic flourishing, and expectations. Our intimacy with others can be impacted by our personal history, romantic or sexual trauma, and general difficulties with communication or self-understanding. As a default orientation to someone we do not know well, emotion compression acknowledges these factors. We help other people to establish a relationship with us by trying not to buffet them with hurtful expressions of emotion.

These points are amplified when we consider how jealousy might sustain romantic privilege. If we have less romantic privilege or are subject to social oppression, our feelings are unlikely to be taken seriously, or will be viewed in stereotypical terms. Emotional compression can help us to express our jealousy in different ways, which help us to secure uptake.

If we have romantic privilege, or contribute to social oppression, emotional compression helps us to reduce the negative impact of our jealousy. We can work to temper the way we express our feelings, striving to be more measured rather than aggressive or accusatory, even if we struggle to unpick our sense of entitlement or confront our insecurities.

Put another way, much of the interpersonal friction surrounding emotions like jealousy arises due to *how* we express our feelings to others, and not because we feel the way we do. Impulsive, aggressive, accusatory, and suspicious expressions of jealous insecurity can hinder intimacy within a relationship. They also browbeat their recipients, which can contribute to social oppression if some people are habitual recipients of the hostile emotions of other people.

Talk of emotional compression is controversial. Even if we set aside the worry that this ideal asks a lot of us, requiring as it does a degree of control over the ways we express ourselves in the moments when we can feel most disoriented or vulnerable, several other objections come into view.

The idea of emotional compression may also seem in tension with my claim that emotions can function as nudges which respond to various kinds of neglect. Tempered feelings are hardly going to jostle others into noticing, considering, and valuing us.

In response it helps to avoid caricaturing a 'nudge' as a violent outburst or cry for attention. What nudges us is relative to a context. As Táíwò's example of the person who manifests their hurt without tears shows, there are times when quiet disappointment is more arresting than rage. Similarly, emotional compression can amplify emotions of people who are stereotyped as over-emotional.

Talk of context and social position leads us to another concern with emotional compression: that it is a trait associated negatively with men and masculinity. Táíwò is attentive to this worry noting that 'When men's lack of emotional self-knowledge is combined with the toxic presence of homophobic and misogynist norms that complicate homosocial forms of support – contributing to noncommunication of one's emotions – it's no surprise that the burden of emotional support so often and so disproportionately falls on women.'[45] Táíwò's discussion of compression takes place within the broader context of stoicism. Modern appropriations of stoicism connect it to restricted masculinity, because people mistakenly bundle together emotional compression and the inability to understand our emotions or the inability to be emotionally available within relationships.[46]

Emotional compression, as a mechanism of emotion management, needs to be decoupled from these negative associations. Men can manage their emotions while also working to understand and address the harmful dimensions of masculine ideals. The ability to temper and modulate how their feelings are expressed will have value in that very process because hard, or potentially confronting, conversations are easier to sustain when people are not also being barraged by turbulent emotions.

Toxic stoicism aside, we might also worry, as Natasha McKeever put it to me, that emotion compression is worryingly similar to the emotional labour which disproportionately impacts women. Táíwò himself describes compression as a form of emotional labour, although he thinks it is a virtuous form.

The use of the idea of emotional labour has expanded in recent years, but I have in mind something of its original meaning established by Arlie Hochschild, a sociologist who studied gendered service workers such as airhostesses.[47] She noted that one feature of the airhostess role was to project an air of calm competence to reassure jittery passengers. Similar efforts are visible in other spaces, from schools and hospitals to the family, where women are expected to manage their own emotions in order to put other people at ease.

Hochschild's primary interest was the way in which this dynamic has been commercialized and forms a part of the modern capitalist service economy, but we can also worry about the emotional labour that may seep into our intimate relationships. Of concern is the idea that this burdens some groups, especially women, to the advantage of the privileged, as they are expected to engage in this labour without reciprocation. In suggesting that emotional compression is a valuable form of emotional management, and one that might help us to approach jealousy, am I not actually endorsing emotional labour?

Táíwò's approach to this question is to say that what is problematic about emotional labour is not the strategy of emotion management, but the ends to which it is directed. He sees emotional compression as an important tool to help us to achieve valuable ends, and I have echoed some of these ideas above. But we can also distinguish between different kinds of compression in a way which helps to reply to the concern about problematically gendered labour.

In one kind, that visible in Táíwò's examples, we compress our emotions to obscure their presence. A frustrated hostess might feign amusement at a customer's bad joke, for example. But this is not an essential feature of emotional compression, for we can also temper the expression of a feeling without hiding it or pretending we feel something else. The example of the woman experiencing jealousy makes this clear; she does not obscure the fact that she is jealous, nor does she pretend to feel good for her partner – instead, she tries to express her emotion in a less impulsive or accusatory way.

Another difference concerns the goal of our emotional compression. The airhostess has external goals in mind, such as ensuring a flight is not disrupted. In our relationships, however, we manage the expression of our feelings not to pursue some independent aim, but so they are more accessible to other people and to improve our intimacy. The benefits of doing this are spread between us and the other person, they are not purely external or instrumental.

Whether we call it emotional labour or not, emotional compression which does not obscure what we feel, and which does not have external goals in mind, strikes me as especially valuable, and should be less concerning to those who think we should try to minimize the amount of emotional labour people perform.

Finally, it is crucial to remember that emotional compression is a skill – it is a strategy, not a default mode of emotion expression. As with all skills, attention to context is vital. At some moments, compression contributes positively to our relationship dynamic by making our emotions more approachable. In other moments, perhaps when we are expected to compress or when we are subject to stereotypes, then unmodulated anger, joy, or jealousy are especially impactful. Although some of us might find one strategy predominates more, given the nature of our relationship or the social expectations we are subject to, within a relationship as a whole we will sometimes compress, sometimes not, and the ability to gauge when to do so is ultimately a skill we can develop.

Emotional compression helps us to manage our expression of feelings such as jealousy. At times, however, we struggle. Romantic relationships expose our fears and vulnerability in ways that undermine our self-control. We cannot always cope with jealousy, and need support from our partners.

Intimate emotional support clearly takes many forms. Here I want to explore *holding*, an important dynamic which helps us to nurture each other in our relationships. Holding is an important response to the turbulent and disorientating experience of feelings like jealousy. I focus on it, as opposed to other more specific forms of emotion management, because it helps us appreciate the significance of our indirect forms of support and the importance of sustaining nurturing environments.

Holding is a rich concept in the work of paediatrician and psychoanalyst Donald Winnicott. Winnicott was interested in the dynamic between mother and child, but then extended his observations into adult life. I will describe what he has in mind in the infant case, before setting out a conception of holding which has relevance in our intimate adult relationships.

Winnicott uses the term 'holding' to refer both to a state and to an activity.[48] He was interested in the ways mothers hold their children: holding's most literal form, and the psychological extensions of this state. This embrace comforts physically and psychologically. The child is warmed and protected, and feels secure.[49] Fellow psychoanalyst Thomas Ogden describes the mother's cradling in these initial days as an 'unconscious effort to get out of the infant's way'.[50] Mothers provide a place of safety in which infants can slowly come to develop a sense of worldly presence on their own terms.

Winnicott also refers to the holding *environments* parents sustain while their infants develop. A holding environment is one in which an infant is able to explore situations, internal and external, with limited risk, and come to integrate their mental life by developing the capacity to be alone in the presence of other people. This idea has clear resonances with some of the states associated with a secure attachment bond.

Crucially, the provision of a holding environment is not just a matter of curating physical space. Central to safe exploration is the parent's *reliability*. Winnicott views this as sensitive empathetic attunement to the infant, not rigid wariness.[51] This sense of reliability is similar to Walker's conception of integrity developed in the previous chapter; it is not simply a matter of being predictable, but requires flexible attention.

Parents also pursue the ongoing psychological task of being there for an infant in order to 'gather [their] bits together' – that is, to attend to, understand, retain, and reflect back the infant's various preoccupations and relations to objects so they can be picked up when required, and woven over time into a functional unit.[52] In holding, parents are 'that human place in which [the other] is becoming whole'.[53]

Holding does not just permeate the parent–infant relationship but continues into adult dynamics. For example, Winnicott draws explicit parallels between the situations of an infant and of an adult in therapy. Although an analyst is unlikely to physically soothe a patient, they hold them in providing a supportive environment and by retaining their various states of mind, making them available for later reassembly.

One of Winnicott's main insights is that providing a holding environment is often more important than offering astute interpretations of a patient's actions or mental life.[54] We need to express ourselves, safe in the understanding that those aspects of mind will become available later for examination. This is perhaps unsurprising because we are often unreceptive to reflection and reasoning in moments of difficulty, but the idea pushes against more rationalistic views of our ability to reason with ourselves and so change our feelings.

I read Winnicott for his insights into the ways in which we sustain each other's 'going on being'.[55] This process is central to our close relationships, from parenting to romantic life. Here is what I take from reading Winnicott.

Fundamentally, holding is the dynamic process of being present for someone without disrupting their efforts to make sense of themselves and form their own identity. Recognition of and respect for their separateness are therefore central to the holding dynamic. We hold another person so they can be themselves without censure, not to assimilate them into our identity.

To maintain a nondisruptive holding presence, we have to be able to withstand a partner's strong feelings and their defensiveness. Their anger, insecurity, or even euphoria can be felt as emotional impositions which we might be tempted to deflect or evade. When we withstand a partner's emotions, however, we allow them to resonate. This does not require us to feel the same way ourselves, or to endorse their feelings, but simply allow them to play out on their terms. This ability requires us to respect them as a separate person, which, in turn, means we need to have confidence in ourselves and our relationship – confidence, that is, that our intimacy will persist despite momentary strong feelings

Providing continuity is also central to holding. When we hold someone, we are a source of memory who helps them to gather aspects of their self together over time. We need to be receptive to parts of their mental life – their feelings, thoughts, desires, habits, and stories, no matter how trivial. As a source of memory, we help someone to become more accessible to themselves.

Holding helps other people make sense of their experiences. We are on hand to provide interpretations and sources of perspective. When a child falls over, for example, our response feels its way into their pain. How surprising! How sore! Although we do not tell them how to feel, they can take up these reactions in making sense of their tumble. With friends, too, we are sources of interpretations which help them to make sense of their experiences. Holding them in this way is not the same as imposing an interpretation, or promoting our own story. We do not enforce our 'interpretive sovereignty' as Dover called it, but instead attend without agenda – a process which can require us to tolerate discomfort or ambivalence.

Although holding requires us to grapple with someone's states of mind, the notion is richer and less cognitive than attempts to just understand what someone is thinking. Recognition of bodily presence is also vital. Our physical presence, and touch, are themselves sources of important continuity which can help someone to cope with disorientation. Physical comfort helps people to make sense of their fear or pain.

Holding also makes someone's skills and abilities available to them. We help someone to experience their skills in action, or their ability to tackle a task, when we withstand their frustrations or anger in the process. Our holding someone enables them to feel secure, and so to feel more confident in their abilities.[56]

Holding is therefore about agency as much as it is about states of mind or identity. From a child learning to explore an environment on their own in the presence of the parent, to someone on belay as they learn to climb, or a lover on the couch with a partner as they grapple with an insecurity, we are held in a variety of situations in a way which allows us to draw on our emerging abilities.

The agential aspect of holding is largely relational, although I set aside here the interesting possibility that we might hold ourselves. When we hold another, we try to withstand difficult emotions and thus avoid being overwhelmed or incapacitated by the feelings of the people we interact with. When we are held, we are able to return to the 'bits' of ourselves kept in place by other people, and to experience our emotions. This is vital when our sense of who we are, what we want, and what we are doing is itself emerging over time in relation to other people.

One way to think of holding is as a significant way that we facilitate others' 'going on being' which cuts across different kinds of emotion regulation. To hold someone skilfully is partly a process of modifying their situation. We create a sense of calm and safety for someone through our use of space, body language, tone, and attention. But when we hold someone, we also support them as they appraise their situation or states of mind, we make available different perspectives for consideration, and we return facets of their mental life and/or life stories for reabsorption.

As Winnicott's psychoanalytic insights show, much holding is in tension with the activity of providing interpretations. But this does not mean we are detached from someone. Examples of analysts or teachers can prompt the concern that holding involves keeping people at arm's length, or aspiring for dispassionate neutrality. This is wrong twice over. First, it overlooks empathetic, engaged, and loving aspects of those professions. Second, it downplays Winnicott's original focus on the mother's concern for her child: a situation which cannot be described as detached.

Nor should talk of parenting or therapy make us think holding is infantilizing. To wrongly infantilize someone is to ignore their agency at the expense of our own. To hold, in contrast, is to facilitate ways of enabling another to arrive at their sense of identity and agency on their terms: we might not like where they end up.

Holding is a dynamic central to romantic life, and something we are often doing without realizing. It is especially valuable when someone is experiencing disorienting or recalcitrant feelings, such as jealousy. In those situations, reasoning is often ineffective; we might already *know* there is no threat, or we are wrong about a rival, or that our partner loves us, yet still feel terrible. In those moments, a calm presence helps us to confront our vulnerability. Our partner's ability to withstand our outbursts, rather than becoming defensive or dismissive, helps to prevent spirals of emotional tension or hostility. Being held by a partner, perhaps experiencing their physical presence, helps our feelings to resonate, or enables us to see the difficult parts of ourselves, like our fears or lack of control, in a way which we can evaluate later. Some moments of romantic jealousy are so messy and complex that we benefit from a partner who can hold together our various thoughts when we are unable to confront them. Later on, in a cooler moment, they might offer us various potential interpretations of our experience which can be useful as we work to digest our feelings and evaluate our situation.

Ideally, people in a relationship hold each other; they provide a stable presence, nurturing environment, sense of physical continuity, and source of memory, which help the other make sense of their states of mind, confront their behaviour, and consolidate their identity. The dynamic is mutually reinforcing. The more we try to provide this continuity, the better placed someone else will be to hold us, and vice versa.

Conclusion

Jealousy resists easy analysis. I have argued we should take a broader look at jealousy as it might be fitting in more contexts than we suppose. Striving to remove jealousy is not appropriate for everyone, especially if their emotions are responding to oppressive social contexts or relationships. Management of our emotions is more important. I looked at the positive role of emotional compression as a way of reducing the negative impact of our jealous experiences. My examination of holding was broader. We are often unable to target specific emotions or outbursts and have to grapple instead with patterns of feeling over time. This involves reflection and realistic conversation, but also the creation of holding environments. To form a holding environment, we may have to suspend the desire to probe, understand, and excerpt difficult feelings, and focus on creating contexts which enable other people to tolerate uncertainty.

Although I have focused on jealousy, much of my discussion applies to other difficult emotions in romantic life. Within relationships, our emotional responses to someone and our shared situation often settle into dynamics. Examples might include aversive patterns, such as indifference, anxiety, or withdrawn emotionality; confrontational patterns, of jealousy or anger; simmering patterns, of resentment or contempt; and disruptive patterns, of sadness or elation.

An emotion can be difficult, in the context of a relationship, without feeling bad or having negative moral connotations. So-called 'new relationship energy', for example, is what nonmonogamous people call the positive feeling of interest and engagement with a new romantic partner against the background of settled relationships. Similar in nature to the limerent stages of romantic love,[57] new relationship energy can be heady, distracting, and disruptive. It is challenging precisely because it feels good for the person experiencing it but is typically not felt by that person's other partners.

Difficult emotions shape our romantic agency. Patterns of anger undermine intimacy; patterns of insecurity stall communication; patterns of fear make us resist new experiences; new relationship energy can cloud empathy. All these emotions might require forms of management, both direct and indirect. Doing so helps us to reduce our defensiveness and yearning for unrealistic romantic changes. Ideally, we would manage our feelings alongside people who work to manage theirs. Difficult emotions will be a fixed feature of romantic life, but one that need not impede our romantic agency.

8
Grasping the Good

... sometimes people deliberately take a myopic view, and fill their eyes with things seen microscopically in order not to see macroscopically. (Marylin Frye)[1]

Insularity

In all good relationships we will have to manage our emotions. My discussion of compression and holding only scratched the surface of this important topic. Often, these processes require us to look inwards. We reflect on our feelings and patterns of behaviour and try to control our reactions. Look inwards for too long, however, and we risk becoming insular; indeed, we might make great progress in tackling our negative feelings yet struggle to appreciate the positive features of our romantic lives. Even worse, our self-directed efforts to manage our feelings could stop us attending fully to the people we care about. The term 'management' itself has to be used carefully. We do not want to be subject to a kind of relationship managerialism, in which our partners care about our inner lives only in times of conflict or disorientation. Put in terms of romantic agency, the worry could be that, as presented so far, emotion management *preserves* romantic agency but does little to *extend* it.

We might want more from our intimate relationships, however, and think that our efforts to cultivate better characters are not simply aimed at tackling problems but might also improve our lives. Such a possibility is part of the appeal of unconventional romantic lifestyles and practices, like polyamory or relationship anarchy, which promise to change how we relate to other people and perhaps offer us new patterns of feeling altogether.

To accompany any efforts at emotional management, I will argue we need to cultivate the distinct ability to see and appreciate the good things ourselves and our partners experience in our romantic life together. I will call this general ability 'grasping the good', for short. There are two dimensions to grasping the good. *Compersion* is our ability to appreciate the flourishing experienced by other people in our romantic lives. *Contentment* is our ability to appreciate our own good. Sustained efforts to be compersive and content can form a character trait which corrects against an insular approach to romantic life. We should try to develop this trait.

Compersion

Compersion is a term used initially to describe the experiences of nonmonogamous people who found themselves feeling joy when their partners were intimate with other people. My analysis of compersion, set out in detail elsewhere, is that it is an emotional response to the flourishing of another person, not their fleeting good feelings.[2] Instead, it is an emotion which comprehends someone within the broader context of their life. To be compersive, we have to believe our partner is flourishing, they have to think they are flourishing, and our emotion also encompasses the person who helps our partner to flourish. We do not have to personally want to experience what our partner experiences, and nor is compersion similar in tone to what our partner feels when they thrive with someone else.

Compersion needs to be distinguished from apparently similar emotions. Compersion is not pride, for example, because we must understand how other people think about their situation, which is not required when we feel pride.

Nor is compersion a form of masochistic enjoyment, because compersion is not painful and masochistic experiences hurt in some sense, even if they are experienced positively overall.

Compersion could be seen as a natural result of caring for someone or being attached to them, so it makes no sense to *try* to feel compersive. But this overlooks that our attachment is often in conflict with other-directed attitudes such as compersion. Monique Wonderly, for instance, points out that attachment needs are often intensely *self*-regarding: 'felt attachment needs are not in the first instance about seeking pleasure, nor are they centrally concerned with the flourishing of another person or object. When one is attached, what one needs is engagement with a particular person or object. In this respect, felt attachment necessity is importantly self-regarding.'[3] Our sense that we need someone in our life often makes it hard for us to appreciate that person's personality or needs. Their feelings and flourishing can easily go unnoticed. Compersion is often a hard-won achievement within loving relationships and we may actually find it easier to be compersive towards people to whom we are not attached, like more 'casual' lovers.

But what about care? Certainly, care for someone involves the desire to see them flourish. But this desire is often clouded by other emotions and desires in romantic life, such as desire for self-preservation, or to avoid loss. Merely caring about someone does not mean we will feel good about them. We should resist an account of love, understood in terms of care or concern, which is not compatible with these experiences.[4]

Compersion is not unique to romantic life – we can feel it towards our friends, or family, or colleagues, but it is arguably rarer in romantic life because it is not something we are expected to feel or socialized into feeling. Our romantic culture has us braced against rivals, threats, and the possibility of being duped and hurt. Romantic practices are often individualistic and competitive. We anticipate feeling jealous, insecure, and envious because romantic life feels like a zero-sum game.

Our difficulty in attending to the good of other people, even our romantic partners, reflects broader social attitudes. Marilyn Frye perceptively described the gendered aspects of this tension in her contrast between two modes of perceiving and engaging with the world which she terms the 'arrogant eye' and the 'loving eye'.[5]

Someone who looks arrogantly is individualistic, dominating, and goal-oriented. (Such a person might also be drawn to agonistic play, in Lugones' sense.) Their 'expectation creates in the space about [them] a sort of vacuum mould into which the other is sucked and held'.[6] Seeing with a loving eye, in contrast, is an achievement. This way of seeing 'does not make the object of perception into something edible, does not try to assimilate it, does not reduce it to the size of the seer's desire, fear and imagination, and hence does not have to simplify'.[7] To see lovingly is to acknowledge and respect the separateness of persons.

The ideal of a certain kind of attentiveness is central to Frye's thinking about love, just as it is to the work of novelist and philosopher Iris Murdoch. For Frye, the ability to attend to other people requires us to have a clear sense of ourselves:

> The loving eye is one that pays a certain sort of attention. This attention can require a discipline but *not* a self denial ... What is required is that one know what are one's interests, desires, and loathings, one's projects, hungers, fears and wishes, and that one know what is and what is not determined by these. In particular, it is a matter of being able to tell one's own interests from those of others and of knowing where one's self leaves off and another begins.[8]

Our attention to others is here linked closely to realism about ourselves – realism that may require work to overcome defensiveness or motivated self-ignorance. Once we are aware of who we are, we can avoid viewing others through the lens of our own interests and concerns.

A further distinction is required, however, because we might attend to a partner's flourishing, not be defensive, and yet fail to *affirm* what we see. Imagine things from your perspective. You want your partner to try to see you as you are, and would be dismayed if they made no effort to do so. You also want them to see you accurately, to not be so defensive or egoistic that they cannot acknowledge the joy and satisfaction in your life. They might do these things, however, but stop short at actually affirming what brings you joy. That lack of affirmation can feel alienating.

The distinct value of affirmation became apparent to me in considering E. M. Hernandez's discussion of gender pronouns.[9] Hernandez exposes the difference between avoiding being wrong about someone (avoiding misgendering them) and actively affirming their gender identity on their terms. Hernandez thinks affirmation of gender pronouns is valuable as a form of attention to oppressed people. It helps to counter the ways in which some gender identities have been marginalized, for example, and the specific practice of affirming gender identity can help to foster broader practices of attending to people in other ways too.

Affirming the good experienced by those we love has value in similar ways to Hernandez's thoughts about pronouns. Affirming the flourishing of nonmonogamous people helps to counter the ways in which their lifestyles have been denigrated through negative stereotypes and oppressive norms. Doing this also constitutes a form of respect, as we try to apprehend and appreciate what makes other people happy. In being guided by their sense of what matters, not ours, we recognize their authority over self-understanding. Some view this partial deference to another's understanding of themselves as central to loving another person.[10] More generally, the activity of trying to attend to a partner's flourishing and affirm what we see plays a role in contesting the individualism and emotional restrictedness characteristic to our romantic culture.

To feel compersion is to affirm the intimacy our partners experience with other people. But we can also affirm these aspects of someone's life without feeling compersion. In practice, compersion can remain out of reach, not least because we are so primed to experience insecurity or hostility when people thrive without us. Compersion occupies one point on a broader spectrum of attitudes. Mere acknowledgement that someone else makes our partner flourish is another point on the spectrum; affirmation of what we acknowledge is yet another. We can acknowledge our partner's flourishing while still experiencing recalcitrant jealousy or a sense of envy.

I find it useful to think of compersion as the possible end of an independently valuable journey of appreciation in our intimate lives. We are usually selective in our appreciation of how other people flourish, and struggle with the idea that our partners may experience intimacy without us. But we can work to appreciate this intimacy and understand what brings people satisfaction. These efforts are especially useful when people we care about have desires which lie beyond the socially recognized limits of hetero-monogamous possibility. Our personal efforts to appreciate and affirm romantic flourishing help us to resist some of the most entrenched romantic norms which restrict the kinds of relationships we can imagine.

Should we prioritize managing our difficult emotions or our attempts to grasp the good? These efforts can conflict because attempts to appreciate what brings a loved one joy might generate a range of uncomfortable emotions like insecurity, jealousy, and envy. There is no straightforward answer to this question. The fact that our romantic agency is fragile supports efforts to manage our emotions, but my remarks about the value of realism also speak in favour of attending to someone in an accurate way, without being defensive. Also relevant is my concern that overly demanding ideals in romantic life risk entrenching conventional relationships and preventing potentially valuable exploration. One way to take romantic risks with integrity is to try to attend fully to someone and affirm what makes them flourish, even if this makes us uncomfortable.

Contentment

We could appreciate how our partner flourishes romantically while not appreciating the good things in our own dating life or relationships. It is easy to yearn for something different, to be mindful of the many potential matches on dating apps, or to fixate on the possibility of a different kind of relationship. When we are restless like this, we focus on what might be better, and overlook what is already good.

Realism can seem like an antidote to restlessness. A better grasp of our personal limitations and the shape and impact of social norms and ideals on our character might seem to help us to focus on what is good in our romantic life. But this antidote is limited. We can be realistic about our situation but crave change. The problem here is that our grasp of the facts is only one part of the picture. We also need to know how best to interpret those facts, and we do so relative to various benchmarks.

Cheshire Calhoun has an analysis of the disposition towards contentment which is especially relevant to romantic life and so worth exploring here. Calhoun thinks there are many ways that we can be appreciative, and there might be several different kinds of 'virtue of appreciation'.[11] Central to her view, however, is the idea that our sense of whether a situation is good enough is always formed relative to an 'expectation frame'. An expectation frame is 'an operating view about what we are, loosely speaking, "entitled" to expect in the way of degree of goodness'.[12] Being content is not the same as being pleased about something because evaluations of contentment involve some counterfactual comparisons between how things are and how they might be or might have been.

Our expectation frame is shaped by our beliefs – by our understanding of society, personal morality, normality, and other values.[13] The way we think about dating, for example, will be shaped by our beliefs about love, romantic success, gender roles, relationship expectations, and so on. This is so even if we remain unaware of precisely what our beliefs are, or how they combine to shape our expectations. Because people have different beliefs, their expectation frames will differ, and so they may evaluate the same event in different ways.

Calhoun suggests we are disposed to be content when we view imperfect situations through expectation frames which allow us to think they are good enough.[14] She thinks this disposition may be a virtue because we can shape and develop the expectation frame we use, and because this process corrects against our impulse to neglect the good things in our life.[15]

Dissatisfaction, according to Calhoun, stems from our cultural norms and practices. She thinks our culture is competitive and consumerist in ways which entrench personal doubts. If we notice what is good in our current situation at all, we question its value and remain curious about other options. We are also prone to assuming that other people have it better, or that distant alternatives are preferable; we 'continuously push the good-enough out of the present and into an aspirational future'.[16]

These doubts are forceful in romantic life. Our romantic culture makes it hard for us to accept the inevitable imperfections in our relationships or the fact that all intimacy involves compromise or forms of loss. Our expectation frames are skewed around ideals of 'the one' or concerns about 'settling', for example. Compatibility culture can also have us doubting whether we are 'right' for our partner. Given the range of choice proffered by dating apps, it is easy to assume someone else would be better for our partners than we are. This faceless array of others can also heighten doubts about our intimate and sexual experiences. Perhaps they are not as exciting or fulfilling as those experienced by other people. These comparisons erode contentment.

We address dissatisfaction by trying to be content. To do this, we must adopt a more realistic expectation frame, accept some imperfection, and accept the impact of luck. The disposition towards contentment is both practical, since it can lead us to do or omit things, such as refraining from breaking up with someone, and what Calhoun calls 'quasi-practical', in that it provides 'the rationale for internal activities of gratefully appreciating the goods and reflecting on how things might have gone worse'.[17]

Contentment is therefore not simply the disposition to accept, or be resigned towards, our present situation. It involves active affirmation of the good in our situation. This affirmation is similar to what is involved in compersion. We might even be tempted to view contentment as a kind of self-compersion, but contentment is broader because we can be content with specific goods in our lives, even if we are not flourishing overall.

Contentment and compersion form two aspects of our attempt to grasp the good in romantic life. But talk of grasping the good, and contentment in particular, prompts an obvious and serious objection: surely some of us should not be content with our situation. If there are larger problems, it seems to wrong to suggest that we work on being content with the good things in our relationship. We can experience occasional joy even in a relationship marred by a lack of intimacy or respect. Being disposed to contentment could sustain a relationship we would be better off leaving.

More generally, might the emphasis on contentment help us to sustain domination and inequality because it stops us from seeking better, more equitable, and respectful forms of interaction? This worry might be heightened by Calhoun's suggestion that contentment involves an 'inclination ... to nonresistance ... to the imperfections of our condition', as sometimes we should resist imperfections.[18] But she has several resources to respond to the worry.

First, contentment is typically focused on how things have unfolded to date, and this is always compatible with a desire for things to improve in the future. We can simultaneously strive to modify an unrealistic expectation frame, perhaps by becoming less comparative, while also encouraging partners to become less entitled. It makes sense to try to redress gendered inequality while becoming more comfortable with good but imperfect relationships.

Second, being content often characterizes our *emotional* orientation to an imperfect situation, rather than a disposition that prevents us from setting ambitious goals or seeking to change a situation.[19] We can acknowledge that a relationship, say, is positive in many ways, while hoping it may become more equal, and while taking a playful attitude towards the ways in which it is currently imperfect.

These points reinforce the idea that being content is quasi-practical. Much of our intimate life is concerned less with action and more with our attitudes towards each other. We can grasp the good in our situation without becoming servile or neglecting our wider interests. The attempt to attend to, appreciate, and affirm what is good is mainly a corrective against the comparative pressures in the other direction, rather than a process which motivates us to accept harm. Indeed, recognition of the genuine goods in our relationships will likely reinforce our desire to seek more of them. As we learn to be content with moments of satisfaction, say, rather than hankering after an unrealistic vision of romantic intensity, we might be motivated to seek satisfying relationships and be less swayed by episodic love-bombing.

Another pressing objection concerns the connection between grasping the good and realism. I have positioned realism as a central virtue in romantic life. Is trying to see the good in our situation, and to appreciate the flourishing of others, just to wear rose-tinted glasses or embrace a 'positive vibes only' attitude? I think not, and have several responses to this worry.

First, grasping the good can be a response to the same pressure to which realism responds – namely, the tendency to be swayed by defensiveness or unrealistic expectations and points of comparison. When we feel compersion, for example, we must grasp accurately what is good about the life of our partner rather than seeing what we want to see.

Second, the disposition to be content concerns the kinds of counterfactual comparisons we are prone to make. In cultivating this disposition, we work to alter our point of reference, not our appreciation of how things are. There is always some indeterminacy about how things might have been, and, given this interpretive free space, we try to respond positively not negatively. There is room for disagreement as to whether there is some objective sense of the expectation frame which is suitable for any given situation. (Calhoun seems to think not.[20]) Either you think there is, in which case it is a separate question whether our attempts to be content are realistic. Or you think there is not, in which case the matter of realism is less relevant when thinking about contentment. Either way, striving to be content by becoming less comparative poses no threat to being realistic about what our romantic life is like.

Finally, being disposed to be content is not to embrace a 'positive vibes' mentality. Such a mentality is best understood as a commitment to a certain kind of relationship – one that emphasizes enjoyment and ease of interaction over vulnerability and potential conflict. We might think that such relationships lack some important goods, or that romantic life rarely unfolds in that way. But there is nothing inherently unrealistic about wanting to relate to people in that way. To do so might limit our pool of potential partners, or the duration of our relationships, but we could be aware of those consequences. These concerns are simply independent from the matter of whether we are being realistic or content.

Grasping the good corrects against the twin distortions of a self-absorbed romantic culture, on the one hand, and excessive striving for fulfilment on the other. To grasp the good is to look with Frye's loving eye; to have a rough sense of who we are, and where the boundary lies between us and other people; it is to appreciate and then affirm the good things within our relationships, and to see the good which might lie beyond those relationships in the lives of the people we care about.

Trying to grasp the good is risky. We might deceive ourselves into thinking we are being content when we are actually excusing mistreatment by a partner. As I discussed in chapter 6, however, risks in romantic life have to be embraced, but can be done so with integrity. The view of integrity I favoured was relational: one open to influence by others. This point is crucial when considering contentment because the disposition is best cultivated with other people. This makes it that bit harder to remain deluded for too long.

Conclusion

Trying to grasp the good matters for several reasons. Experiencing positive emotions, of joy or contentment, has a beneficial effect on our feelings and inclinations. When we feel good, we are likely to engage in exploratory or playful behaviours which can, in turn, make us feel even better.[21] Put in terms of romantic agency, feelings of contentment or compersion can help to reinforce a sense of joyful confidence and security which supports further intimacy.

Because our romantic agency is nurtured by other people, our ability to grasp the good in romantic life also helps them. Compersion towards a partner, for example, can help them to come to notice, and then appreciate, their own flourishing – a task which might be hard to achieve in a mononormative and amatonormative society where even open-minded people can be resistant to the idea that they can flourish without a single loving domestic partner. Grasping the good also helps people to incorporate their self-image into a broader narrative. When we see that someone is loved by people other than us, and affirm that love, we can help *them* to fit that affection into their identity, and also make space for it in our shared romantic story. As an attitude towards situations, grasping the good helps us to resist pressure to keep things unsaid, downplay them, or explain them away.

Trying to grasp the good, particularly in trying to be compersive, is central to an effort to see one another generously.[22] Such generous seeing is preferable to a romantic culture which prizes vigilance in the face of threats and competition. When we attend with generosity, we are better able to be playful, rather than shut down and protective.

Finally, and most importantly, trying to grasp the good is crucial if we want to change our modern romantic context. Even if we cannot substantially change our romantic life due to danger or our temperament, and even if we are not in a position to publicly advocate for social change, there is independent value in the personal attempt to see and affirm the good we have. This is a perceptual and emotional shift which has a practical impact on the lives of others, and which may have a broader social impact beyond that. Compersion pushes against possessiveness and entitlement; contentment pushes against romantic restlessness.

Conclusion

At the beginning of the twenty-first century we face what is, in many ways, a more chaotic and sometimes destructive set of ideas about love, sex, marriage, and relationships than at any time in previous history. (Mary Evans)[1]

Summary

I began with a picture of our romantic culture, which shapes who we are and how we love. Our practices and values are changing, but remain shaped by entrenched norms which privilege amorous, monogamous, and sexually restrained relationships. For some, these shifts move us towards more equal and autonomous relationships. For others, the more private intimacy becomes, the more disoriented and anxious we feel. Some of us might even agree with Evans' more gloomy view, expressed at the start of this chapter.

Unconventional intimate arrangements, such as polyamory or relationship anarchy, could offer us new ways to relate to each other. But we often face principled objections from other people, or personal resistance from our emotions. Concerns about practicality, greed, fairness, jealousy, and so on, are easily answered, but our engrained habits and emotional wariness are more challenging.

These difficulties motivated my shift of focus towards our romantic agency. Our ability to sustain intimacy as we would like is shaped by the romantic choices we make, and the ways in which we nurture our relationships. This ability is central to real romantic freedom. Having permission to explore unconventional arrangements is valuable only if we have the social and psychological resources to act.

Our romantic agency is shaped by many different factors. I tried to resist stark divisions between monogamous and nonmonogamous relationships, for example, as they have many similarities and the personal impact of any particular relationship form is so varied. Instead, I tried to isolate some agential themes: the possibility of intimate specialization, of ongoing romantic appreciation, of more checks and balances, of rejecting common norms or rules.

Several traits help us to protect our romantic agency, whichever romantic lifestyle we pursue. Realism helps us to correct against the seductions of romantic ideals and to appreciate the mutuality and uncertainty integral to romantic relationships. Integrity helps us to remain accountable as we take romantic risks and face uncertainty. Playfulness stops us from being too serious, or uncreative. Emotional compression and holding help us to manage our jealousy. Efforts to grasp the good help us to appreciate intimacy. These traits and practices reinforce each other.

Cultivation

What can we do to cultivate our romantic agency? We can divide our efforts into three strands: understanding, exploration, and nurturance.

First, understanding. Often, we do not know what we are working with. We have a poor grasp of ourselves – our desires, habits, and ideals. This opacity can increase in relationships where our obscurities mingle with those of our partners, or the shared narratives which structure our thoughts and action. Trying to understand ourselves is therefore valuable.

Our goal is to understand our desires, capacities, and limitations. We need to appreciate how we have been shaped by our social context. These efforts to understand ourselves proceed at different levels of resolution. On the one hand, we evaluate ourselves in reference to general beliefs about romantic success, legitimate expectations, or self-worth, which are often widely shared. On the other hand, we are also shaped by highly particular experiences and our unique idiolects. Teasing apart these factors is a challenge. General frameworks for thinking about intimacy – say, the loose distinction between 'committed' and 'casual' relationships – can coexist with very specific ideas about what a good relationship looks like, such as those inherited from our parents or friends. We start to make sense of our starting point through observation, listening, open conversation, and realistic comparisons.

Understanding ourselves is hard. Self-knowledge is often in short supply. Coming to appreciate the gap between who we are and who we realistically might become is especially challenging. Exploration is vital if we are to make sense of this gap, and come to know our capabilities.

Exploration takes different forms, not all of which are practical. Take the critical evaluation of our beliefs, for example. We can ask ourselves whether we actually endorse our implicitly held views about romantic life. Exploration is often in imagination as we try to view the familiar from different perspectives. Are other forms of intimacy available? Could we be more creative?

Exploration does not require us to reject what is familiar. Sometimes we just embrace conventional norms in a slightly looser way. Reflection on monogamy, for example, could have us seeing that norm as something more contingent, historical, and flexible, rather than a rigid default. Exploration in imagination can open space for irony and humour. We might remain monogamous, but with a sense of the strangeness of such a lifestyle.

Narrative exploration is also crucial. It is increasingly common for people to talk of the need to interrogate and unlearn some of our romantic beliefs and ideals. We are prompted to take a hard look at our entitlement, or views about gendered roles in intimate settings. But we can place individual ideas under the microscope without considering the broader stories to which they contribute. It is easy to accept that one person can love two more, say, while still thinking that relationships must 'progress' to be valuable, or that romantic love is more important than friendship. Often we tinker with details without questioning the wider stories which frame our understanding of intimacy. Other stories are possible, however, and we have some freedom to tell new ones. Coming to appreciate that we have this discretion can be transformative.

Exploration is not only discursive. Sexuality is one aspect of romantic life where experimentation is beneficial. On the one hand, sexual behaviour offers a chance for playfulness in the face of vulnerability as we improvise together. On the other hand, sexual norms and ideals can be constraining and lead to behavioural clichés rather than free expression. Sexual exploration helps us to understand our desires, and the receptiveness of our body and imagination. The activity of experimenting with someone can yield confidence in our bodily presence.

Romantic exploration can be solitary or shared. Single people, or people dating, can also explore the outlines of their core beliefs and values, consider new ways to relate to old norms, and try out different modes of communication. These processes can be confronting. We may discover gaps in our abilities in considering new beliefs, norms, ways of relating to familiar ideas, and forms of communication. The attempt to attend to someone or to affirm what they desire or value can be harder than gliding along on default. Similarly, exploration with other people can unearth previously unseen points of tension or conflict, whether in desire, value, narrative sensibility, or capacity for intimacy.

Sustaining a nurturing environment is so important when we consider the difficulties we have in understanding ourselves and exploring alternatives. Few of us can be philosophized into feeling secure. Critical thinking rarely eradicates our jealousy, or ironic habits. Our attachment to someone can persist even when they hurt us and we know we should leave.

We foster a nurturing environment in different ways. In some contexts, it might involve the literal search for a calm space where intimacy has room to develop away from external pressure. In other contexts, a nurturing environment is linked to a calm state of mind. Being a reliable but unintrusive presence can help to bring about this security;

we try to attend to someone, withstand their frustrations and silliness, and hold them together. When we are nurtured like this, our fears have less of a hold and we are better placed to start telling our own romantic story, rather than existing on default.

Our wider communities contribute towards a nurturing environment. Solidarity is fostered through the support of like-minded people, whether friends, family, or even therapists and counsellors. Solidarity helps us in our efforts to understand and explore romantic life, reject familiar norms or practices, or adopt new postures towards familiar ideals.

Domination

Social changes can further nurture our romantic agency. Full consideration of the breadth of social policy is for another book, but before concluding I want to return briefly to domination. In chapter 2, I suggested that domination, where people have the ability to interfere in our lives in an arbitrary way, can be a feature of romantic life which limits our freedom.

Domination is inherently bad.[2] Domination is also instrumentally bad. People who live under conditions of domination are practically and psychologically more likely to be hesitant, even if they have kind partners.

It is hard to track how specific romantic configurations or policies sustain domination. We should worry especially about dynamics which increase our dependency, or which make it harder for us to leave a relationship, or where the care and support we receive is conditional on someone's whims. These dynamics can arise in many forms of relationship.

A reasonable moral constraint on our choice of relationship structure, however, is that it does not exacerbate domination – that is, it does not improve the ability of one person to be able to wield arbitrary power over another. We can embrace this constraint even if we think that romantic relationships *always* expose us to some arbitrary domination in virtue of our vulnerability or attachment. At the very least, we do not want our relationships to make this domination worse.

When thinking about the practical ways in which domination can be minimized, several themes emerge which cut across changes that we can make and changes that require wider intervention or state support. I think of them as abilities which constitute forms of 'antipower' that help us respond to the possibility that other people might wield arbitrary power over us, and vice versa.[3] In no particular order, I call them the ability to be *seen*, the ability to *reconsider*, the ability to *leave*, and the ability to *recover*. I will describe them here as they give a sense of some of the social changes which might support our romantic agency.

The ability to be seen relates to some of the agency-supporting features of romantic life I considered in chapter 3. Some nonmonogamous dynamics help us to corroborate our intimate identity, and increase the accountability of our partners. The sense of accountability is anchored in the idea that plural romantic dynamics benefit from increased exposure and oversight. This openness can help to reduce romantic domination. We can resist the idea that romantic life is purely private, and embrace romantic accountability. Accountability can take different forms, from communication with other people in a polyamorous network, or between various partners and their partners, through to openness with friends and family. To be open, we need to reduce the social grip of amatonormativity and sex negativity. The more we think of romantic life as walled-off from other kinds of care and relationship, the more space there is for domination and abuse.

We can also adjust our approach to commitment by embracing practices of provisional or revisable commitment. Most easily achievable is to accept that our needs and desires will change, and resist making commitments which ignore this fact. This change of emphasis away from the 'happy ever after' finality of the monogamous ideal can become part of everyday relationship education. Practically, we can structure our relationships around periods of reflection and readjustment. Some of us may find it helpful to think in terms of relationship 'retrospectives' or 'reviews', in which we consider how our relationship has unfolded over a year and seek to be explicit about any changes we might implement.[4] We can also campaign to encourage the state to offer renewable or temporary forms of marriage.[5] These would offer people the legal rights, responsibilities, and protections of a marriage regime, but only for a period of time. As that time ends, there would be the option to renew, end, or perhaps amend the marriage. This makes explicit the idea that the relationships and their constitutive boundaries may require adjustment. State provision of this option would help to encourage a more considered approach to relationships.

The ability to reconsider romantic relationships is useless if we struggle to leave them on the basis of our reconsiderations. If we would struggle to leave someone, they are better placed to wield arbitrary power over us. To combat this, we need the real freedom to exit.[6] Governments should remove laws which make it difficult for people to reconfigure their romantic life – for example laws which give men more power than women, make marriages hard to dissolve, or limit change of domestic arrangement. But real freedom to exit requires more than this, because financial or social difficulties are often the main barrier to us leaving a relationship. There are different ways these barriers could be overcome. At the personal level, we could resist fully blending our finances, or form legal contracts to protect separate assets. We might even prefer to live apart. Governments could fund transitional housing for people leaving a domestic arrangement, or provide one-off payments to help us to readjust, or re-examine the provision of state security and provide a universal basic income to ensure we are never beholden to the income of a romantic partner.[7] All of these practices and policies help to limit dependency.

The real freedom to rethink or walk away from an intimate relationship will help us to avoid some forms of domination and may nurture our romantic agency. But the ability to be intimate, and to experience romantic life under our own direction, can be set back by harmful relationships. Negative experiences can linger and we may struggle to reassert our romantic life. Our ability to date and form new relationships can be hindered by diminished self-esteem, spiralling envy, or bodily doubt. These experiences make us more vulnerable to domination and the impact of arbitrary power. This is why the ability to recover from a troubled relationship is vital. In part this is connected to the ability to be seen: wider romantic oversight means we are less likely to struggle on our own with an inaccurate sense of our abilities, or an eroded sense of self-worth. But the ability to recover requires active intervention. State-funded counselling and relationship support, for example, can help us to rediscover our romantic agency. Extended relationship education would also help us to better navigate difficult relationship changes or break-ups. Governments could re-examine employment law and the regulation of working life to provide time and support for employees whose lives have been upended by a break-up or divorce.

Tackling domination in romantic life is a complex and multifaceted task, and more research is required to understand how best to proceed. Invoking state support is rarely straightforward, and raises important concerns about equality, invasiveness, and overreach. These worries are amplified by existing relationship norms and legal frameworks which favour some forms of intimate life over others and distribute romantic privilege unevenly. To address domination and support romantic agency requires more than supporting the existing marriage regime, for example, and will require hard thinking about romantic life in general and the situation of people who do not want legal recognition of their relationships. Many of these themes are also being discussed by relationship anarchists who want to provide forms of oversight and resist domination without invoking the state. In future work, I hope to contribute to those discussions.

Talk of domination and romantic agency also prompts an objection about relationships where we might choose to adopt a subordinate role. This can happen for a variety of reasons – perhaps we want to occupy a gender or sexual role, or prefer hierarchical nonmonogamy where we seek additional partners on a 'secondary' basis, or desire a relationship which gives our partner more latitude than we have. These arrangements seem to entrench domination by giving someone greater opportunity to wield arbitrary power over others. But if steps are taken to prevent these arrangements, are we not failing to allow people to direct relationships as they wish?

Several points are worth making in response. First, it would be a significant achievement if we were able to move the default social setting away from one of inequality or romantic domination and place the justificatory burden on people who want apparently unequal or dominating relationships.

Second, it is integral to some of these dynamics that we *want* the others involved to endorse our shared situation, rather than having roles or rules enforced externally. This means our arrangement is compatible with wider social efforts to reduce domination, just as wider efforts to promote safety are compatible with individual acts of risk-taking under certain conditions. In any case, we need to think carefully about the connections between particular relationship configurations and romantic agency.

Final Thoughts

I called this book *Romantic Agency* because I wanted to draw attention to the ways in which our relationships require activity. Relating to someone is an ongoing effort which draws on our abilities to sustain intimacy. These abilities must be nurtured. We might have to help each other to excavate them from underneath the tangled layers of social norms, personal expectations, and bad habits, and unhelpful patterns of thought or feeling.

Hopefully, my discussion of romantic life helps you to think about your own situation. Whether you are married, just starting a relationship, dating, or happily single, there is value in taking stock of your desires, values, and intimate abilities.

This reflection can be confronting. You might look at your life, and wish it was more intimate. Or realize you have been following convention rather than pursuing your own vision of romantic flourishing. You may see that you are hostile to people who have unconventional relationships, but realize this resentment is anchored in doubts about your life or discomfort with your desires. Maybe it is time to be more realistic about what you actually want.

One question to ask is whether you feel able to act on your desires. If not, what holds you back? You might have an answer, only to realize you would struggle to communicate it to the people you love. Perhaps you are defensive, or they are unreceptive. Or perhaps the romantic story that excites you is too radical.

Relationships evolve and often end. How does that fact shape your thinking? Are your partners free to change? What does commitment mean to you? Do you want to be more playful, or make greater room for risks?

How do your emotions shape your romantic choices and practices? Perhaps entitlement or fear underpins moments of jealousy, or perhaps you struggle to stop comparing yourself to other people. Might there be ways of tempering your feelings, or creating more nurturing spaces for a partner? Are you able to appreciate what brings them joy, and be content with your own intimate flourishing?

Power saturates romantic life. How much romantic privilege do you have? Is it easy for you to be open about your desires, to enter and leave relationships, and to feel secure? Question whether you could do more to affirm unconventional forms of love around you.

This book opened with Berlant's observation that romantic love and relationships seem like transformative possibilities. In practice, however, transformations are often scary and elusive. Our ability to translate our desires into action meets resistance, both internal and external. Our embodied selves rebel with their challenging feelings, saturating moods, and frustrating habits. Our social world enforces its sedimented layers of norms, rituals, and standards.

Luck and temperament mean that we encounter this resistance in different places. For some of us, dating and the search for a partner is where the gap between desire and ability looms largest. Others find that relationships, the ceaseless activity of finding a home for love, are what strain our capacity for intimacy. Still others of us struggle most as break-ups harm our identity, interrupt our story, and disorder our action.

Wherever they arise, moments of friction can spark something new. With courage, we start talking to each other and talking is often transformative. Gadamer is right that genuine conversations are those we never really intend to have. Writing this book was such a conversation. Hopefully you can have similar discussions, look beyond familiar norms and practices, and discover how to nurture your romantic agency.

Notes

Introduction
1. Cited in Ann Brooks, *Love and Intimacy in Contemporary Society: Love in an International Context* (London: Routledge, 2019), 3.
2. Benjamin Bagley, '(The Varieties of) Love in Contemporary Anglophone Philosophy', in *The Routledge Handbook of Love in Philosophy* (Abingdon: Routledge, 2018), 453–64.
3. Luke Brunning and Natasha McKeever, 'Asexuality', *Journal of Applied Philosophy* 38, no. 1 (2021): 497–517.
4. Bennett W. Helm, *Love, Friendship, and the Self: Intimacy, Identification, and the Social Nature of Persons* (Oxford University Press, 2009), 4.
5. Ásta, *Categories We Live By: The Construction of Sex, Gender, Race, and Other Social Categories* (Oxford University Press, 2018).
6. Jasmine Gunkel, 'What Is Intimacy?', *The Journal of Philosophy* (forthcoming).
7. R. C. Otter, 'Perfectionist Argument for Legal Recognition of Polyamorous Relationships', in *Philosophical Foundations of Children's and Family Law*, ed. Elizabeth Brake and Lucinda Ferguson (Oxford University Press, 2018), 95–114.

1 Modern Romance
1. Eva Illouz, *The End of Love: A Sociology of Negative Relations* (New York: Oxford University Press, 2019), 228.
2. Dr E. J. M. Bowlby, *Attachment: Volume One of the Attachment*

and Loss Trilogy (London: Pimlico, 1997); Monique Lisa Wonderly, 'On Being Attached', *Philosophical Studies* 173, no. 1 (2016): 223–42.
3. Edward Harcourt, 'Two Routes from Secure Attachment to Virtue', in *Attachment and Character*, ed. Edward Harcourt (Oxford University Press, 2021), 137–53.
4. Monique Wonderly, 'Agency and Varieties of Felt Necessity', *Ethics* 132, no. 1 (2021): 155–79.
5. Ibid., 164.
6. Arthur Aron et al., 'The Self-Expansion Model of Motivation and Cognition in Close Relationships', in *The Oxford Handbook of Close Relationships*, ed. Jeffry Simpson and Lorne Campbell (Oxford University Press, 2013), 91–115.
7. Thomas Fuchs, 'Presence in Absence: The Ambiguous Phenomenology of Grief', *Phenomenology and the Cognitive Sciences* 17, no. 1 (2018): 43–63.
8. Susan J. Brison, *Aftermath: Violence and the Remaking of a Self* (Princeton University Press, 2002).
9. Timothy D. Wilson, *Strangers to Ourselves: Discovering the Adaptive Unconscious* (London: Belknap, 2002).
10. Lisa M. Diamond, *Sexual Fluidity: Understanding Women's Love and Desire* (Cambridge, Mass.: Harvard University Press, 2008).
11. Luke Brunning, 'Virtuous Chameleons: Social Roles, Integrity, and the Value of Compartmentalization', in *The Ethics of Social Roles*, ed. Alex Barber and Sean Cordell (Oxford University Press, 2023), 298–320.
12. Quill R. Kukla, *City Living: How Urban Spaces and Urban Dwellers Make One Another* (New York: Oxford University Press, 2022).
13. Justin Oakley and Dean Cocking, *Virtue Ethics and Professional Roles* (Cambridge University Press, 2001), 25.
14. Aaron Ben-Ze'ev, *The Subtlety of Emotions* (Cambridge, Mass.: MIT Press, 2000), 25.
15. Jesse Prinz, 'Moral Sedimentation', in *Neuroexistentialism*, ed. Gregg Caruso and Owen Flanagan (New York: Oxford University Press, 2018), 89.
16. Ibid., 92.
17. Jonathan Webber, *Rethinking Existentialism* (Oxford University Press, 2018), 123–4.
18. Elizabeth Brake, *Minimizing Marriage: Marriage, Morality, and the Law* (New York: Oxford University Press, 2012), 88.
19. Ani Ritchie and Meg Barker, '"There Aren't Words for What We Do or How We Feel So We Have to Make Them

Up": Constructing Polyamorous Languages in a Culture of Compulsory Monogamy', *Sexualities* 9, no. 5 (2006): 584–601.
20 Luke Brunning, *Does Monogamy Work?* (London: Thames & Hudson, 2020), 88.
21 Elizabeth F. Emens, 'Manogamy's Law: Compulsory Monogamy and Polyamorous Existence', *New York University Review of Law & Social Change* 29, no. 2 (2004): 291.
22 Michael Warner, *The Trouble with Normal: Sex, Politics, and the Ethics of Queer Life* (Cambridge, Mass.: Harvard University Press, 2000), 23.
23 Stephanie Coontz, *Marriage, a History: How Love Conquered Marriage* (New York: Penguin, 2006).
24 Nathan Rambukkana, *Fraught Intimacies: Non/Monogamy in the Public Sphere* (Vancouver: University of British Columbia Press, 2015), 22.
25 Stephen Macedo, *Just Married: Same-Sex Couples, Monogamy, and the Future of Marriage* (Princeton University Press, 2017), 202.
26 Warner, *The Trouble with Normal*, 23.
27 Anna Clark, *Desire: A History of European Sexuality* (London: Routledge, 2008); Faramerz Dabhoiwala, *The Origins of Sex: A History of the First Sexual Revolution* (London: Allen Lane, 2012); William M. Reddy, *The Making of Romantic Love: Longing and Sexuality in Europe, South Asia, and Japan, 900–1200 CE* (University of Chicago Press, 2012).
28 Illouz, *The End of Love*, 9.
29 Ron Lesthaeghe, 'The Unfolding Story of the Second Demographic Transition', *Population and Development Review* 36, no. 2 (2010): 211–51.
30 Coontz, *Marriage, a History*.
31 Marie Bergström, *The New Laws of Love: Online Dating and the Privatization of Intimacy* (Cambridge: Polity, 2021).
32 Anthony Giddens, *The Transformation of Intimacy: Sexuality, Love and Eroticism in Modern Societies* (Cambridge: Polity, 1992), 58.
33 Illouz, *The End of Love*, 153.
34 Ibid., 8.
35 Ibid., 93.
36 Ibid., 9.
37 Ibid., 136.
38 Ibid., 158.
39 Ibid., 94.
40 Troy Jollimore, *Love's Vision* (Princeton University Press, 2011).
41 Sharon Lamb, Sam Gable, and Doret de Ruyter, 'Mutuality

in Sexual Relationships: A Standard of Ethical Sex?', *Ethical Theory and Moral Practice* 24, no. 1 (2021): 271–84.
42 Lisa Tessman, *Burdened Virtues: Virtue Ethics for Liberatory Struggles*, Studies in Feminist Philosophy (New York: Oxford University Press, 2005).
43 Illouz, *The End of Love*, 228.
44 Celeste Vaughan Curington, Jennifer Hickes Lundquist, and Ken-Hou Lin, *The Dating Divide: Race and Desire in the Era of Online Romance* (Oakland: University of California Press, 2021).
45 Bergström, *The New Laws of Love*, 92.
46 Giddens, *The Transformation of Intimacy*, 189.
47 Ibid., 185.
48 Ibid., 194.
49 Ibid., 189–90.
50 Ibid., 192.
51 Ibid., 202.
52 Illouz, *The End of Love*, 147.

2 Opening Up

1 Rebecca Kukla, 'That's What She Said: The Language of Sexual Negotiation', *Ethics* 129, no. 1 (2018): 96–7.
2 Bernard Williams, 'Justice as a Virtue', in *Essays on Aristotle's Ethics*, ed. Amélie Oksenberg Rorty (Berkeley: University of California Press, 1980), 92.
3 Ben-Ze'ev, *The Subtlety of Emotions*, 315.
4 Mark Regnerus, *Cheap Sex: The Transformation of Men, Marriage, and Monogamy* (New York: Oxford University Press, 2017), 179.
5 Martha C. Nussbaum, 'Objectification', *Philosophy & Public Affairs* 24, no. 4 (1995): 249–91.
6 Rae Langton, 'Autonomy-Denial in Objectification', in *Sexual Solipsism: Philosophical Essays on Pornography and Objectification* (Oxford University Press, 2009), 223–40.
7 John Witte, *The Western Case for Monogamy over Polygamy* (New York: Cambridge University Press, 2015), 362.
8 Herbert Marcuse, *Eros and Civilization: A Philosophical Inquiry into Freud*, 2nd edition (London: Routledge, 1987).
9 Iris Marion Young, *Justice and the Politics of Difference* (Princeton University Press, 2011), 16–17.
10 Ann Tweedy, 'Polyamory as a Sexual Orientation', *University of Cincinnati Law Review* 79, no. 4 (2011): 1461–1515.
11 For some discussion of this, see Christian Klesse, 'Polyamory: Intimate Practice, Identity or Sexual Orientation?', *Sexualities* 17, no. 1/2 (2014): 81–99.

12 Regnerus, *Cheap Sex*, 182.
13 Ibid., 181–2.
14 Ibid., 184.
15 Richard A. Posner, *Sex and Reason* (Cambridge, Mass.: Harvard University Press, 1992).
16 Joseph Henrich, Robert Boyd, and Peter J. Richerson, 'The Puzzle of Monogamous Marriage', *Philosophical Transactions of the Royal Society B: Biological Sciences* 367, no. 1589 (2012): 657–69.
17 Andrew March, 'Is There a Right to Polygamy? Marriage, Equality and Subsidizing Families in Liberal Public Justification', *Journal of Moral Philosophy* 8, no. 2 (2011): 262.
18 Ibid., 263.
19 Ibid., 263.
20 Ibid., 267.
21 John Rawls, *A Theory of Justice: Original Edition*, reissue edition (Cambridge, Mass.: Harvard University Press, 2005), 11–22.
22 Greg Matos, 'The Rise of Lonely, Single Men', *Psychology Today*, 2022, www.psychologytoday.com/gb/blog/the-state-our-unions/202208/the-rise-lonely-single-men.
23 Emily A. Vogels and Colleen Mcclain, 'Key Findings about Online Dating in the U.S.', Pew Research Center (blog), www.pewresearch.org/short-reads/2023/02/02/key-findings-about-online-dating-in-the-u-s.
24 Mara L. Haupert et al., 'Prevalence of Experiences with Consensual Nonmonogamous Relationships: Findings from Two National Samples of Single Americans', *Journal of Sex & Marital Therapy* 43, no. 5 (2017): 424–40.
25 Anna Brown, 'Bisexual Adults Are Far Less Likely than Gay Men and Lesbians to Be "Out" to the People in Their Lives', Pew Research Center (blog), accessed 10 August 2023, www.pewresearch.org/short-reads/2019/06/18/bisexual-adults-are-far-less-likely-than-gay-men-and-lesbians-to-be-out-to-the-people-in-their-lives.
26 Travis Mitchell, 'Rising Share of U.S. Adults Are Living Without a Spouse or Partner', Pew Research Center's Social & Demographic Trends Project (blog), 5 October 2021, www.pewresearch.org/social-trends/2021/10/05/rising-share-of-u-s-adults-are-living-without-a-spouse-or-partner.
27 Brunning and McKeever, 'Asexuality'.
28 Rhaina Cohen, 'What If Friendship, Not Marriage, Was at the Center of Life?', *The Atlantic*, 2020, www.theatlantic.com/family/archive/2020/10/people-who-prioritize-friendship-over

-romance/616779/; Geoffroy de Lagasnerie, *3. Une aspiration au dehors* (Paris: Flammarion, 2023).
29 Harry Chalmers, 'Is Monogamy Morally Permissible?', *The Journal of Value Inquiry* 53, no. 2 (2019): 225.
30 Ibid., 225.
31 Ibid., 241.
32 Justin Leonard Clardy, 'Monogamies, Non-Monogamies, and the Moral Impermissibility of Intimacy Confining Constraints', *Journal of Black Sexuality and Relationships* 6, no. 2 (2019): 17–36.
33 Harry Chalmers, 'Monogamy Unredeemed', *Philosophia* 50 (2022): 1009–34.
34 Luke Brunning, 'The Distinctiveness of Polyamory', *Journal of Applied Philosophy* 35, no. 3 (2018): 513–31; Brunning, *Does Monogamy Work?*
35 Natasha McKeever, 'Is the Requirement of Sexual Exclusivity Consistent with Romantic Love?', *Journal of Applied Philosophy* 34, no. 3 (2017): 354.
36 Kyle York, 'Why Monogamy Is Morally Permissible: A Defense of Some Common Justifications for Monogamy', *The Journal of Value Inquiry* 54, no. 4 (2020): 539–52.
37 Elaine Scarry, *On Beauty and Being Just* (Princeton University Press, 1999), 80.
38 Hallie Liberto, 'The Problem with Sexual Promises', *Ethics* 127, no. 2 (2017): 383–414.
39 Ibid., 397.
40 Kukla, 'That's What She Said', 96–7.
41 Ibid., 96.
42 Ibid., 96.
43 Ibid., 96–7; Emily C. R. Tilton and Jonathan Jenkins Ichikawa, 'Not What I Agreed To: Content and Consent', *Ethics* 132, no. 1 (2021): 127–54.
44 Philip Pettit, *Republicanism: A Theory of Freedom and Government*, Oxford Political Theory (Oxford University Press, 1997); Philip Pettit, *Just Freedom: A Moral Compass for a Complex World* (New York: W. W. Norton & Company, 2014); Frank Lovett, *A General Theory of Domination and Justice* (Oxford University Press, 2010).
45 Pettit, *Just Freedom*, 28–54.
46 Philippe van Parijs, *Real Freedom for All: What (If Anything) Can Justify Capitalism?* (Oxford University Press, 1995).
47 Pettit, *Just Freedom*, 37–8.
48 Ibid., 40.
49 Lovett, *A General Theory of Domination and Justice*, 119.

50 Pettit, *Just Freedom*, 53.
51 Lovett, *A General Theory of Domination and Justice*, 44–5.
52 Pettit, *Just Freedom*, 49.
53 Ibid., 91.
54 Chalmers, 'Is Monogamy Morally Permissible?', 225.
55 Young, *Justice and the Politics of Difference*.
56 Natasha McKeever and Andrew Kirton, 'Trust, Attachment, and Monogamy', in *The Moral Psychology of Trust*, ed. M. Alfano, D. Collins, and I. Vidmar Jovanovic (London: Lexington Books, 2023), 295–312.

3 Romantic Agency

1 Talbot Brewer, *The Retrieval of Ethics* (Oxford University Press, 2011), 64.
2 Kukla, *City Living*, 15.
3 James C. Scott, *Seeing Like a State: How Certain Schemes to Improve the Human Condition Have Failed*, Revised edition (New Haven: Yale University Press, 1999), 103–47.
4 L. A. Paul, *Transformative Experience* (Oxford University Press, 2014).
5 Samuel Scheffler, *Equality and Tradition: Questions of Moral Value in Moral and Political Theory* (New York: Oxford University Press, 2012).
6 Benjamin Bagley, 'Loving Someone in Particular', *Ethics* 125, no. 2 (2015): 477–507.
7 Ibid., 504.
8 Peter Goldie, *The Mess Inside: Narrative, Emotion, and the Mind* (Oxford University Press, 2012).
9 Pilar Lopez-Cantero, 'Being in Love: A Narrative Account' (unpublished dissertation, University of Manchester, 2020); Luke Brunning, 'Multiple Loves and the Shaped Self', in *The Moral Psychology of Love*, ed. B. Brogaard and A. Pismenny (Lanham, Md.: Rowman & Littlefield, 2022), 151–70.
10 Giovanna Colombetti and Joel Krueger, 'Scaffoldings of the Affective Mind', *Philosophical Psychology* 28, no. 8 (2015): 1157–76.
11 Diana Tietjens Meyers, 'Decentralizing Autonomy: Five Faces of Selfhood', in *Autonomy and the Challenges to Liberalism* (New York: Cambridge University Press, 2005), 38.
12 Eileen John, 'Love and the Need for Comprehension', *Philosophical Explorations* 16, no. 3 (2013): 285–97.
13 Peggy Orenstein, *Girls & Sex – Navigating the Complicated New Landscape* (London: Oneworld Publications, 2016), 108.

4 Shaping Intimacy

1. Jane Jacobs, *The Death and Life of Great American Cities* (London: Bodley Head, 2020), 45.
2. Robert Nozick, 'Love's Bond', in *The Examined Life: Philosophical Meditations* (New York: Simon & Schuster, 1989), 68–86.
3. Iris Murdoch, *Existentialists and Mystics: Writings on Philosophy and Literature*, new edition (London: Penguin, 1999), 215.
4. Luke Brunning, 'The Avoidance Approach to Plural Value', *Theoria* 66, no. 160 (2019): 53–70.
5. M. Kalmijn, 'Friendship Networks over the Life Course: A Test of the Dyadic Withdrawal Hypothesis Using Survey Data on Couples', *Social Networks* 25, no. 3 (2003): 231–49.
6. Kenneth Savitsky et al., 'The Closeness–Communication Bias: Increased Egocentrism among Friends versus Strangers', *Journal of Experimental Social Psychology* 47, no. 1 (2011): 269–73.
7. Sherri Irvin and Sheila Lintott, 'Sex Objects and Sexy Subjects: A Feminist Reclamation of Sexiness', in *Body Aesthetics*, ed. Sherri Irvin (Oxford University Press, 2016), 313.
8. Jessica Fern, *Polysecure: Attachment, Trauma and Consensual Nonmonogamy* (Portland: Thorntree Press, 2020).
9. Edna St Vincent Millay, *Letters of Edna St. Vincent Millay* (New York: Harper, 1952), 142.
10. Jacobs, *The Death and Life of Great American Cities*, 45.
11. Emma Glassman-Hughes, 'What Is Kitchen Table Polyamory?', *Cosmopolitan*, 18 January 2022: www.cosmopolitan.com/sexopedia/a38807618/kitchen-table-polyamory.
12. Pettit, *Republicanism*, 171–206.
13. Andie Nordgren, 'The Short Instructional Manifesto for Relationship Anarchy', *The Anarchist Library*, 2006, https://theanarchistlibrary.org/library/andie-nordgren-the-short-instructional-manifesto-for-relationship-anarchy; Ole Martin Moen and Aleksander Sørlie, 'The Ethics of Relationship Anarchy', in *The Routledge Handbook of Philosophy of Sex and Sexuality* (New York: Routledge, 2022), 341–56.
14. Luke Brunning, Natasha McKeever, and Sophie Goddard, 'Relationship Anarchy', n.d. (unpublished paper).
15. Nordgren, 'The Short Instructional Manifesto for Relationship Anarchy'.
16. Moen and Sørlie, 'The Ethics of Relationship Anarchy'.
17. Brake, *Minimizing Marriage*.
18. Elizabeth Brake, ed., *After Marriage: Rethinking Marital Relationships* (New York: Oxford University Press, 2016).

19 James C. Scott, *Two Cheers for Anarchism – Six Easy Pieces on Autonomy, Dignity, and Meaningful Work and Play* (Princeton University Press, 2014).
20 Lee Shevek, 'Process-Centered Love', The Anarchist Library, 2019, https://theanarchistlibrary.org/library/lee-shevek-process-centered-love.
21 Mark D. Finn, 'The Psychological Architecture of the Stable Couple Relationship', *Theory & Psychology* 22, no. 5 (2012): 614.
22 Peter Kropotkin, *Mutual Aid* (London: Penguin, 2022).
23 Elisabeth Sheff, *The Polyamorists Next Door: Inside Multiple-Partner Relationships and Families* (Lanham, Md.: Rowman & Littlefield Publishers, 2013).
24 Fern, *Polysecure*; Mycah Katz and Ellen Katz, 'Reconceptualizing Attachment Theory through the Lens of Polyamory', *Sexuality & Culture* 26 (2021): 792–809.
25 Ruth Kinna, *The Government of No One* (Penguin, 2020), 254.
26 Rambukkana, *Fraught Intimacies*, 113.

5 Realistic Conversation

1 Hans-Georg Gadamer, *Truth and Method*, trans. Joel Weinsheimer and Donald G. Marshall (London: Bloomsbury Academic, 2013), 401.
2 Ibid., 375.
3 Ibid., 401.
4 Daniela Dover, 'The Conversational Self', *Mind* 131, no. 521 (2022): 193–230.
5 Ibid., 201.
6 Ibid., 202.
7 Andrea C. Westlund, 'Deciding Together', *Philosopher's Imprint* 9, no. 10 (2009).
8 Ibid., 7.
9 Dover, 'The Conversational Self', 202; Westlund, 'Deciding Together', 11.
10 Westlund, 'Deciding Together', 7.
11 Ibid., 12.
12 Dover, 'The Conversational Self', 197.
13 Brewer, *The Retrieval of Ethics*, 37.
14 Julia Annas, *Intelligent Virtue* (Oxford University Press, 2011).
15 John Christman, 'Autonomy and Personal History', *Canadian Journal of Philosophy* 21, no. 1 (1991): 1–24; John Christman, *The Politics of Persons: Individual Autonomy and Sociohistorical Selves* (Cambridge University Press, 2009).

16 F. H. Bradley, *Ethical Studies* (Cambridge University Press, 2012), 68.
17 Lisa Bortolotti, 'Optimism, Agency, and Success', *Ethical Theory and Moral Practice* 21, no. 3 (2018): 526–7.
18 Ibid., 527.
19 Sandra L. Murray, John G. Holmes, and Dale W. Griffin, 'The Benefits of Positive Illusions: Idealization and the Construction of Satisfaction in Close Relationships', *Journal of Personality and Social Psychology* 70, no. 1 (1996): 79–98.
20 Bortolotti, 'Optimism, Agency, and Success', 527.
21 Valerie Tiberius, *The Reflective Life: Living Wisely with Our Limits* (Oxford University Press, 2008), 151–4.
22 Ibid., 152.

6 Romantic Risks

1 Margaret Walker, *Moral Understandings: A Feminist Study in Ethics*, 2nd edition (New York: Oxford University Press, 2007), 125.
2 Raja Halwani, *Virtuous Liaisons: Care, Love, Sex, and Virtue Ethics* (Chicago, Ill.: Open Court, 2003).
3 Ibid., 241.
4 Ibid., 242.
5 Brunning, 'The Distinctiveness of Polyamory', 518–21.
6 Marcuse, *Eros and Civilization*; Laura Kipnis, *Against Love: A Polemic* (New York: Vintage, 2004).
7 Halwani, *Virtuous Liaisons*, 238.
8 Charles Larmore, *The Autonomy of Morality* (Cambridge University Press, 2008).
9 Walker, *Moral Understandings*, 129.
10 Kathryn Addelson, *Moral Passages: Towards a Collectivist Moral Theory* (London: Routledge, 1994), 104.
11 Damian Cox, Marguerite La Caze, and Michael Levine, 'Integrity', in *The Stanford Encyclopedia of Philosophy*, ed. Edward N. Zalta, Fall 2021 (Metaphysics Research Lab, Stanford University, 2021), https://plato.stanford.edu/archives/fall2021/entries/integrity.
12 Luke Brunning, 'Cultivating an Integrated Self', in *Ethics and Self-Cultivation*, ed. Matthew Dennis and Werkhoven Sander (London: Routledge, 2018), 174–96.
13 Brunning, 'The Avoidance Approach to Plural Value'.
14 Brunning, 'Cultivating an Integrated Self', 179.
15 Cheshire Calhoun, 'Standing for Something', *The Journal of Philosophy* 92, no. 5 (1995): 235–60.
16 Ibid., 259.

17 Margaret Walker, 'Moral Luck and the Virtues of Impure Agency', *Metaphilosophy* 22, no. 1/2 (1991): 14–27.
18 Walker, *Moral Understandings*, 122–3.
19 Ibid., 116.
20 Ibid., 113.
21 Ibid., 125.
22 Ibid., 122.
23 Ibid., 124.
24 Ibid., 124.
25 Ibid., 125.
26 Ibid., 136.
27 Ibid., 127.
28 Goldie, *The Mess Inside*, 151.
29 Edward Harcourt, 'Nietzsche and the "Aesthetics of Character"', in *Nietzsche's On the Genealogy of Morality: A Critical Guide*, ed. Simon May, Cambridge Critical Guides (Cambridge University Press, 2011), 265–84.
30 Walker, *Moral Understandings*, 136.
31 Calhoun, 'Standing for Something', 260.
32 Hilde Lindemann Nelson, 'Resistance and Insubordination', *Hypatia* 10, no. 2 (1995): 23–40.
33 Moen and Sørlie, 'The Ethics of Relationship Anarchy'.
34 Anca Gheaus, 'The (Dis)Value of Commitment to One's Spouse', in *After Marriage*, ed. Brake, 204–24.
35 Bernard Suits, *The Grasshopper: Games, Life and Utopia* (Peterborough, Ont.: Broadview Press, 2014); C. Thi Nguyen, *Games: Agency as Art* (New York: Oxford University Press, 2020).
36 Glenn Mac Trujillo, 'No Laughing Matter: Playfulness and a Good Life', 2019, https://ir.vanderbilt.edu/handle/1803/12933.
37 Ibid., 74.
38 Maria Lugones, *Pilgrimages/Peregrinajes: Theorizing Coalition against Multiple Oppressions* (Lanham, Md.: Rowman & Littlefield Publishers, Inc., 2003).
39 Ibid., 96.
40 Ibid., 95.
41 Ibid., 95.
42 Tiberius, *The Reflective Life*, 96–7.
43 Vida Yao, 'Grace and Alienation', *Philosopher's Imprint* 20, no. 16 (2020): 1–18.
44 Luke Brunning and Per-Erik Milam, 'Letting Go of Blame', *Philosophy and Phenomenological Research* 106, no. 2 (2023): 720–40.
45 Regina Rini, *The Ethics of Microaggression* (Abingdon: Routledge, 2020).

46 Daniel Nolan, 'Temporary Marriage', in *After Marriage*, ed. Brake, 180–203.
47 Carrie Jenkins, *Sad Love: Romance and the Search for Meaning* (Cambridge: Polity, 2022).
48 A. Lorde, 'Uses of the Erotic: The Erotic as Power', in *Sister Outsider* (London: Penguin, 2019), 43–50.
49 Marcuse, *Eros and Civilization*.
50 McKenzie Wark, 'Charles Fourier's Queer Theory', 2015, www.versobooks.com/blogs/1896-charles-fourier-s-queer-theory.
51 Neil Strauss, *The Game: Undercover in the Secret Society of Pickup Artists* (Edinburgh: Canongate Books, 2007).
52 Kate Manne, *Down Girl: The Logic of Misogyny* (New York: Oxford University Press, 2017).
53 Martha C. Nussbaum, 'Winnicott on the Surprises of the Self', *Massachusetts Review* 47, no. 2 (2006): 381.

7 Jealousy

1 Anna Welpinghus, 'Jealousy: A Response to Infidelity? On the Nature and Appropriateness Conditions of Jealousy', *Philosophical Explorations* 20, no. 3 (2017): 323.
2 Ben-Ze'ev, *The Subtlety of Emotions*; Jerome Neu, *A Tear Is an Intellectual Thing: The Meanings of Emotion* (Oxford University Press, 2000).
3 Kristján Kristjánsson, *Justifying Emotions: Pride and Jealousy* (London: Routledge, 2002); Jesse J. Prinz, *Gut Reactions: A Perceptual Theory of Emotion* (Oxford University Press, 2006).
4 Luke Brunning, 'Compersion: An Alternative to Jealousy?', *Journal of the American Philosophical Association* 6, no. 2 (2020): 229–30.
5 Charlie Kurth, 'Inappropriate Emotions, Marginalization, and Feeling Better', *Synthese* 200, no. 2 (2022): 154.
6 Justin D'Arms and Daniel Jacobson, 'The Moralistic Fallacy: On the "Appropriateness" of Emotions', *Philosophy and Phenomenological Research* 61, no. 1 (2000): 65–90.
7 Hichem Naar, 'The Fittingness of Emotions', *Synthese* 199, no. 5 (2021): 13601–19; Justin D'Arms, 'Fitting Emotions', in *Fittingness: Essays in the Philosophy of Normativity*, ed. Chris Howard and R. A. Rowland (Oxford University Press, 2022), 105–29.
8 Young, *Justice and the Politics of Difference*.
9 Kristjánsson, *Justifying Emotions*; Kristján Kristjánsson, *Virtuous Emotions* (Oxford and New York: Oxford University Press, 2018).
10 Kristjánsson, *Virtuous Emotions*, 103.

11 Ibid., 117.
12 Ibid., 105.
13 Ibid., 104.
14 Ibid., 105.
15 Ibid., 105.
16 Catherine Wesselinoff, 'Is Jealousy Justifiable?', *European Journal of Philosophy*, 2022: 703–10.
17 Stephen L. Darwall, 'Two Kinds of Respect', *Ethics* 88, no. 1 (1977): 36–49.
18 Ibid., 38.
19 Neu, *A Tear Is an Intellectual Thing*, 48.
20 Welpinghus, 'Jealousy'.
21 Tessman, *Burdened Virtues*; Myisha Cherry, *The Case for Rage: Why Anger Is Essential to Anti-Racist Struggle* (New York: Oxford University Press, 2021).
22 Welpinghus, 'Jealousy', 333.
23 Tyler Paytas, 'Aptness Isn't Enough: Why We Ought to Abandon Anger', *Ethical Theory and Moral Practice*, 2022: 1–17.
24 Brunning, 'Compersion', 239.
25 Paytas, 'Aptness Isn't Enough'.
26 Brunning, 'Compersion', 239.
27 Ibid., 239.
28 Ibid., 239.
29 Tessman, *Burdened Virtues*; Amia Srinivasan, 'The Aptness of Anger', *Journal of Political Philosophy* 26, no. 2 (2018): 123–44; Alfred Archer and Georgina Mills, 'Anger, Affective Injustice, and Emotion Regulation', *Philosophical Topics* 47, no. 2 (2019): 75–94; Nabina Liebow and Trip Glazer, 'White Tears: Emotion Regulation and White Fragility', *Inquiry* (2019), 1–21; Cherry, *The Case for Rage*.
30 Srinivasan, 'The Aptness of Anger'.
31 Ibid., 133.
32 Ibid., 142.
33 Liebow and Glazer, 'White Tears'.
34 Cherry, *The Case for Rage*.
35 Martha C. Nussbaum, *Anger and Forgiveness: Resentment, Generosity, Justice* (Oxford University Press, 2016); Myisha Cherry, 'Political Anger', *Philosophy Compass* 17, no. 2 (2022): 1–11.
36 Kurth, 'Inappropriate Emotions, Marginalization, and Feeling Better'.
37 James J. Gross, 'The Emerging Field of Emotion Regulation: An Integrative Review', *Review of General Psychology* 2, no. 3 (1998): 271–99; James J. Gross, 'Emotion Regulation:

Taking Stock and Moving Forward', *Emotion* 13, no. 3 (2013): 359.
38 James J. Gross and Ross A. Thompson, 'Emotion Regulation: Conceptual Foundations', in *Handbook of Emotion Regulation*, ed. J. J. Gross (New York: The Guilford Press, 2007).
39 Olúfẹ́mi O. Táíwò, 'Stoicism (as Emotional Compression) Is Emotional Labor', *Feminist Philosophy Quarterly* 6, no. 2 (2020): 1–26.
40 Ibid., 5.
41 Ibid., 6.
42 Ibid., 9.
43 Ibid., 12.
44 Ibid., 13.
45 Ibid., 16.
46 Ibid., 18.
47 Arlie Hochschild, *The Managed Heart: Commercialization of Human Feeling*, 3rd edition (Berkeley, Calif., and London: University of California Press, 2012).
48 Thomas H. Ogden, 'On Holding and Containing, Being and Dreaming', *The International Journal of Psychoanalysis* 85, no. 6 (2004): 1349–64.
49 D. W. Winnicott, *Through Paediatrics to Psychoanalysis: Collected Papers*, 1st edition (London: Routledge, 1975), 303; D. W. Winnicott, *The Maturational Processes and the Facilitating Environment: Studies in the Theory of Emotional Development*, 1st edition (Princeton: Routledge, 1990), 43–6.
50 Ogden, 'On Holding and Containing, Being and Dreaming', 1351.
51 Winnicott, *The Maturational Processes and the Facilitating Environment*, 48–9.
52 Winnicott, *Through Paediatrics to Psychoanalysis*, 150.
53 Ogden, 'On Holding and Containing, Being and Dreaming', 1352.
54 Winnicott, *The Maturational Processes and the Facilitating Environment*, 240.
55 Winnicott, *Through Paediatrics to Psychoanalysis*, 303.
56 Monique Wonderly, 'On the Affect of Security', *Philosophical Topics* 47, no. 2 (2019): 165–81.
57 Dorothy Tennov, *Love and Limerence: The Experience of Being in Love*, 2nd edition (Lanham, Md.: Scarborough House, 1998).

8 Grasping the Good
1 Marilyn Frye, *The Politics of Reality: Essays in Feminist Theory* (Trumansburg, NY: Crossing Press, 1983), 6–7.
2 Brunning, 'Compersion'.
3 Wonderly, 'Agency and Varieties of Felt Necessity', 169.

4 Pilar Lopez-Cantero, 'Non-Harmonious Love', *International Journal of Philosophical Studies* 30, no. 3 (2022): 276–97.
5 Frye, *The Politics of Reality*, 66–76.
6 Ibid., 69.
7 Ibid., 76.
8 Ibid., 75.
9 E. M. Hernandez, 'Gender-Affirmation and Loving Attention', *Hypatia* 36, no. 4 (2021): 619–35.
10 John, 'Love and the Need for Comprehension'.
11 Cheshire Calhoun, 'What Good Is Commitment?', *Ethics* 119, no. 4 (2009): 347.
12 Ibid., 334.
13 Ibid., 335.
14 Ibid., 340.
15 Ibid., 336.
16 Ibid., 346.
17 Ibid., 339.
18 Ibid., 332.
19 Ibid., 349.
20 Ibid., 334.
21 Barbara L. Fredrickson, 'Positive Emotions Broaden and Build', in *Advances in Experimental Social Psychology*, vol. XLVII, ed. Patricia Devine and Ashby Plant (San Diego: Academic Press, 2013), 1–53.
22 Jollimore, *Love's Vision*.

Conclusion

1 Mary Evans, *Love: An Unromantic Discussion*, 1st edition (Cambridge, UK, and Malden, Mass.: Polity, 2002), 119.
2 Lovett, *A General Theory of Domination and Justice*, 134–6.
3 Philip Pettit, 'Freedom as Antipower', *Ethics* 106, no. 3 (1996): 576–604.
4 Karl, 'Relationship Retros', Medium (blog), 2019, https://medium.com/@glovguy/relationship-retros-625ee5a27d5f.
5 Nolan, 'Temporary Marriage'; Vicki Larson, 'Why All Women Need Renewable Marriage Contracts', Medium (blog), 15 October 2022, https://omgchronicles.medium.com/why-all-women-need-renewable-marriage-contracts-1ce134c89890.
6 Élise Rouméas, 'The Right to a Fair Exit', *Politics, Philosophy & Economics*, 2023.
7 Phillipe van Parijs and Yannick Vanderborght, *Basic Income: A Radical Proposal for a Free Society and a Sane Economy*, illustrated edition (Cambridge, Mass.: Harvard University Press, 2017).

References

Addelson, Kathryn. *Moral Passages: Towards a Collectivist Moral Theory*. London: Routledge, 1994.
Annas, Julia. *Intelligent Virtue*. Oxford University Press, 2011.
Archer, Alfred, and Georgina Mills. 'Anger, Affective Injustice, and Emotion Regulation'. *Philosophical Topics* 47, no. 2 (2019): 75–94.
Aron, Arthur, Gary W. Lewandowski Jr, Debra Mashek, and Elaine N. Aron. 'The Self-Expansion Model of Motivation and Cognition in Close Relationships'. In *The Oxford Handbook of Close Relationships*, edited by Jeffry Simpson and Lorne Campbell, 91–115. Oxford University Press, 2013.
Ásta. *Categories We Live By: The Construction of Sex, Gender, Race, and Other Social Categories*. Oxford University Press, 2018.
Bagley, Benjamin. 'Loving Someone in Particular'. *Ethics* 125, no. 2 (2015): 477–507.
———. '(The Varieties of) Love in Contemporary Anglophone Philosophy'. In *The Routledge Handbook of Love in Philosophy*, 453–64. Abingdon: Routledge, 2018.
Ben-Ze'ev, Aaron. *The Subtlety of Emotions*. Cambridge, Mass.: MIT Press, 2000.
Bergström, Marie. *The New Laws of Love: Online Dating and the Privatization of Intimacy*. Cambridge: Polity, 2021.
Bortolotti, Lisa. 'Optimism, Agency, and Success'. *Ethical Theory and Moral Practice* 21, no. 3 (2018): 521–35.

Bowlby, Dr E. J. M. *Attachment: Volume One of the Attachment and Loss Trilogy*. London: Pimlico, 1997.
Bradley, F. H. *Ethical Studies*. Cambridge University Press, 2012.
Brake, Elizabeth, ed. *After Marriage: Rethinking Marital Relationships*. New York: Oxford University Press, 2016.
———. *Minimizing Marriage: Marriage, Morality, and the Law*. New York: Oxford University Press, 2012.
Brewer, Talbot. *The Retrieval of Ethics*. Oxford University Press, 2011.
Brison, Susan J. *Aftermath: Violence and the Remaking of a Self*. Princeton University Press, 2002.
Brooks, Ann. *Love and Intimacy in Contemporary Society: Love in an International Context*. London: Routledge, 2019.
Brown, Anna. 'Bisexual Adults Are Far Less Likely than Gay Men and Lesbians to Be "Out" to the People in Their Lives'. Pew Research Center (blog). www.pewresearch.org/short-reads/2019/06/18/bisexual-adults-are-far-less-likely-than-gay-men-and-lesbians-to-be-out-to-the-people-in-their-lives.
Brunning, Luke. 'Compersion: An Alternative to Jealousy?' *Journal of the American Philosophical Association* 6, no. 2 (2020): 225–45.
———. 'Cultivating an Integrated Self'. In *Ethics and Self-Cultivation*, edited by Matthew Dennis and Werkhoven Sander, 174–96. London: Routledge, 2018.
———. *Does Monogamy Work?* London: Thames & Hudson, 2020.
———. 'Multiple Loves and the Shaped Self'. In *The Moral Psychology of Love*, edited by B. Brogaard and A. Pismenny, 151–70. Lanham, Md.: Rowman & Littlefield, 2022.
———. 'The Avoidance Approach to Plural Value'. *Theoria* 66, no. 160 (2019): 53–70.
———. 'The Distinctiveness of Polyamory'. *Journal of Applied Philosophy* 35, no. 3 (2018): 513–31.
———. 'Virtuous Chameleons: Social Roles, Integrity, and the Value of Compartmentalization'. In *The Ethics of Social Roles*, edited by Alex Barber and Sean Cordell, 298–320. Oxford University Press, 2023.
Brunning, Luke, and Natasha McKeever. 'Asexuality'. *Journal of Applied Philosophy* 38, no. 1 (2021): 497–517.
Brunning, Luke, Natasha McKeever, and Sophie Goddard. 'Relationship Anarchy', n.d. (unpublished paper).
Brunning, Luke, and Per-Erik Milam. 'Letting Go of Blame'. *Philosophy and Phenomenological Research* 106, no. 2 (2023): 720–40.

Calhoun, Cheshire. 'Standing for Something'. *The Journal of Philosophy* 92, no. 5 (1995): 235–60.
———. 'What Good Is Commitment?' *Ethics* 119, no. 4 (2009): 613–41.
Chalmers, Harry. 'Is Monogamy Morally Permissible?' *The Journal of Value Inquiry* 53, no. 2 (2019): 225–41.
———. 'Monogamy Unredeemed'. *Philosophia* 50 (2022): 1009–34.
Cherry, Myisha. 'Political Anger'. *Philosophy Compass* 17, no. 2 (2022): 1–11.
———. *The Case for Rage: Why Anger Is Essential to Anti-Racist Struggle*. New York: Oxford University Press, 2021.
Christman, John. 'Autonomy and Personal History'. *Canadian Journal of Philosophy* 21, no. 1 (1991): 1–24.
———. *The Politics of Persons: Individual Autonomy and Sociohistorical Selves*. Cambridge University Press, 2009.
Clardy, Justin Leonard. 'Monogamies, Non-Monogamies, and the Moral Impermissibility of Intimacy Confining Constraints'. *Journal of Black Sexuality and Relationships* 6, no. 2 (2019): 17–36.
Clark, Anna. *Desire: A History of European Sexuality*. London: Routledge, 2008.
Cohen, Rhaina. 'What If Friendship, Not Marriage, Was at the Center of Life?' *The Atlantic*, 2020. www.theatlantic.com/family/archive/2020/10/people-who-prioritize-friendship-over-romance/616779.
Colombetti, Giovanna, and Joel Krueger. 'Scaffoldings of the Affective Mind'. *Philosophical Psychology* 28, no. 8 (2015): 1157–76.
Coontz, Stephanie. *Marriage, a History: How Love Conquered Marriage*. New York: Penguin, 2006.
Cox, Damian, Marguerite La Caze, and Michael Levine. 'Integrity'. In *The Stanford Encyclopedia of Philosophy*, edited by Edward N. Zalta, Fall 2021. Metaphysics Research Lab, Stanford University, 2021. https://plato.stanford.edu/archives/fall2021/entries/integrity.
Curington, Celeste Vaughan, Jennifer Hickes Lundquist, and Ken-Hou Lin. *The Dating Divide: Race and Desire in the Era of Online Romance*. Oakland: University of California Press, 2021.
Dabhoiwala, Faramerz. *The Origins of Sex: A History of the First Sexual Revolution*. London: Allen Lane, 2012.
D'Arms, Justin. 'Fitting Emotions'. In *Fittingness: Essays in the Philosophy of Normativity*, edited by Chris Howard and R. A. Rowland, 105–29. Oxford University Press, 2022.

D'Arms, Justin, and Daniel Jacobson. 'The Moralistic Fallacy: On the "Appropriateness" of Emotions'. *Philosophy and Phenomenological Research* 61, no. 1 (2000): 65–90.

Darwall, Stephen L. 'Two Kinds of Respect'. *Ethics* 88, no. 1 (1977): 36–49.

Diamond, Lisa M. *Sexual Fluidity: Understanding Women's Love and Desire*. Cambridge, Mass.: Harvard University Press, 2008.

Dover, Daniela. 'The Conversational Self'. *Mind* 131, no. 521 (2022): 193–230.

Emens, Elizabeth F. 'Manogamy's Law: Compulsory Monogamy and Polyamorous Existence'. *New York University Review of Law & Social Change* 29, no. 2 (2004): 277–376.

Evans, Mary. *Love: An Unromantic Discussion*, 1st edition. Cambridge, UK and Malden, Mass.: Polity, 2002.

Fern, Jessica. *Polysecure: Attachment, Trauma and Consensual Nonmonogamy*. Portland: Thorntree Press, 2020.

Finn, Mark D. 'The Psychological Architecture of the Stable Couple Relationship'. *Theory & Psychology* 22, no. 5 (2012): 607–25.

Fredrickson, Barbara L. 'Positive Emotions Broaden and Build'. In *Advances in Experimental Social Psychology*, vol. XLVII, edited by Patricia Devine and Ashby Plant, 1–53. San Diego: Academic Press, 2013.

Frye, Marilyn. *The Politics of Reality: Essays in Feminist Theory*. Trumansburg, NY: Crossing Press, 1983.

Fuchs, Thomas. 'Presence in Absence: The Ambiguous Phenomenology of Grief'. *Phenomenology and the Cognitive Sciences* 17, no. 1 (2018): 43–63.

Gadamer, Hans-Georg. *Truth and Method*, translated by Joel Weinsheimer and Donald G. Marshall. London: Bloomsbury Academic, 2013.

Gheaus, Anca. 'The (Dis)Value of Commitment to One's Spouse'. In *After Marriage: Rethinking Marital Relationships*, edited by Elizabeth Brake, 204–24. Oxford University Press, 2016.

Giddens, Anthony. *The Transformation of Intimacy: Sexuality, Love and Eroticism in Modern Societies*. Cambridge: Polity, 1992.

Glassman-Hughes, Emma. 'What Is Kitchen Table Polyamory?' *Cosmopolitan*, 18 January 2022. www.cosmopolitan.com/sexopedia/a38807618/kitchen-table-polyamory.

Goldie, Peter. *The Mess Inside: Narrative, Emotion, and the Mind*. Oxford University Press, 2012.

Gross, James J. 'Emotion Regulation: Taking Stock and Moving Forward'. *Emotion* 13, no. 3 (2013): 359.

———. 'The Emerging Field of Emotion Regulation: An Integrative Review'. *Review of General Psychology* 2, no. 3 (1998): 271–99.

Gross, James J., and Ross A. Thompson. 'Emotion Regulation: Conceptual Foundations'. In *Handbook of Emotion Regulation*, edited by J. J. Gross. New York: The Guilford Press, 2007.

Gunkel, Jasmine. 'What Is Intimacy?'. *The Journal of Philosophy* (forthcoming).

Halwani, Raja. *Virtuous Liaisons: Care, Love, Sex, and Virtue Ethics*. Chicago, Ill.: Open Court, 2003.

Harcourt, Edward. 'Nietzsche and the "Aesthetics of Character"'. In *Nietzsche's On the Genealogy of Morality: A Critical Guide*, edited by Simon May, 265–84. Cambridge Critical Guides. Cambridge University Press, 2011.

———. 'Two Routes from Secure Attachment to Virtue'. In *Attachment and Character*, edited by Edward Harcourt, 137–53. Oxford University Press, 2021.

Haupert, Mara L., Amanda N. Gesselman, Amy C. Moors, Helen E. Fisher, and Justin R. Garcia. 'Prevalence of Experiences with Consensual Nonmonogamous Relationships: Findings from Two National Samples of Single Americans'. *Journal of Sex & Marital Therapy* 43, no. 5 (2017): 424–40.

Helm, Bennett W. *Love, Friendship, and the Self: Intimacy, Identification, and the Social Nature of Persons*. Oxford University Press, 2009.

Henrich, Joseph, Robert Boyd, and Peter J. Richerson. 'The Puzzle of Monogamous Marriage'. *Philosophical Transactions of the Royal Society B: Biological Sciences* 367, no. 1589 (2012): 657–69.

Hernandez, E. M. 'Gender-Affirmation and Loving Attention'. *Hypatia* 36, no. 4 (2021): 619–35.

Hochschild, Arlie. *The Managed Heart: Commercialization of Human Feeling*, 3rd edition. Berkeley and London: University of California Press, 2012.

Illouz, Eva. *The End of Love: A Sociology of Negative Relations*. New York: Oxford University Press, 2019.

Irvin, Sherri, and Sheila Lintott. 'Sex Objects and Sexy Subjects: A Feminist Reclamation of Sexiness'. In *Body Aesthetics*, edited by Sherri Irvin, 299–318. Oxford University Press, 2016.

Jacobs, Jane. *The Death and Life of Great American Cities*. London: Bodley Head, 2020.

Jenkins, Carrie. *Sad Love: Romance and the Search for Meaning*. Cambridge: Polity, 2022.

John, Eileen. 'Love and the Need for Comprehension'. *Philosophical Explorations* 16, no. 3 (2013): 285–97.

Jollimore, Troy. *Love's Vision*. Princeton University Press, 2011.

Kalmijn, M. 'Friendship Networks over the Life Course: A Test of the Dyadic Withdrawal Hypothesis Using Survey Data on Couples'. *Social Networks* 25, no. 3 (2003): 231–49.

Karl. 'Relationship Retros'. Medium (blog), 2019. https://medium.com/@glovguy/relationship-retros-625ee5a27d5f.

Katz, Mycah, and Ellen Katz. 'Reconceptualizing Attachment Theory through the Lens of Polyamory'. *Sexuality & Culture* 26 (2021): 792–809.

Kinna, Ruth. *The Government of No One*. London: Penguin, 2020.

Kipnis, Laura. *Against Love: A Polemic*. New York: Vintage, 2004.

Klesse, Christian. 'Polyamory: Intimate Practice, Identity or Sexual Orientation?' *Sexualities* 17, no. 1/2 (2014): 81–99.

Kristjánsson, Kristján. *Justifying Emotions: Pride and Jealousy*. London: Routledge, 2002.

———. *Virtuous Emotions*. Oxford and New York: Oxford University Press, 2018.

Kropotkin, Peter. *Mutual Aid*. London: Penguin, 2022.

Kukla, Quill R. *City Living: How Urban Spaces and Urban Dwellers Make One Another*. New York: Oxford University Press, 2022.

Kukla, Rebecca. 'That's What She Said: The Language of Sexual Negotiation'. *Ethics* 129, no. 1 (2018): 70–97.

Kurth, Charlie. 'Inappropriate Emotions, Marginalization, and Feeling Better'. *Synthese* 200, no. 2 (2022): 155.

Lagasnerie, Geoffroy de. *3: Une aspiration au dehors*. Paris: Flammarion, 2023.

Lamb, Sharon, Sam Gable, and Doret de Ruyter. 'Mutuality in Sexual Relationships: A Standard of Ethical Sex?' *Ethical Theory and Moral Practice* 24, no. 1 (2021): 271–84.

Langton, Rae. 'Autonomy-Denial in Objectification'. In *Sexual Solipsism: Philosophical Essays on Pornography and Objectification*, 223–40. Oxford University Press, 2009.

Larmore, Charles. *The Autonomy of Morality*. Cambridge University Press, 2008.

Larson, Vicki. 'Why All Women Need Renewable Marriage Contracts'. Medium (blog), 15 October 2022. https://omgchronicles.medium.com/why-all-women-need-renewable-marriage-contracts-1ce134c89890.

Lesthaeghe, Ron. 'The Unfolding Story of the Second Demographic

Transition'. *Population and Development Review* 36, no. 2 (2010): 211–51.
Liberto, Hallie. 'The Problem with Sexual Promises'. *Ethics* 127, no. 2 (2017): 383–414.
Liebow, Nabina, and Trip Glazer. 'White Tears: Emotion Regulation and White Fragility'. *Inquiry*, 2019, 1–21.
Lopez-Cantero, Pilar. 'Being in Love: A Narrative Account'. Unpublished dissertation, University of Manchester, 2020.
———. 'Non-Harmonious Love'. *International Journal of Philosophical Studies* 30, no. 3 (2022): 276–97.
Lorde, A. 'Uses of the Erotic: The Erotic as Power'. In *Sister Outsider*, 43–50. London: Penguin, 2019.
Lovett, Frank. *A General Theory of Domination and Justice*. Oxford University Press, 2010.
Lugones, Maria. *Pilgrimages/Peregrinajes: Theorizing Coalition against Multiple Oppressions*. Lanham, Md.: Rowman & Littlefield Publishers, Inc., 2003.
Macedo, Stephen. *Just Married: Same-Sex Couples, Monogamy, and the Future of Marriage*. Princeton University Press, 2017.
Manne, Kate. *Down Girl: The Logic of Misogyny*. New York: Oxford University Press, 2017.
March, Andrew. 'Is There a Right to Polygamy? Marriage, Equality and Subsidizing Families in Liberal Public Justification'. *Journal of Moral Philosophy* 8, no. 2 (2011): 246–72.
Marcuse, Herbert. *Eros and Civilization: A Philosophical Inquiry into Freud*, 2nd edition. London: Routledge, 1987.
Matos, Greg. 'The Rise of Lonely, Single Men'. *Psychology Today*, 2022. www.psychologytoday.com/gb/blog/the-state-our-unions/202208/the-rise-lonely-single-men.
McKeever, Natasha. 'Is the Requirement of Sexual Exclusivity Consistent with Romantic Love?' *Journal of Applied Philosophy* 34, no. 3 (2017): 353–69.
McKeever, Natasha, and Andrew Kirton. 'Trust, Attachment, and Monogamy', in *The Moral Psychology of Trust*, edited by M. Alfano, D. Collins, and I. Vidmar Jovanovic, 295–312. London: Lexington Books, 2023.
Meyers, Diana Tietjens. 'Decentralizing Autonomy: Five Faces of Selfhood'. In *Autonomy and the Challenges to Liberalism*, 27–55. New York: Cambridge University Press, 2005.
Millay, Edna St Vincent. *Letters of Edna St. Vincent Millay*. New York: Harper, 1952.
Mitchell, Travis. 'Rising Share of U.S. Adults Are Living Without a Spouse or Partner'. Pew Research Center's Social & Demographic

Trends Project (blog), 5 October 2021. www.pewresearch.org/social-trends/2021/10/05/rising-share-of-u-s-adults-are-living-without-a-spouse-or-partner.

Moen, Ole Martin, and Aleksander Sørlie. 'The Ethics of Relationship Anarchy'. In *The Routledge Handbook of Philosophy of Sex and Sexuality*, 341–56. New York: Routledge, 2022.

Murdoch, Iris. *Existentialists and Mystics: Writings on Philosophy and Literature*, new edition. London: Penguin, 1999.

Murray, Sandra L., John G. Holmes, and Dale W. Griffin. 'The Benefits of Positive Illusions: Idealization and the Construction of Satisfaction in Close Relationships'. *Journal of Personality and Social Psychology* 70, no. 1 (1996): 79–98.

Naar, Hichem. 'The Fittingness of Emotions'. *Synthese* 199, no. 5 (2021): 13601–19.

Nelson, Hilde Lindemann. 'Resistance and Insubordination'. *Hypatia* 10, no. 2 (1995): 23–40.

Neu, Jerome. *A Tear Is an Intellectual Thing: The Meanings of Emotion*. Oxford University Press, 2000.

Nguyen, C. Thi. *Games: Agency as Art*. New York: Oxford University Press, 2020.

Nolan, Daniel. 'Temporary Marriage'. In *After Marriage: Rethinking Marital Relationships*, edited by Elizabeth Brake, 180–203. Oxford University Press, 2016.

Nordgren, Andie. 'The Short Instructional Manifesto for Relationship Anarchy'. *The Anarchist Library*, 2006. https://theanarchistlibrary.org/library/andie-nordgren-the-short-instructional-manifesto-for-relationship-anarchy.

Nozick, Robert. 'Love's Bond'. In *The Examined Life: Philosophical Meditations*, 68–86. New York: Simon & Schuster, 1989.

Nussbaum, Martha C. *Anger and Forgiveness: Resentment, Generosity, Justice*. Oxford University Press, 2016.

———. 'Objectification'. *Philosophy & Public Affairs* 24, no. 4 (1995): 249–91.

———. 'Winnicott on the Surprises of the Self'. *Massachusetts Review* 47, no. 2 (2006): 375.

Oakley, Justin, and Dean Cocking. *Virtue Ethics and Professional Roles*. Cambridge University Press, 2001.

Ogden, Thomas H. 'On Holding and Containing, Being and Dreaming'. *The International Journal of Psychoanalysis* 85, no. 6 (2004): 1349–64.

Orenstein, Peggy. *Girls & Sex – Navigating the Complicated New Landscape*. London: Oneworld Publications, 2016.

Otter, R. C. 'Perfectionist Argument for Legal Recognition of

Polyamorous Relationships'. In *Philosophical Foundations of Children's and Family Law*, edited by Elizabeth Brake and Lucinda Ferguson, 95–114. Oxford University Press, 2018.

Parijs, Philippe van. *Real Freedom for All: What (If Anything) Can Justify Capitalism?* Oxford University Press, 1995.

Parijs, Phillipe van, and Yannick Vanderborght. *Basic Income: A Radical Proposal for a Free Society and a Sane Economy*, illustrated edition. Cambridge, Mass.: Harvard University Press, 2017.

Paul, L. A. *Transformative Experience*. Oxford University Press, 2014.

Paytas, Tyler. 'Aptness Isn't Enough: Why We Ought to Abandon Anger'. *Ethical Theory and Moral Practice*, 2022: 1–17.

Pettit, Philip. 'Freedom as Antipower'. *Ethics* 106, no. 3 (1996): 576–604.

———. *Just Freedom: A Moral Compass for a Complex World*. New York: W. W. Norton & Company, 2014.

———. *Republicanism: A Theory of Freedom and Government*. Oxford Political Theory. Oxford University Press, 1997.

Posner, Richard A. *Sex and Reason*. Cambridge, Mass.: Harvard University Press, 1992.

Prinz, Jesse. 'Moral Sedimentation'. In *Neuroexistentialism*, edited by Gregg Caruso and Owen Flanagan, 87–108. New York: Oxford University Press, 2018.

Prinz, Jesse J. *Gut Reactions: A Perceptual Theory of Emotion*. Oxford University Press, 2006.

Rambukkana, Nathan. *Fraught Intimacies: Non/Monogamy in the Public Sphere*. Vancouver: University of British Columbia Press, 2015.

Rawls, John. *A Theory of Justice: Original Edition*, reissue edition. Cambridge, Mass.: Harvard University Press, 2005.

Reddy, William M. *The Making of Romantic Love: Longing and Sexuality in Europe, South Asia, and Japan, 900–1200 CE*. University of Chicago Press, 2012.

Regnerus, Mark. *Cheap Sex: The Transformation of Men, Marriage, and Monogamy*. New York: Oxford University Press, 2017.

Rini, Regina. *The Ethics of Microaggression*. Abingdon: Routledge, 2020.

Ritchie, Ani, and Meg Barker. '"There Aren't Words for What We Do or How We Feel So We Have To Make Them Up": Constructing Polyamorous Languages in a Culture of Compulsory Monogamy'. *Sexualities* 9, no. 5 (2006): 584–601.

Rouméas, Élise. 'The Right to a Fair Exit'. *Politics, Philosophy & Economics*, 2023.

Savitsky, Kenneth, Boaz Keysar, Nicholas Epley, Travis Carter, and Ashley Swanson. 'The Closeness–Communication Bias: Increased Egocentrism among Friends versus Strangers'. *Journal of Experimental Social Psychology* 47, no. 1 (2011): 269–73.

Scarry, Elaine. *On Beauty and Being Just*. Princeton University Press, 1999.

Scheffler, Samuel. *Equality and Tradition: Questions of Moral Value in Moral and Political Theory*. New York: Oxford University Press, 2012.

Scott, James C. *Seeing Like a State: How Certain Schemes to Improve the Human Condition Have Failed*, revised edition. New Haven: Yale University Press, 1999.

———. *Two Cheers for Anarchism – Six Easy Pieces on Autonomy, Dignity, and Meaningful Work and Play*. Princeton University Press, 2014.

Sheff, Elisabeth. *The Polyamorists Next Door: Inside Multiple-Partner Relationships and Families*. Lanham, Md.: Rowman & Littlefield Publishers, 2013.

Shevek, Lee. 'Process-Centered Love'. *The Anarchist Library*, 2019. https://theanarchistlibrary.org/library/lee-shevek-process-centered-love.

Srinivasan, Amia. 'The Aptness of Anger'. *Journal of Political Philosophy* 26, no. 2 (2018): 123–44.

Strauss, Neil. *The Game: Undercover in the Secret Society of Pickup Artists*. Edinburgh: Canongate Books, 2007.

Suits, Bernard. *The Grasshopper: Games, Life and Utopia*. Peterborough, Ont.: Broadview Press, 2014.

Táíwò, Olúfẹ́mi O. 'Stoicism (as Emotional Compression) Is Emotional Labor'. *Feminist Philosophy Quarterly* 6, no. 2 (2020): 1–26.

Tennov, Dorothy. *Love and Limerence: The Experience of Being in Love*, 2nd edition. Lanham, Md.: Scarborough House, 1998.

Tessman, Lisa. *Burdened Virtues: Virtue Ethics for Liberatory Struggles*. Studies in Feminist Philosophy. New York: Oxford University Press, 2005.

Tiberius, Valerie. *The Reflective Life: Living Wisely with Our Limits*. Oxford University Press, 2008.

Tilton, Emily C. R., and Jonathan Jenkins Ichikawa. 'Not What I Agreed To: Content and Consent'. *Ethics* 132, no. 1 (2021): 127–54.

Trujillo, Glenn Mac. 'No Laughing Matter: Playfulness and a Good Life', 2019. https://ir.vanderbilt.edu/handle/1803/12933.

Tweedy, Ann. 'Polyamory as a Sexual Orientation'. *University of Cincinnati Law Review* 79, no. 4 (2011), 1461–1515.

Vogels, Emily A., and Colleen Mcclain. 'Key Findings about Online Dating in the U.S.' Pew Research Center (blog). www.pewresearch.org/short-reads/2023/02/02/key-findings-about-online-dating-in-the-u-s.
Walker, Margaret. 'Moral Luck and the Virtues of Impure Agency'. *Metaphilosophy* 22, no. 1/2 (1991): 14–27.
———. *Moral Understandings: A Feminist Study in Ethics*. 2nd edition. New York: Oxford University Press, 2007.
Wark, McKenzie. 'Charles Fourier's Queer Theory', 2015. www.versobooks.com/blogs/1896-charles-fourier-s-queer-theory.
Warner, Michael. *The Trouble with Normal: Sex, Politics, and the Ethics of Queer Life*. Cambridge, Mass.: Harvard University Press, 2000.
Webber, Jonathan. *Rethinking Existentialism*. Oxford University Press, 2018.
Welpinghus, Anna. 'Jealousy: A Response to Infidelity? On the Nature and Appropriateness Conditions of Jealousy'. *Philosophical Explorations* 20, no. 3 (2017): 322–37.
Wesselinoff, Catherine. 'Is Jealousy Justifiable?' *European Journal of Philosophy*, 2022: 703–10.
Westlund, Andrea C. 'Deciding Together'. *Philosopher's Imprint* 9, no. 10 (2009).
Williams, Bernard. 'Justice as a Virtue'. In *Essays on Aristotle's Ethics*, edited by Amélie Oksenberg Rorty, 189–200. Berkeley: University of California Press, 1980.
Wilson, Timothy D. *Strangers to Ourselves: Discovering the Adaptive Unconscious*. London: Belknap, 2002.
Winnicott, D. W. *The Maturational Processes and the Facilitating Environment: Studies in the Theory of Emotional Development*. 1st edition. Princeton: Routledge, 1990.
———. *Through Paediatrics to Psychoanalysis: Collected Papers*. 1st edition. London: Routledge, 1975.
Witte, John. *The Western Case for Monogamy over Polygamy*. New York: Cambridge University Press, 2015.
Wonderly, Monique. 'Agency and Varieties of Felt Necessity'. *Ethics* 132, no. 1 (2021): 155–79.
———. 'On Being Attached'. *Philosophical Studies* 173, no. 1 (2016): 223–42.
———. 'On the Affect of Security'. *Philosophical Topics* 47, no. 2 (2019): 165–81.
Yao, Vida. 'Grace and Alienation'. *Philosopher's Imprint* 20, no. 16 (2020).
York, Kyle. 'Why Monogamy Is Morally Permissible: A Defense of

Some Common Justifications for Monogamy'. *The Journal of Value Inquiry* 54, no. 4 (2020): 539–52.

Young, Iris Marion. *Justice and the Politics of Difference*. Princeton University Press, 2011.

Index

abilities, romantic agency and, 58–62
accountability, 81–4, 111, 112, 114, 116, 180, 184
agency, pure agents, 111–12
airhostesses, 158–9
alternative lifestyles, 6, 104, 106, 127
amatonormativity, 12–15, 16, 30, 37, 44, 84, 116, 177
anarchists, 126, 127, 186
anarchization of relationships, 72, 84–8, 103, 168, 179, 186
Annas, Julia, 95
appraisal respect, 138
appreciation, intimacy and, 77–80
Armand, Émile, 127
aromanticism, 4, 29, 35, 36–7, 40, 117
asexuality, 3, 4, 35, 36, 40, 117
autonomy, 17, 20–1, 40, 66, 96, 179

Bagley, Benjamin, 64–5, 74
Ben-Ze'ev, Aaron, 11
Berlant, Lauren, 1, 59–60, 121, 188
Bex-Priestley, Graham, 79
Bortolotti, Lisa, 99–100
Bradley, F. H., 98, 110
Brake, Elizabeth, 12
Brewer, Talbot, 58, 64, 94

Calhoun, Cheshire, 111, 118, 121, 173–5, 176
capitalism, 15, 158–9
celibacy, 3
Chalmers, Harry, 41–3, 46, 48, 49, 51, 53, 54, 55, 57
Cherry, Myisha, 149
Christman, John, 96
cognitive behavioural therapy, 134
commitment
  concept, 8
  contentment, 176
  integrity and, 110, 112, 117–19
  marriage, 14

Index

nonmonogamy and, 26, 75
practicalities, 123
provisional, 184–5
social expectations, 137
value, 5, 16, 118–20
vulnerability and, 115
compersion, 7, 145, 168–72, 174, 176, 177, 178
configurations, meaning, 5
consumerism, 2, 27, 173
contentment, 12, 168, 172–7, 178
conversation
  negotiations and, 91–4
  realism, 6–7, 89–102
  requirements, 90–5
  taking someone seriously, 90–1, 93, 126
courage, 95, 188
COVID-19 pandemic, 1
critical theorists, 127
cultivation
  exploration, 181–2
  methods, 180–3
  nurturing environment, 182–3
  self-knowledge, 180–1
culture
  competitiveness, 169, 178
  consumerism, 173–4
  contentment and, 173–4
  individualism, 169, 171
  modern romance, 56, 70
  narratives, 116–17
  playfulness and, 128
  realism and, 96, 129

D'Arms, Justin, 132
Darwall, Stephen, 138
dating apps, 2, 16, 17, 20, 39, 174
dating shows, 16–17
democracy
  freedom and, 55
  power and, 33

romance and, 20–2, 23, 27
detachment strategies, 18
disorientation, 6, 17–19, 65, 87, 160, 163, 167
domination
  anger, 140
  contentment and, 175
  emotion cultivation, 148
  freedom and, 50, 52–5, 87
  Giddens, Anthony 20–1, 67
  harm, 183
  law and, 185, 186
  minimizing, 7, 22, 81–3, 129, 183–7
  play and, 123
Dover, Daniela, 90–1, 92, 93, 126, 162

emotion cultivation, 132, 134, 136, 146–9, 151, 152
emotional compression, 153–60
emotional labour, 153, 158–9
erotophobia, 13
error-friendliness, 124–5, 128–9
Evans, Mary, 179
experimentation, 5, 16, 36, 89, 100, 103, 105–6, 108, 182
exploration
  constraints, 107, 109, 172
  forms, 181–2
  infants, 161, 163
  lifestyles, 6, 104, 106
  narrative exploration, 181–2
  nonmonogamy, 51, 54–5, 105, 106, 130
  openness to, 125–7
  playfulness, 7, 123, 125–7, 177
  process, 85–6, 96
  sexual identity, 45
  solidarity and, 183
  transformation, 63
  value, 5, 180

fairness, nonmonogamy and, 32–40, 56–7
Fournier, Charles, 127
freedom
    concepts, 49–50
    conditions, 49–50
    non-domination, 50, 53–5, 67
    nonmonogamy, 46–55
    republican concept, 49, 50–1, 52–3, 54
    resources, 49–50, 51–2
Frye, Marylin, 167, 169–70, 177

Gadamer, Hans-Georg, 89, 90, 92, 188
gender
    domination and, 185
    labour, 159
    nonmonogamy and, 53
    patriarchy, 28–9
    possessiveness and, 45
    pronouns, 171
    social norms, 13, 30, 128, 169–70, 173, 181
Gheaus, Anca, 119
Giddens, Anthony, 16, 20–2, 23, 24, 55, 67, 80, 82
Goldman, Emma, 127
greed
    nonmonogamy and, 27–32, 56–7
    reluctance to share, 31–2
group dynamics, 82–3

Halwani, Raja, 104–5, 107, 109
Hernandez, E. M., 171
Hochschild, Arlie, 158–9
holding, 160–5
honesty, cruelty and, 87
hookup culture, 14–15

idealizations, 98, 99–100
Illouz, Eva, 9, 16, 17, 18, 20, 21–2, 23, 24

improvisation, 64–5, 74, 182
individualism, 15–16, 27, 65, 74, 76, 88, 108, 169–70, 171
insularity, 167–8
integrity
    benefits, 180
    concept, 110–15
    disruption and, 117–18
    nonmonogamy and, 116
    playfulness and, 121–9
    realism and, 117
    risks and, 7, 110–21
intimacy
    anarchization, 84–8
    appreciation, 77–80
    hierarchies, 83–4
    monogamy and, 6, 72–7
    oversight, 80–4
    privatization, 16
    shaping, 71–88
    specialization, 72–7
intimate privilege, 14

Jacobs, Jane, 71
Jacobson, Daniel, 132
jealousy
    analysis, 130–7
    anger, 131, 135, 144, 147–9, 152
    compression, 153–60, 180
    definition, 131
    deservingness, 137–41, 147
    fittingness, 133–7, 141–2, 143–6, 151–2
    holding, 160–5
    management, 152–65
    pluralism, 139–41, 152
    Rakes and Saints, 149–51
    removing, 134–5, 141–52
    value, 131–2

kindness, 50, 95
Kinna, Ruth, 87
Kollontai, Alexandra, 127

Index

Kristjánsson, Kristján, 135–7, 138, 140
Kukla, Quill, 25, 47–8, 52, 59–60, 75

leisure, 122
Liberto, Halle, 47, 48
Lindemann, Hilde, 118
Locke, John, 33
loneliness, 38
Lorde, Audre, 149
Lugones, Maria, 122–3, 128, 170

Macedo, Stephen, 14
March, Andrew, 33, 34–5
Marcuse, Herbert, 127
marriage
  domination, 50, 186
  entitlement, 137
  forms, 33–4
  hierarchy, 83
  same-sex marriage, 14
  shifts, 15, 84
  temporary forms, 127, 185
Marxists, 127
Matos, Greg, 38, 193n22
McKeever, Natasha, 44–5, 118, 158
Mense, Anna, 124
methodology, 7–8
Meyers, Diana, 66
Mill, John Stuart, 5
misogyny, 128, 157–8
monogamy
  anarchization, 84–8
  appeal, 72–3
  appreciation, 77–80
  benefits, 43–4, 56
  fairness, 32–40, 56–7
  freedom and, 46–55
  intimacy and, 6, 72–7
  mononormativity, 13, 14, 25, 106, 181

moral norm, 40–6
nonmonogamy. *See* nonmonogamy
possessiveness, 32
promises, 47–8, 52
restrictions, 46–55
sexual exclusivity, 44–5
specialization, 72–7
symbolic value, 44–5
Montesquieu, Charles de, 29
moral damage, 19, 22–3, 56, 76, 106
Murdoch, Iris, 73–4, 170
mutual aid, 86

narratives
  exploration, 181–2
  integrity and, 114
  nonmonogamy, 117
  romantic agency and, 65–6
  simple stories, 114, 117, 118
negotiations, conversation and, 91–4
neoliberalism, 21, 23
nonmonogamy
  accountability, 184
  alternative, 25–7
  anarchization, 84–8
  appreciation, 77–80
  effect, 6
  forms, 72
  freedom, 46–55
  greed, 27–32, 56–7
  integrity and, 116
  moral damage, 56
  oversight and, 80–4
  practicality, 26–7, 43
  resources, 86
  romantic agency and, 69
  sexual orientation, 29–30
  unfairness, 32–40, 56–7
  virtue and, 104–5

O'Shea, Tom, 54, 55

Ogden, Thomas, 160
online dating, 2, 16, 17, 20, 39, 174
optimism, realism and, 98–102
oversight, intimacy and, 80–4

past, influence, 10, 67
patriarchy, 21, 28, 32, 106, 139
Paul, L. A., 63
Paytas, Tyler, 144
Pettit, Philip, 49–50, 52
plans, risks, 104–10
playfulness
  agonistic play, 123
  benefits, 180
  concept, 122–3
  error-friendliness, 124–5
  exploration, 125–7
  integrity and, 7, 121–9
  ironic distance, 124
  loving play, 123
  perspectival seriousness, 123–4
  requirements, 123–7
  risks, 7, 121–9
policies, meaning, 5
polyamory. *See* nonmonogamy
polyandry, 33
polygamy, 29, 33, 127
polygyny, 33
possessiveness, 28, 32, 45, 46, 132, 147, 178
Prinz, Jesse, 12
psychoanalysts, 127, 128, 160

Rambukkana, Nathan, 14
Rawls, John, 36
realism
  autonomy and, 96
  conversation, 6–7, 89–102
  doubts, 103–4
  grasping the good and, 176
  idealizations, 98, 99–100
  integrity and, 117
  optimism and, 98–102
  particular versus general, 96–7, 98–9, 117
  positive illusions, 99–100
  requirements, 95–7
  risks and, 129
  simple stories and, 114, 117, 118
  virtue, 95–7, 176, 180
recognition respect, 138
Regnerus, Mark, 28, 32–3, 36, 37
Reich, Wilhelm, 127
republicanism, 20, 49, 50–1, 52–3, 54
respect, concept, 138
risks
  competence and, 103–4
  experimentation, 107–9
  integrity and, 7, 110–21
  plans, 104–10
  playfulness, 7, 121–9
  realism and, 129
  self-knowledge and, 105–6
  unconventional lifestyles, 107
Roman republic, 49
romance
  casualization, 17
  democracy and, 20–2, 23
  disorientation, 17–19
  emotional modernity, 16
  expertise, 18
  forms, 118–19
  individualism, 15–16, 27
  meaning, 3–5
  modern structures, 6, 9–24
  rituals, 17
  selves and, 9–12
  shifts, 15–17
  social norms, 12–15
romantic agency
  abilities, 58–62
  cultivation, 180–3

flourishing, 61–2
fragility, 61, 68–9, 76
meaning, 2, 59–60
narratives, 65–6
passive shaping, 66
past influences, 10, 67
relationality, 60–1, 62–8
spatial agency, 59–60
styles, 60
summary, 179–80
value shaping, 63–5
See also specific aspects
Ross, Otto, 127

Scarry, Elaine, 46
Schadenfreude, 133, 146
Scott, James C., 85
selves
  comparisons, 11–12
  context, 12
  ensemble subjectivity, 114
  modern romance and, 9–12
  mutability, 11
  opacity, 11
  past and, 10
  sedimentation, 12
  self-knowledge, 180–1
  social world, 12
  understanding, 180–1
  vulnerability, 9–10, 110, 115
sex
  exclusivity and possessiveness, 44–5
  hookup culture, 14–15
  male possessiveness, 44–5
  promises, 47–8, 52
  romance and, 3–4
  See also intimacy; jealousy
sex negativity, 13, 14, 15
society
  amatonormativity, 12–15,
    16, 30, 37, 44, 84, 116, 177
  romantic norms, 12–15
  shifts, 15–17, 84
solidarity, 134, 150, 183
spatial agency, 59–60
specialization, intimacy and, 72–7
Srinivasan, Amia, 148
St Vincent Millay, Edna, 80
stoicism, 153, 158

Táíwò, Olúfémi, 154, 155, 157–8, 159
Tessman, Lisa, 19, 76, 106, 140
Tiberius, Valerie, 101
transformations, overview, 1–3
Trujillo, Glenn, 122
Tweedy, Ann, 29

United States
  gay marriage, 14
  nonmonogamy, 39–40

value shaping, 63–5

Walker, Margaret, 103, 111–16, 118, 121, 161
Warner, Michael, 13, 15
Welpinghus, Anna, 130, 137, 140–1
Wesselinoff, Catherine, 137
Westlund, Andrea, 91, 92
Winnicott, Clare, 128
Winnicott, Donald, 128, 160–2, 164
women. *See* gender
Wonderly, Monique, 10, 169

York, Kyle, 45